Annie Keary

The Nations Around

Annie Keary

The Nations Around

ISBN/EAN: 9783337190712

Printed in Europe, USA, Canada, Australia, Japan

Cover: Foto ©ninafisch / pixelio.de

More available books at **www.hansebooks.com**

THE NATIONS AROUND.

The Nations Around

BY A. KEARY,

AUTHOR OF "EARLY EGYPTIAN HISTORY."

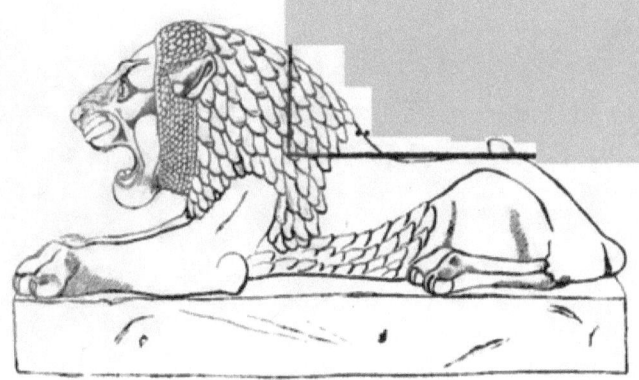

MACMILLAN & CO
PUBLISHERS
1870.

PREFACE.

THE following sketch of the early history of the great Eastern Empires, whose territories surrounded, and sometimes included, Palestine, is entitled "The Nations Around," because the writer's aim has been to dwell chiefly on the periods and circumstances which brought these people into connexion with the Hebrews, and to regard their history somewhat in the reflected light of the interest which attaches to all that concerns the heroes of the sacred narrative. This has been done in the double hope of making some points of the Bible history clearer to some readers, and of awakening a more lively interest in the history of "The Nations Around the Jews," than is usually felt when they are regarded quite independently.

One great distinction between the history of the early ages of the world, as we gather it from the Bible narrative or from the records on Egyptian tombs and Chaldean and Assyrian cylinders, is, that while one account brings us face to face with real men and women, and lets us know their thoughts on the deepest subjects—their joys and sorrows, their struggles and temptations, in the most momentous and in the most ordinary events of their lives—the other continually disappoints by bringing before us long lists of names indeed, and minute particulars of the outward forms of living, but no one life that we can really enter into, scarcely one name that at all vividly represents a person to us. The prosaic outward details of one history require contact with the other to make them attract and interest us. That contact brings life to them. When we hang the minute knowledge of ancient manners and customs, buildings and costumes, that may be learnt from Egyptian and Assyrian records, round the familiar heroes of Bible stories, like an ornamental frame round a beloved portrait, we discover, as we might not otherwise have discovered, how much value and interest such knowledge has for us.

CONTENTS.

CHAPTER I.
ABRAHAM	PAGE 1

CHAPTER II.
ABRAHAM'S FATHER	15

CHAPTER III.
ABRAHAM'S WANDERINGS	33

CHAPTER IV.
ABRAHAM IN EGYPT	42

CHAPTER V.
THE BOOK OF THE DEAD	54

CHAPTER VI.
ISRAEL IN EGYPT	69

CHAPTER VII.
EGYPTIAN ROMANCE	85

CHAPTER VIII.
THE KINGDOMS OF CANAAN	99

CHAPTER IX.
THE FISHERIES	106

CHAPTER X.
THE HIGH PLACES OF BAAL	120

CHAPTER XI.
HIRAM, KING OF TYRE	130

CHAPTER XII.
"BEHOLD, I AM AGAINST THEE, O TYRUS"	142

CHAPTER XIII.
THE ASSYRIAN	PAGE 149

CHAPTER XIV.
AN ASSYRIAN PALACE 165

CHAPTER XV.
A CHAPTER OF HISTORY 174

CHAPTER XVI.
SENNACHERIB, KING OF ASSYRIA 199

CHAPTER XVII.
THE BURDEN OF NINEVEH 219

CHAPTER XVIII.
THAT GREAT CITY BABYLON 229

CHAPTER XIX.
THE EAGLE WITH GREAT WINGS 243

CHAPTER XX.
THE LAND OF CAPTIVITY 258

CHAPTER XXI.
THE SIEGE 273

CHAPTER XXII.
WEIGHED IN THE BALANCE AND FOUND WANTING 288

CHAPTER XXIII.
THE MEANING OF THE SIGNS 305

CHAPTER XXIV.
THE BURIED PALACES 318

LIST OF ILLUSTRATIONS.

LION FROM SARGON'S TEMPLE.	*Vignette on Title-page.*	
JUDGMENT PICTURE FROM THE BOOK OF THE DEAD.	*To face*	60
THE TEMPLE OF KARNAC (*from a Photograph*) . . .	,,	83
SARGON'S PALACE WALL	,,	197

THE NATIONS AROUND.

CHAPTER I.

ABRAHAM.

WE are accustomed to think of the Children of Israel as a peculiar people set apart from the nations around them to occupy an exceptional position in the history of mankind. From the time when the first Hebrew (the passer over) crossed the great river, and at the call of the Divine Voice left the gods his fathers had worshipped, and the people among whom he had passed his youth, they were set apart—the chosen guardians of a treasure that was not yet to be openly displayed. They were the city set upon a hill, the candle in the candlestick that required to be kept distinct and bright, the eye which must remain single or the whole body would be full of darkness. Their history is more than anything else the history of the efforts which their lawgivers and prophets made to preserve them from being corrupted by the example of the nations that dwelt around them; of the calamities that overtook them when they fell into heathen practices, and of the wonderful national vitality which enabled them, after the most complete conquest and apparent absorption by their enemies, to gather themselves together and come out once more as distinctly Hebrews—people who were morally separated for ever from the rest of mankind—as they were before their long residence in foreign lands.

And yet, distinct and individual as is their history, we cannot fail to see that the nations around did play a very conspicuous part in it. The geographical position of Palestine made its inhabitants peculiarly subject to attacks from their stronger neighbours, and also liable at times to be courted as allies by one or another of them. Like the Low Countries and Italy in Europe, it was for centuries the battle-ground of rival empires. The road from the Nile valley to the Euphrates lay through the broad lowlands of Philistia, and along the narrow strip of coast to the north, where the Phœnician towns were situate. Above the road, like a succession of great fortresses, rose the rugged highlands of Judah, with the hills of Ephraim; and beyond the valley of Esdraelon (so often chosen as a battle-field by the highlanders) came the fastnesses of the northern tribes, losing themselves at length in the Lebanon mountain range. The armies of Egypt and Assyria had to pass along the seacoast road whenever either nation attacked the other; and their safe passage advancing or retreating might have been perilled by even a small body of troops holding the heights above.

The possession of these strongholds rendered the

alliance of the Jews a matter of some importance to the Assyrians, Babylonians, and later Egyptians, and also caused them to be objects of hatred and vengeance to the conqueror in the frequent struggles between these great rival powers, whenever the Jews had espoused the losing side. Israel was at different periods brought into closest contact with both the Southern and the Eastern Empire. Slaves for four hundred years in Egypt, captives for seventy years in Babylon, they were twice in the course of their history subject to the influence of a foreign civilization in some respects more advanced than their own. It is impossible but that some traces of the ideas and customs of the alien people among whom they dwelt so long, should have interwoven themselves with their traditions, coloured their literature, and helped to shape their subsequent national character and history.

It will interest us to consider the position of the two nations who exercised this influence over the Israelites, at the time when the foundation for the future sacred destiny of the Hebrew people was laid, by the Divine command given to their forefather Abraham to come out from the home of his fathers, and live as a pilgrim in the land which his descendants were hereafter to possess. In spite of the call that drew him away from all the associations of his early years, some traces of the thoughts and traditions of the nation among whom his youth was passed must, one would suppose, have remained with Abraham and been transmitted to his descendants, giving them an affinity with the parent people. **Abraham was** the first Hebrew; he crossed over the **river** and separated himself from the dwellers in the rich level lands of Mesopotamia, where the **most** renowned cities in the world sprang up; **but he was born in** one of those cities—Ur of the **Chaldees—where his** father dwelt for many years and (says tradition) carried on a trade among that people. We cannot but suppose **that** whatever degree of civilization they had attained to, whatever thoughts about the future and God, whatever traditions about the beginnings of things were current among them, must **have** been familiar to Abraham; must, up to the time when God called him, have formed the staple of his religious beliefs.

The first point of contact between the Hebrews and the nations whose neighbourhood affected them **in** after times was therefore with the Chaldeans; and **if** we wish **to** form a conception **of** the degree of attainment in the various **arts** of life which formed, so to speak, the starting-point of Hebrew civilization, we must study the remains of the very ancient cities of Lower Chaldea, which the Second Dynasty of Chaldean kings was adorning with palaces **and** temples while Terah was dwelling **in** one **of** them. The locality **of** Abraham's birth has long been a subject of dispute among the learned, and it cannot even now be considered a settled question, though the discovery of the remains of a very ancient city in Lower Chaldea, the clay bricks of which are inscribed with the name of Ur, and which was evidently **a noted** city in Terah's time, worthy to be **described by** his descendants as

"Ur of the Chaldees," seems to make the pretensions urged in favour of other sites less worthy of consideration than formerly. Even if we may not feel any degree of certainty respecting the precise spot in Chaldea where Abraham was born, we have the authority of the Bible for the fact that it was in a city *of the Chaldees*, evidently a noted and important one to be so particularized. And as there is a certain similarity of structure common to all the very early cities of that people, we shall not be transgressing against probability if, in attempting to describe the appearance which this ancient town of Ur presented in former times, we allow ourselves to believe we are picturing the sights familiar to Abraham when a boy. At all events, whether he was ever within its walls or not, it was there, with the grandest of its temples and the fairest of its palaces standing up newly finished for every one to see, at the time when Terah and Abraham and Sarai and Lot still worshipped the gods and followed the customs of their forefathers.

What we have thought the beginning to the Hebrew people—that time which looks to us so very distant and sacred, when so much freshness and mystery still seem to hang over the earth, and lingering airs of paradise to make life full of beauty and sweetness— does not, as far as we can make out from the remains of the cities that existed at that period, appear to have been in any sense a beginning to the people among whom Abraham was born. Ur, now called Mugheir by the wandering Arab tribes that pitch their tents among its ruins, was in Terah's time a flourishing seaport town situate at what was then the head of the Persian Gulf. The country on which it stood had known changes, had been colonized and conquered and reconquered, and had a far back history of its own before the buildings began to be erected on it, whose inscriptions give us faint glimmerings into that primal darkness.

Our knowledge of the city and its inhabitants of long ago is almost entirely drawn from inscriptions graven on the foundation bricks of temples and tombs which explorers in Lower Mesopotamia have disinterred from what is now a gigantic sand grave, hiding the relics of the past in its heart. The Arabs call this heap of ruins the "mother of bitumen," from the remains, seventy feet high, of a gigantic temple, the unburnt bricks of which are cemented with bitumen. The springs which supplied the bitumen to the ancient temple builders still exist in the neighbourhood of Mugheir, and are visited by the Arabs, who procure from them the cement they use in the erection of their frail reed huts.

The country round the ruins, as far as the eye can reach on every side, is now a flat, monotonous desert. For some months of the year it is flooded with water up to the edge of the sand mounds that enclose the ruins. When the waters retire, the swampy ground yields a rank growth of coarse grass and gigantic dark-stemmed reeds; later on in the summer, the scorching heat of the sun withers up rushes and grass, and bakes the earth till the whole landscape is one uniform dust colour—a picture of desolation.

To the south of the Mugheir ruins, however, are still to be found groups of palm-trees, which, by their pertinacity in continuing to flourish amidst the general desolation, bear witness to the peculiar adaptability of this district to the growth of the palm which is spoken of by ancient writers. Still further away there stretches now a wide district of low-lying, swampy land, which is supposed to have been added on to the country by the retirement of the waters of the Persian Gulf since the commencement of the historic period.

In Abraham's time, this town of Ur was the capital city and principal seaport of a kingdom ruled over by the Second Dynasty of Chaldean monarchs, and comprising a territory about as great in extent as the whole of ancient Greece.

The country stretching northwards to the Sinjar hills, and westward to the Arabian desert, was the plain of Shinar, where Nimrod's cities, Erech and Accad and Calneh and Babel—perhaps with its unfinished tower still standing—were in the course of being enlarged and embellished. The paralysis that fell on the building energies of mankind after the confusion of tongues had passed away; and the ancient cities in Abraham's time rose conspicuous from the level plain, with many-terraced temples and brick palaces lifting their heads above the small, frail, reed constructions of the very earliest architecture. The open country, level and featureless as now, was invested with a certain beauty by the luxuriant vegetation with which it was clothed. The city of Ur itself stood in a grove of palm-trees, and the neighbouring towns, of which several **could** be descried from the second terrace of its gigantic temple, had their gardens, where palms, **acacias**, and pomegranates, lovely with delicate white and rich crimson blossoms, relieved the monotonous grey colouring of the unburnt brick buildings.

Long level lines of embankments of the numerous watercourses crossed the fields in every direction, and wherever these ended sandy tracts of desert, or swamps covered **with** gigantic reeds, harbouring innumerable wild birds, appeared to diversify the scene.

The waters of the Persian Gulf, as far as the eye could reach, would be dotted with sails—the large square sail which **we** see in pictures on Egyptian tombs, for **Ur** traded with Ethiopia, and there appears to have been a close connection in early times between the cities on the Persian Gulf and Egypt and Ethiopia.

The city, of grey, unburnt brick, shaded by rows of tall palm-trees, and enclosed within high battlemented walls, would look pleasant and cool rising up from the sunny waters and the busy harbour. There would be a great diversity, even in that early time, in **the** character **of** the houses that clustered round the shore. The poorer ones were probably little better than such rude constructions of reeds woven together and plastered over with bitumen as the Arabs who live in the marsh **lands** near Mugheir construct for themselves at the present day; but there would be many more imposing edifices, buildings of two and even three stories high, for the most part of unburnt brick, with flat roofs, the dull monotony of grey wall broken here and there by layers of dark blue and red bricks, let in in alternate bands, or by the interposition of dark polished reeds between the clay bricks, that had the effect of courses of black marble. The interior of these houses must have been somewhat dark and dull, for the walls were immensely thick and the rooms small, and lighted only by windows close to the roof; but the Chaldeans were always a people who loved to live in the open air, and when not engaged in outdoor occupations they probably spent their time on the roofs of their houses, protected by awnings, and only used the inside chambers for sleeping apartments and for storerooms. The handsomest houses had inscriptions, and perhaps rude pictures over their doorways, and were supported by buttresses of red or dark blue burnt brick; but the object in the town, which attracted every eye, and served as a landmark to sailors far out at sea, and to travellers approaching Ur from the plains or the desert, was the gigantic temple, erected probably during Abraham's youth by King Urukh, the great builder of the first monarchy, in honour of Hurki, the moon god. It could not, as far as we can judge by its remains, have ever had any beauty of architectural design or ornamentation to recommend it, but its gigantic proportions, and the long flights of wide shallow steps that led up to its several terraces, must have given it a grand and imposing appearance. It stood on an artificial mound thirty feet high, probably in the centre of the town, which may have been laid out in gardens or planted with rows of trees—a four-sided, oblong-shaped building, its angles exactly facing the four cardinal points of the compass. The sides, which were faced with burnt brick of a dark red colour, sloped upwards pyramid-wise to the height of thirty-seven feet: this composed the first story, the roof of which was approached from all the four sides by immense flights of steps nine feet wide, stretching up from the platform below. A second story rested on this first structure, but it was so much smaller in size that a wide terrace was left between its base and the outer ledge of the first building.

What a favourite walk this terrace must have been with the inhabitants of Ur, in the cool of the evening and late on into the night, when the heavenly bodies, which they regarded with so much awe, were shining with the peculiar brilliancy that the clear air of that climate imparts to them. And what a view they must have had from thence at sunrise, looking southwards over the brightening waters of the Gulf, and north, east, and west, over the richly cultivated level land where the horizon line was broken by other massive towers rising as high, or even higher, into the blue heaven. The second story did not stand quite in the middle of the roof of the first; it approached the north-western edge by about ten feet nearer than the south-eastern, on which side it is supposed (for no trace of such a thing now remains) that a flight of steps, rising thirty or forty feet, led up to the roof of the second story, on which at length there rested the edifice to which all this immense pile was but the approach—a single comparatively small chamber, richly ornamented, where stood the shrine of the moon god. Probably none but the priests and the king, who in Chaldea as in Egypt united the characters of priest and monarch, ever mounted this last flight of steps, or was permitted to enter the secret chamber that had been lifted away from the common earth up towards heaven at the cost of so much labour. There does not appear to have been anything inside the two lower stories but solid brickwork; and, hidden away in the four corners of the basement-story (luckily for us), the four cylindrical pillars of sun-dried clay, graven all over with minute cuneiform writing, from which Sir Henry Rawlinson has deciphered the history of the building, the name of the city, and many other important matters as well.

Like the ancient Egyptian cities with which we are acquainted, the architecture of Ur did not end with the dwelling-places and temples of the living; there was rising up round it, increasing year by year, and beginning to look important even in Abraham's time, also a city of the dead. At a little distance from where the brick houses and reed huts ended, a succession of low mounds began, stretching out on all sides of the town to the open country. These were the tenements of the dead; within these artificial elevations the bodies of the departed, enclosed in clay coffins of various constructions, were ranged tier above tier—each mound being probably the burial-place of a family or tribe. Some of the hillocks enclosed vaulted chambers built of burnt brick, within which the dead body, dressed as in life, was laid, reposing on the right side, the arms falling crosswise towards each other, the fingers of one hand resting on a copper bowl, while at the head and foot were disposed dishes of delicate food, vases of wine, valued articles of furniture, and ornaments that had decked the person of the deceased in his lifetime. Other bodies, also richly dressed and surrounded with their treasures, were disposed singly on what may be called enormous dishes of coarse clay, and roofed in with a clay cover cemented to the dish with bitumen. The common cheap form of burial was to enclose the body within two large clay vessels cemented together with bitumen; these coffins were ranged in layers one above the other, separated by tiers of unburnt brick, and roofed in with brick-work when the mound was completed.

In later times of Chaldean history, when the shores of the Persian Gulf had ceased to be the seat of empire, the inhabitants of Higher Mesopotamia appear to have regarded these first settlements of their ancestors with such peculiar veneration as to make them the burial-places of the whole country. Ur and Erech were to the Babylonians what the Western hills were to the people of Egypt, and the Valley of Jehoshaphat to the Jews—the chosen last home of the entire nation. And so when the grand temple and the unburnt brick houses had come to be little thought of and the waters of the Persian Gulf had left the busy harbour choked with sand, the city behind the city grew and grew.

Erech, now called Warka, a ruin about twenty miles from Mugheir, was a still more celebrated burial-place than Ur. It is supposed to be the place to which the Babylonian priests referred when they told Alexander the Great that all the old Babylonian kings were taken away to be buried in the marsh-lands of the low country. Some trace of its old character lingers about it yet, for the Arabs who live near shun the place after dark, considering it to be the favourite haunt of spirits.

The inhabitants of Ur and of the other cities of Southern Chaldea in ancient times appear to have comprised several distinct races of people. In the inscriptions on the bricks and cylinders the early kings designate their subjects as the four nations, or the four tongues. Sir Henry Rawlinson conjectures that these four elements in the population of the Persian Gulf cities correspond to the followers of the four kings who, in Abraham's time, invaded Palestine from Lower Mesopotamia. Chedorlaomer, the chief power in the country, was more especially followed by the Hamite descendants of the first settlers on the shores of the Gulf, who originally came from Ethiopia. Tidal, king of nations, led the tribes of a wandering Scythian people, who, at some far back period, had penetrated into Chaldea from the north. Arioch and Amraphel were the chiefs of the Aryan and Shemite races, who were the original inhabitants of the country.

Specimens of all these races dwelt or sojourned in the cities of Lower Chaldea, and were claimed as subjects by the first Chaldean kings — warlike Scythians; peaceful Shemite shepherds, who resorted to the neighbourhood of the towns with their flocks and herds, as wandering Arab tribes do now to the vicinity of Damascus and other large towns in times of war or famine; Cushite traders whose "cry was in the ships."

CHAPTER II.

ABRAHAM'S FATHER.

TERAH was, as we know, a Shemite, and may probably have been driven to take shelter in or near Ur, with his possessions, on the breaking out of some war or the appearance of some fierce marauding Scythian invaders in the districts he and his tribe had been accustomed to wander over. A very old and generally received Arabian tradition, however, describes Terah, or Azer, as he is called by Arabic writers, as having been, not a shepherd king like his son Abraham, but a carver and seller of idols in the town of Ur. Some rabbinical writers even say that he was the high priest and head of an order of idol carvers. No remains of bas-reliefs representing the figures of gods or heroes, such as might have given us an idea of what Terah's idols were like, have as yet been found among the remains of the Persian Gulf cities. But the cylinders discovered in the temples of Ur and Erech, and many of the bricks of the tombs and buildings, are covered with writing in the cuneiform character. If there was an order of priestly idol carvers in Ur, the engraving of these inscriptions which set forth the titles and attributes of the gods, and the services the king had rendered to them, would probably form part of the duties of their office.

The cylinders and bricks of Ur, some of which are now in the British Museum, do not need the supposition that Terah may possibly have had something to do with the graving of them to make them interesting. Apart from the information they give, the discovery of this early writing is important because it enables us to trace some of the stages through which the cuneiform character passed in its progress from rude picture-writing like that which the Mexicans used, to a system of signs, most of which have a settled phonetic value.

The change from writing to printing surely does not mark such an interval in human intelligence as that which divides the men striving to express their thoughts by rude likenesses of the objects with which they were occupied, and those to whom the idea of using signs to convey sounds and so spell words had come. The first man who spelt a word, was not he the greatest of all inventors? Early history, or rather mythology, busies itself about him in its cloudy symbolic way, and presents him to us under many different names and in various characters. He is Oannes, half man and half fish, coming up from the Persian Gulf with the alphabet in his hand for the Chaldeans; he is Ibis-headed Thoth, "the great and great;" "the three times great," recording events with reed pen on papyrus rolls; he is Hermes, with wings on his head and feet; he is grave Odin, ruthlessly tearing out his right eye for the draught of wisdom-water that brought his sixteen runes to his mind. In these, and in many other forms besides, the fame of this man, and the gratitude mankind felt for him, are dimly shadowed forth.

The great step of using signs to express sounds had been made by the Chaldeans long before the time of the earliest inscription that has yet been found. It is supposed that the settlers on the shores of the Persian Gulf brought the knowledge with them from their first home. Oannes or Thoth flourished apparently when the ancient Egyptians and Chaldeans lived together, and the two nations worked out the invention after their separation, each in its own fashion, the Egyptians retaining much more of picture and symbol in their writing than did the Chaldeans.

Urukh's bricks are in the second stage of progress of which we have any examples. On some other bricks, which bear the name of an earlier monarch, the characters have not the wedge-shaped form of ordinary cuneiform writing; they are simply straight lines of a uniform thickness, which in some cases still rudely outline the object for whose name they stand, picturing the thing itself instead of spelling its name. Thus four lines enclosing a space signify a house; an eight-rayed star stands for a god; five lines of different lengths for a hand; a rude drawing of a comb symbolizes the female sex.

In Urukh's time the thick lines had changed into wedges, but the signs for a house, a god, &c., have still a semblance of pictured representation. In later cuneiform writing all trace of resemblance has passed away. Signs are in many cases still placed before spelt words, but they no longer have the smallest likeness to the things themselves; they serve no other purpose apparently than our capital letters, and show that an important word is coming. The sign placed before the name of a god is no longer an eight-rayed star, it is a group of three wedges stuck into each other; the comb, the female determinative, is a heap of wedges with hardly any shape at all; the sign for a house no longer suggests a ground-plan, it is three large wedges with two little ones stuck into them. No one could have guessed that any of these words had ever been pictures if we had not seen on Urukh's bricks, and those of his predecessors, the transitions through which they had passed, and learned that the determinative signs put before words in cuneiform character are actually relics of a time when the two systems of writing—pictorial representation and spelling by letters—were used together to help each other out.

More interesting, however, than the question how the inscriptions are written is, What do they tell us? What sort of events did people four thousand years ago think worthy to be recorded on the foundation-bricks of their temples and graven on clay pillars, which they hid away for better preservation under mountains of earth? One cannot help being disappointed at first to find such carefully preserved histories so meagre and monotonous, recording the same class of events in much the same language over and over again. It is, "Urukh king of Ur is he who has built a temple to the moon god;" or, "The sun god, his lord, has caused Urukh, the pious chief of the land of the Akkad, to build a temple to him;" or, "The moon god, brother's son of Anu, and eldest son of Belus, has caused Urukh, the pious chief of Ur, to build the temple of his holy place." The first Chaldean temple builders have fared just as the pyramid kings would have done if there had been no Herodotus to tell us a few pleasant gossipy stories about them; they have left names behind them, indeed, but the most painstaking and ingenious students of antiquities are puzzled to piece together a history to fit on to the names. Of this Urukh and his son Ilgi, who were contemporaries of Terah and Abraham, little can be said except that they reigned, and began and finished nearly all the great temples in Lower Chaldea.

Yet the inscriptions they caused to be graven, little as they tell us about themselves, deserve some gratitude from us to them, for they throw considerable light on a subject that interests us much more nearly than any king's character or history. From the names of the gods enumerated, and from the titles that accompany the names, we learn something of what people were thinking about God and the gods at that very early time. The Bible tells us that Terah and Abraham, before the Call, worshipped the gods of their fathers; tradition represents Terah as having actually been engaged in the temple worship. We may well be thankful to Urukh's bricks for giving us some contemporary information about what it was they worshipped, what were the notions respecting the Divine nature that Abraham shared before the

Call came that made all things new to him. We have said that the temple inscriptions show us what people, in Urukh's time, were thinking about God and the gods; and though the thought can be only dimly traced, it does appear that even in those early days some such division of the objects of reverence existed. They had gods to whom they reared temples, whom they served fearfully, hoping to secure their co-operation in war, their protection in time of peace; gods whom they identified more or less with the heavenly bodies—the sun, moon, and planets—and to whom they believed the government of all earthly transactions had been entrusted; but above and beyond these, they thought, or rather perhaps we should say felt, that there was some One else; some One the perfection of whose attributes neither the glory of the sun, nor the tranquil loveliness of the moon, nor the sheen of the planets could adequately show forth; some One who dwelt apart, far beyond the reach of the feeble prayers and praises of short-lived men separated from His passionless perfection by such vast intervals of Being. **Il, or Ra,** God, the Lord, the Chaldeans called Him, mentioning Him for the most part by implication only, in connection with other more accessible deities, who were thought to have derived their being **from Him** in far back æons of eternity.

Of this Perfect, Inaccessible One, Il, the God whom no man might venture to approach with prayer or praise, Abraham must have heard in his childhood. He must have known how men thought of Him as of a Being too far off to interest them, or to be interested in them. **Perhaps this** knowledge may have enhanced the wonder **and gratitude in** his heart when the great hour of his life came, and it was revealed to him, one man out of all the world, that the Eternal One was not far off, but close at hand; **so close** that a man **might** hear His voice and hold communion with Him, and be called His friend. For Abraham the vast interval was bridged over, the distant **dweller in** eternity became **the** ever-present Leader and Guide. Il, the first cause, revealed Himself as Elohim, the first, the last, the all, God and the gods, in whom all the powers and attributes that **men** were worshipping under various names, and degrading by dividing, were gathered up.

No temple ever appears to **have** been erected to Il in Lower Chaldea, **but one of the** earliest Chaldean cities, Babel, the gate **of** Il, was called by **His name,** and perhaps placed under His special protection.

The divinities whom the Chaldeans regarded as objects of worship were either personifications of the heavenly bodies **and the** appearances of the sky and atmosphere, or were connected **with** burial rites and the abodes of the dead. Like **the** Egyptian gods, **they** have different degrees **of** importance, and **the** first two orders contain each a group of three who were worshipped together. **The** gods **of the first** order are Anu, Bil, and **Hea.** The first and the last of these appear to be connected with death and life; with "a far-off land," "a great deep," **which** is not the sea, but something vaster **and more** unfathomable.

Anu is the head of the triad, and in him the character of lord of departed spirits is most strongly marked. Erech, the great burial city, is especially dedicated to him. He is a melancholy sort of divinity, and his titles are gloomy enough: "Anu the old," "the original chief," "the ruler of a far-off city," "the lord of darkness and death," "the king of the lower world." He is also strangely enough the lord of the earth and mountains, the storer of the precious metals, and the layer up of treasures.

Bil, the second member of this triad, is supposed to be the deification of Nimrod, the founder of the Chaldean monarchy. He is called the lord of all spirits, alive and dead; the lord of all lands. Kingship is his special attribute. The city where he was chiefly worshipped was Calneh, where the remains of an immense temple dedicated to him have been found.

Hea, the last member of the triad, is a much more interesting personage. His name has an affinity with an Arabic word that signifies at once life and serpent; and Sir H. Rawlinson says that there are very strong grounds for connecting him with the serpent of Scripture and the paradisaical traditions of the tree of knowledge and the tree of life. Berosus calls him Oannes, and relates how, in a very confused early time, when men in Chaldea lived like the beasts of the field, a mystic animal, half man and half fish, but speaking with the voice of a man, rose every morning from the Persian Gulf and spent the day in teaching the Chaldeans letters and arts; acquainting them also with the events of the far back time before the present race of men existed on the earth; with the age of darkness and water; with the four-winged, two-faced monsters, part men and part bulls and lions, who wallowed in the deep before light and the solid land were created—monsters whose images, Berosus says, were preserved on the walls of Chaldean temples down to his day. During the day Oannes held such discourse with men, but he never condescended to eat with them; and at night he always returned to his home in the sea.

Perhaps the memory of some early inventor, whose discoveries gave a great impulse to the advancement of mankind, may have mixed itself up with the Chaldean's conception of this being; yet he is evidently much more than the deification of a hero: mystical thoughts about life—about life, that is, somehow connected with death—seem to be struggling to express themselves in him. He is lord of the abyss, and he is lord of life. The serpent is his symbol and one meaning of his name, and he gives knowledge to mankind. He is the intelligent fish, the god of glory, the god of giving. This looks like a faint reflex of the history related in the third chapter of Genesis, where the serpent, most subtle of the beasts of the fields, tempts the first woman with the fruit of the tree of knowledge.

The members of the second triad are Hurki, San, and Vul; the moon, sun, and atmosphere. The moon god stands before the sun god in Chaldean mythology, and has the greatest honours paid him; perhaps because in a country where, as travellers tell us, the heat is so oppressive that birds sit on the date-trees with their mouths open panting for breath, the night is better loved than the day. Hurki was the great god of Ur; its immense temple was erected in his honour, and the chief religious worship of its inhabitants must have been paid to him. By the priests who had the privilege of entering the sanctuary on the upper terrace of the temple, service was paid to some image, probably a human figure with the new moon on his head; by the people who thronged the lower terraces it was offered to the full "moon walking in brightness," or to the slender silver bow shining faintly in the purple sky. San, the sun god, had a great temple built to him by King Urukh at Ellasar. His symbol was a disk quartered, or filled with a drawing of a four-leaved flower. Vul was called the lord of tempests and of the air, and carried thunder and lightning in his hand. All the gods of these orders have goddesses associated with them, but none of them appears to have had any distinguishing characteristic except Beltis, the wife of Bil, who represents the principle of fertility, and answers to the Egyptian Isis and the Grecian Ceres.

Next in order of reverence to the gods of the second triad come five divinities identified with the five planets visible to the naked eye, which at that time, and for many centuries afterwards, were supposed to exercise peculiar influences over the earth and the fortunes of its inhabitants—Nebo, Ishtar, Nergal, Bel-Merodach, Nin, the Chaldeans called them, assigning to each planet much the same character as it maintained ever afterwards under various names, in the mythologies of different people, down to that far-off northern mythology from whence we get the designations of the last five days of our week.

Nebo—like Hermes, Mercury, and Odin—is the "lover of light," the god who possesses intelligence; he who hears from afar; he who instructs; he who prophesies. Ishtar (Astarte, Ashtoreth, Aphrodite, Venus, Freya) is the queen, the fortunate, the happy, she who rejoices mankind; the mistress of earth and heaven; the lover and mourner of the day.

Nergal (Aria, Ares, Mars, Tyr) is the king of battles, the storm-ruler, the champion. His name comes from two words which signify a man and great. His symbol was a winged, man-headed lion.

Bel-Merodach (Zeus, Jupiter, Thor) has the character of a powerful ruler and judge. He is the "old man of the gods," "the great lord," "the most ancient." The gates of the city, where in old times justice was dispensed, were dedicated to him. In later times Bel-Merodach became a chief object of worship. It was his image (according to Diodorus, a figure "standing and walking") which is mentioned in the apocryphal story of Bel and the Dragon. Nin (Saturn) was the fish-god of whom we see so many pictures on the Ninevite marbles. He has also for his emblem the winged, man-headed bull, the impersonation of strength, two of which were placed as guardians at the entrance of the king's palaces. There is no evidence that he was worshipped in early times, though he occupied so conspicuous a place in the Pantheon of the second empire.

There are some Arabic traditions about Abraham's childhood, which, though probably not more than two thousand years old, have a certain interest for us in connection with the worship which the people of his native city paid to the sun, moon, and planets. Abraham is said to have been persecuted by Nimrod, who in all the traditional stories is supposed to have reigned over Chaldea in the patriarch's time. The king's jealousy had been excited by a dream, in which Abraham's future greatness had been revealed to him; and to save the child's life, his mother was obliged to hide him for many months in a cave. "On stepping for the first time beyond the cave, and seeing a beautiful star, Abraham said, 'This is my God, which has given me meat and drink in the cave.' Yet anon the moon arose in full splendour, exceeding the light of the star, and he said, 'This is not God, I will worship the moon.' But when towards morning the moon waxed more and more pale, and the sun rose, he acknowledged the latter as a divinity, till he also disappeared from the horizon. He then asked his mother, 'Who is my god?' and she replied, 'It is I.' 'And who is thy god?' he inquired further. 'Thy father.' 'And who is my father's god?' 'Nimrod.' 'And Nimrod's god?' She then struck him on the face, and said, 'Be silent.' He was silent, but thought within himself, 'I acknowledge no other God than Him who has created heaven and earth and all that is in them.'"

Abraham's contempt for idols, and the punishment which his open avowal of his belief in one God brought upon him from Nimrod, is the subject of a widely spread Jewish legend.

"Terah was an idol-carver," the story runs, "and when he set out one day on a journey, he appointed Abraham to sell his idols in his stead. 'What is the price of that god?' asked an old man, who entered to make a purchase. 'Old man,' said Abraham, 'may I be permitted to ask thine age?' 'Three score years,' replied the idolater. 'Three score years!' exclaimed Abraham, 'and thou wouldst worship a thing that has been fashioned by the hands of my father's slaves! Woe to the man of sixty who bows down his grey head to the creature of a day!' So the man was ashamed, and went away. After this came a grave sedate matron, with a bowl of flour, and said, 'Set it before them, and beg them to look upon me with favour.' But after she had gone away he took a staff and broke all the idols, and placed the staff in the hands of the largest of them.

"When his father returned he inquired, 'Who has done this?' Abraham said, 'Why should I deny it? There was a woman here with a bowl of fine flour, and she directed me to set it before them. When I did so, the younger gods, who had not tasted food for a long time, greedily stretched out their hands and began to eat before the old god had given them permission; then arose the old one, and demolished them with the staff.' Terah said, 'What fable art thou telling me? Have they any understanding? Do I not know that they can neither eat, nor stir, nor move?' 'And yet,' said Abraham, 'thou payest them divine honours, and wouldst have me worship them!' Whereupon Terah was **angry and** took him and delivered him unto Nimrod, who urged him to worship the fire.

"'Great king,' said Abraham, 'would it not **be** better to worship the water that quenches the fire?'

"'Worship the water then,' said Nimrod.

"'Methinks it would be more reasonable to worship the clouds that carry the water.'

"'Well then, worship the clouds.'

"'Nay, ought **we not** rather to worship the wind which scatters the clouds, and drives them before it?'

"'Worship the wind, and we pardon thee.'

"'Be not angry, great king; is not man even greater, for he endures the wind?'

"'Thou art a babbler,' replied the king; 'I worship the fire, and will cast thee into it. May the God thou adorest deliver thee thence.'"

The Arabic account of Abraham's deliverance from the furnace into which Nimrod threw him on this occasion is pretty, and was probably originally taken from a rabbinical source.

"At the same instant when Abraham was thrown **into** the burning furnace, heaven with all its angels, **and** earth with all its creatures, cried as with one **voice,** 'God of Abraham, Thy friend, who alone worships Thee on earth, is being thrown into a furnace; permit us to rescue him.' But God said, 'I permit every one of you to whom Abraham shall cry for assistance to help **him;** yet **if he turn** only to me, let me, by my own immediate aid, rescue him from death.' Then cried Abraham **from** the midst of the fire, 'There is no God beside Thee! To Thee belong praise and glory!' The flame, meanwhile, had consumed Abraham's robe, when the angel Gabriel stepped before him, and asked, 'Hast thou need of me?' Abraham replied, 'The help of God alone is what I need.' 'Pray, then, to Him, that He may save thee,' replied Gabriel. 'He knows my condition,' said Abraham.

"All the creatures of the earth now attempted to quench the fire; the lizard alone blew upon it, and as a punishment became dumb from that hour. At God's command Gabriel then cried to the fire, 'Become cool, and do Abraham no harm.' The fire lost all its warmth at these words, and God caused a fountain of fresh water to spring up in the midst of the furnace, and roses and other flowers to bloom round the spot where Abraham was lying. He likewise sent him a silken robe from paradise, and an angel in human shape, who kept him company during seven days. So long did Abraham remain in the fire; and these seven days he was accustomed in after years to call the most precious of his life."

These are but legendary tales, interesting to us because they tell us something of the thoughts that gathered round the venerable figure of Abraham in the minds of his Jewish and Arabian descendants; but they have too little agreement with the impression the Bible narrative gives us of the condition of Abraham's family, while dwelling in Ur, for us to consider them as throwing any real light on his early history.

We do not know exactly at what period in Abraham's life the impulse came to Terah to leave the shelter of the grey walls of Ur, and the neighbourhood of the sea, and journey northwards with his family, but it was doubtless just at the moment when the lessons which the civilization of Ur was designed to teach him had been learned, and the influence of the solitary, wandering, shepherd life was needed to prepare Abraham for the revelation that was ultimately to come to him. He could not have been very young; Haran, his elder brother, was dead, having married and left a son, and he himself had apparently been some time married to his relative Sarai.

It is still a very common custom among the Arabs for cousins to marry. The women in the desert go unveiled, and have much greater freedom than their sisters in the towns; but even there the intercourse between men and women is circumscribed, and the man who wishes to know anything of the character of the woman he marries must choose her from among his own connections, the frequenters of his mother's tent, to which, at least in his childhood and early youth, he has had free access. It was probably much the same among the wandering Shemite shepherd tribes in Abraham's time. He chose in Sarai the woman whose character he knew best, and whom he could love most truly.

It would be in the spring-time, after the winter rains were over, when even the uncultivated lands yielded a short-lived growth of thymy, sweet-scented herbage for the nourishment of the flocks and herds, that Terah must have commenced his journey. The circumstances attending the journey of an Arab chieftain across the desert have been so often described that it is not difficult to picture the appearance which Terah and his party presented on their pilgrimage from Ur to Haran. Long lines of camels carrying the tent-furniture and the women and children, the men with staves in their hands walking by the side; the wide straggling flocks, each division following its appropriate guardian; the black goats, the white sheep, the tawny buffalo cows, with the calves following or led by the boys and girls of the tribe; the lowing and bleating, the tinkling of camel-bells filling the air; then the stoppage at night, the pitching of the chieftain's tent, the kindling of the low-burning fires of camel's-dung, the bruising of the corn, the brown faces of the women, with the glow of firelight on them, as they stoop to turn the flat cakes baking on the embers —quiet at last, as the sheep are herded, and the cattle and camels tethered for the night, and intense stillness reigning over the scene till sunrise, with the tent-curtains close drawn, the weary animals reposing in circles round the silent watchers seated by the fires, nothing stirring but the moon in its stately march across the solid-looking purple dome that roofs the unbroken level plain, and the stars rising and falling. During the first part of Terah's journey, while he was still in the neighbourhood of the great cities, his route would lie along embankments raised above the level of the watered fields, in order to prevent the communication between the towns being interrupted when the rivers overflowed in the rainy season. He would pass by several Chaldean walled towns as great, or even greater, than Ur, each with its **city of** tombs encircling it without the walls, and its central temple towering to the sky. As the travellers proceeded northwards, the daily lessening and vanishing one after the other of these elevations would mark the progress of their journey. Then the outline of the Sinjar hills would dawn upon them from the north, the rich alluvial flat of Chaldea would be left behind, and they would enter a country bearing fewer marks of cultivation. A low-lying range of limestone hills would, after many days **of** travel, break the monotonous character of the scenery; and passing **beyond** these, they would gain yet another plain of higher elevation and richer soil — Padan Aram, the well-watered and fair table-land of Syria—the field **of** Aram, as the name signifies. The centre of this fertile district afforded a permanent resting-place to Terah and a portion of the tribe. Josephus tells us that Terah left Ur on account of the sorrow he felt for the loss of his son Haran. **It** was at a place named Haran that, after his wanderings, Terah again settled, and where he passed the remaining years of his life. It seems not improbable that he and his sons were the founders of the town that remained for many generations the head-quarters of the tribe. **They** came to a fertile, tree-shaded spot, rich **in** wells; **and,** weary with wandering, they pitched their tents there. And Terah called **the** place by the name of his dead son, and could not leave it afterwards, **till** death came and restored him to him **he mourned.**

CHAPTER III

ABRAHAM'S WANDERINGS.

It was after Terah's death that the command came to Abraham to leave his own people and his father's house, and go into a strange land that God would show him. The tribe had settled again, and Haran was becoming to them as much a permanent dwelling-place as ever Ur had been; the old heathen beliefs were taking root in the new home. They had not the great moon-god's temple, but they had brought images of their gods with them, and no doubt established rites of worship. This second smaller Ur, with its heathen associations, and population of settled Arabs, was not to be for any length of time a resting-place for Abraham. That voice came to him, whose command made him a stranger and a wanderer all the rest of his life, and for all future ages a memory that lives in Eastern and Western homes alike, under the titles of closest affection, "Father" and "Friend" —the Father of the Faithful, and the Friend of God. It is not the personal history of Abraham with which we are at present concerned, but the condition of the different nations among whom he, the first of the chosen people, sojourned; we must not therefore linger over this crisis in his life, surpassing as is its importance in the world's history. A few verses in the Bible contain the narrative. "Now God had said unto Abraham, Get thee out of thy country, and from thy kindred, and from thy father's house, unto a land that I will show thee. . . . So Abraham departed as the Lord had told him. . . . And Abraham took Sarai his wife, and Lot his brother's son, and all the substance they had gathered; and they went forth to go into the land of Canaan; and into the land of Canaan they came. And the Canaanite was then in the land."

Very little is known about the condition of the inhabitants of Canaan when Abraham came to dwell among them. Later on we have pictures on Egyptian temples and monuments describing the wars of the Egyptian kings in Palestine, which show us a thickly populated country, with high-walled towns perched on every hill-top, and valleys crowded with cattle and shaded with groves of ilex and palm-trees. In Abraham's time these same people were still in the nomadic stage. They were divided then, as afterwards, into hill-tribes and valley-tribes, and the more settled and civilized dwellers by the sea, who, in the north of Palestine, were already laying the foundations of the great maritime cities of Sidon and Aradus, and developing the enterprising spirit that afterwards made the name of Canaanite synonymous with trader. Living among these tribes were remnants of an ancient giant race, whose existence is only known to us by a few obscure allusions to them in the sacred writings, and by the meanings of some names of places in Palestine, which preserved the tradition of their occupation of the country to a late period—Zamzummim, Emim, Anakim, Rephaim, strange, uncouth-sounding names of a race whose origin and history is involved in impenetrable mystery.

The chief seats of these ancient giant tribes appear to have been the high lands on the eastern side of Jordan and the country about Hebron (Kirjath-arba, "the city of the giant Arba"), where, up to the time of Joshua, their descendants were still to be found. The gigantic Og king of Bashan, a descendant of the Zamzummim, ruled over the Amorites, who had superseded the giant people in the east of Palestine; and in the south, the sons of Anak, "great men and tall," were still numerous enough to strike terror into the spies sent by Moses, and to make them seem as grasshoppers in their own sight. While Abraham was living in Palestine the ancient people on the east side of Jordan sustained a great overthrow at the hands of Chedorlaomer, the most warlike king of the first Babylonian empire, who had by this time succeeded Urukh's son Ilgi on the throne. For twelve years they consented to pay tribute and acknowledge the supremacy of the Cushite king. At the end of that time an attempt at rebellion on their part brought Chedorlaomer again into Palestine. In conjunction with three confederate, or more probably tributary, kings, he swept across the country, conquering all before him, from the northern regions about Damascus to the circle of five Canaanitish cities in the south of the Jordan valley, whose ruins lie now beneath the waters of the Dead Sea. Lot, Abraham's nephew, was residing in Sodom when the city was taken by the Chaldeans, and was carried off captive by Chedorlaomer among the other spoil of the city. This peril of his nephew caused Abraham to be once more brought into contact with the people among whom he had lived, and by whom, tradition says, he had been persecuted in his youth. At the head of his armed followers, and aided by his confederates the Amorite chiefs—Mamre and Eshcol and Aner—Abraham pursued the Chaldean army, as they were returning home overladen with spoil, as far north as the neighbourhood of Damascus, conquered them in a night attack, and succeeded in driving them from the country, and despoiling them of the fruits of their former victories. He was met on his return by the kings of the districts whose independence his valour had restored, the king of Sodom, and the mysterious Melchizedek, king of Salem, "priest of the most high God," whose authority as chief priest of the country, maintaining the primitive doctrine of the unity of God amid the growing confusions and idolatries of the Canaanitish tribes, Abraham, the friend and chosen of God, acknowledged by offering him a tithe of the spoil, and received his blessing. Our knowledge of these rulers and their people is entirely confined to what we can learn from the notices of them contained in the Bible narrative. But at one period of Abraham's life he was led into a country and among a people about whose condition, even at that early period, profane history has a great deal to tell us. A famine fell on the land of Canaan while he sojourned there, and, to procure food for his numerous flocks and herds, Abraham journeyed across the desert to the fertile lowlands of Northern Egypt, the natural resort of the pastoral tribes of Palestine and Arabia when the herbage of their chalk hills and sandy plains failed them.

He cannot have been the first Arab chieftain who was driven by stress of famine into Egypt, for the records of the age of the Pyramids show that at a much earlier date than can be assigned to his visit a great amount of intercourse was carried on between the Egyptians and the nomadic people of Arabia and Palestine; but the ease with which he entered the country, and the hospitable entertainment he received, are proofs that he came at a time when the appearance of an Arab tribe pitching their tents on the unenclosed land, still caused no alarm to the peaceful agriculturists of the Delta—possibly gave them pleasure, as affording opportunity for bartering the surplus of their provisions for the gums, spices, honey, skins of wild animals, and precious metals that the wandering people brought with them.

On one of the rock-tombs at Beni Hassan, which, according to the best authorities, were excavated about the time when Abraham was in Egypt, there is a picture of the introduction of a party of Asiatic travellers into the presence of an Egyptian lord, which may not unfitly represent to us some of the occurrences of Abraham's journey. The strangers whom the great man in the picture on the tomb is in the act of welcoming appear to have come from a distant country, for their complexion, dress, and general appearance differ greatly from that of the Egyptians who receive them; and they seem to be people of some consequence, for a herald walks before to usher them into the presence of the lord of the district, who receives them seated on a chair of state. The chief of the strangers, bare-headed, bows low to the Egyptian lord, and offers him a mountain goat as a present; an attendant drags forward another goat; behind come the women and children, escorted by a band of armed men of their tribe, the children seated in panniers across a donkey's back, the women walking unveiled and dressed in handsome dresses of several colours; a man with a lyre in his hand brings up the rear of the procession. The light complexions and aquiline features by which these people are distinguished in the picture show that they are meant for natives of Asia; and as mention is made on the wall of a neighbouring tomb of a famine which the ruler of the district had relieved by a distribution of corn from the hoarded stores in his granaries, their journey may be conjectured to have had the same object as that of Abraham—the search for food.

It was usually a failure of the spring rains that brought scarcity into Canaan; and as Egypt was independent of rain, and indebted only to its great river for its fertility, as its priests long afterwards boasted to Herodotus, the short journey across the rocky desert would bring the travellers fleeing from want into the midst of most cheering plenty. "As the garden of the Lord, like the land of Egypt as thou comest unto Zoan."[1] When the author of Genesis wishes to give us an idea of the beauty of the scene that dazzled Lot's eyes when, long after his return from Egypt, he beheld all the plain of Jordan and chose it for his residence, it is in these words that he sets forth its fertility; evidently recalling to mind the first view of the green rice-fields and rich marsh meadows of Lower Egypt, as they break on the eyes of weary travellers approaching the frontier town of Zoan or Avaris from the desert.

A place for moving tents, or for going forth, the Hebrew and the Egyptian names signify; the first resting-place and the last spot on which wayfarers lingered before they exchanged the well-watered lands on one side of the town for the arid dusty ways that stretched to its opposite horizon. Zoan must have been a town of note when Abraham passed by it, for we are told that it was built seven years before Hebron or Kirjath-arba, one of the oldest cities of Canaan; and there is reason to suppose it was a royal residence as far back as in the times of the Twelfth Dynasty. Its first aspect may have recalled some of the scenes of Abraham's early youth to his mind, for its high walls and houses of unburnt brick would wear the same grey hue as those of Ur, and there would be the quays on the river-side of the town, and the square-sailed boats passing up and down the branch of the Nile on which the city stood, to remind him of his first home.

[1] Zoan, for Zoar, by an easy change of one letter—a probable reading.

The landscape seen from the walls of Zoan, too, would have many features of resemblance with that of Southern Chaldea. There would be the same wide extent of richly cultivated land stretching southwards as far as the eye could reach, intersected with silvery watercourses crossing and recrossing each other among golden patches of corn and green rice-fields, and purple flower-gardens of lupins. Elevations would break the horizon line, where a grey city lifted its palm groves and its temple crown high above the particoloured level, like islands rising out of the sea; but the artificial mounds on which the Egyptian temples stood would be less massive than those of Chaldea, and the buildings themselves more shapely and varied. Groups of low truncated pyramids, with here and there one of greater dimensions, would attract the eye, stretching westward from every palm grove in which a cluster of houses was hidden; and in the vicinity of the town, among the cultivated fields, solitary farmhouses with their gardens, vineyards, fish-ponds, and long rows of round-topped granaries, would form a feature of beauty and prosperity in the landscape which the less secure country of Southern Chaldea in Urukh's time could not have matched. To the north of the city lay the field of Zoan, as the wide extent of marsh country lying between the city of Zoan and the coast was called. In this open country the Arab tribes coming from the desert in search of food would pitch their tents, and here Abraham probably chiefly resided during his sojourn in Egypt.

Dotted over by vast herds of cattle and countless flocks of sheep, these monotonous, peaceful marsh lands, whose level surface was only broken here and there by a single palm-tree, or patch of graceful flowering reeds bowing their heads in the sea-breeze, had a beauty of their own not inferior to that of the more cultivated part of the country. They were, at all events, much esteemed and loved by the ancient Egyptians; for Herodotus tells us that when Mycerinus, the king who built the Third Pyramid, wished to make the most of the short term of life the oracle allotted to him, he determined to spend his time "in moving about in the marsh country, and visiting all the places that he had heard were agreeable sojourns."

In some part of this favoured district lay the land of Goshen, which in after-times was assigned to Abraham's descendants to wander over with their flocks and herds. Here, dwelling somewhat apart from the Egyptians, the Children of Israel grew into a great and powerful people under the protection of the royal dynasty whom Joseph had served; here they were subsequently oppressed and enslaved; and here, "in the field of Zoan," were wrought the "wonders of the Lord" that brought about their deliverance. The Pharaoh of the Exodus was evidently residing in Zoan when Moses came to him from Midian, and when the children of Israel on the night of the Passover escaped from the country; and it is probable that the Egyptian king of Abraham's time was holding a summer court in his pleasant northern capital when his princess praised Sarah's beauty before him, and when the incidents recorded in Genesis, which brought Abraham into connection with the Egyptian monarch, took place.

CHAPTER IV.

ABRAHAM IN EGYPT.

THE Egyptian kings of the early dynasties are so little more to us than mere names, that we should hardly care to know which name to assign to the ruler Abraham saw. Our knowledge of Egyptian manners and customs in these early times is gathered almost wholly from the pictures and inscriptions on certain groups of monuments which were erected at periods separated from each other by considerable spaces of time. A few hundred years in the intervals between the periods thus illustrated would alter little in any portrait of Egyptian life we could frame for ourselves.

The most ancient series of scene-pictures in the long illustrated gallery of national history which Egyptian builders have left behind them is to be found on the walls of the tombs round the Pyramids, which were finished and closed up long before Abraham's time. The second group of pictures was painted on the rock tombs of Beni Hassan some centuries later, when the Twelfth Dynasty of kings were ruling in Egypt; one of whom Baron

Bunsen believes to have been contemporary with Abraham. Both these groups of pictures show us a country enjoying a milder and more patriarchal form of government, and inhabited by a people of simpler manners, than we find described in the next series of records; but even when studying the remains of the earliest epoch, we do not find ourselves concerned with a society in a very primitive state of cultivation. As was the case with the Chaldean records, we are plunged at once into the middle of a history, and the beginning flies back from us into deeper and deeper distance as we pursue our investigations. The Egyptians among whom Abraham came—if (as Josephus tells us) he left the Field of Zoan and journeyed southwards as far as Heliopolis—were a busy, enterprising, inventive people, divided into several distinct ranks of society, skilled in most of the arts of civilized life, and having among them an educated class, wise already with all the learning Moses acquired.

In leaving the unenclosed marsh-lands—which were in Abraham's time wandered over, perhaps to a certain extent claimed, by tribes of nomadic people from Asia—and entering the arable land lying southward up the narrowing Nile valley, the traveller passed at once from the primitive pastoral stage of society into the second more complex agricultural stage, crossing a division of some centuries of progress in all the arts of life, rather than a few miles of space. The contrast between the simple tent-life of the Arabs, with its few monotonous occupations and easily-supplied wants, and the mode of existence prevailing in an Egyptian country-house, would be the more striking because of the patriarchal habits of that early period brought within the compass of one household the practice of all the various industries and arts by which the luxuries of the great people of the country were supplied. The rich lords who possessed the land of the country, before the sale of estates under Joseph made the king and the priests the only landed proprietors in Egypt, were to a certain extent little kings—each on his own territory.

Every one of the country-houses dotted over the rich land between Zoan and Memphis was a centre of active, laborious life, where evidence of all the conquests that skill had made over nature might be observed.

The contrast between rich and poor was then as ever in Egypt extremely great. There was in every territory the great chief, to whom everything belonged absolutely; who came out, as the pictures on the tombs show us, leaning on his staff to watch his harvesters cutting off the heads of his ripe Indian corn and carrying it away in baskets to the threshing-floor; and his smiths forging bronze knives and spear-heads for him to use on his hunting-expeditions; and his carpenters building handsome boats for his family to sail in on the river, and carving elegant tables and easy-chairs for the house; and his scribes numbering his flocks and herds, and taking account of the wealth in his granaries. And under him there were the serfs, to whom nothing belonged, who herded the cattle, and rowed the boats, and stooped low under the heavy loads of corn, and sweated at the forge and in the workshops. But the well-cultivated soil brought forth an abundance of food for all; and perhaps the interest and variety of the employments in which the servants of these great households engaged made up to them a little for their dependence.

They came into the amusements as well as into the work; for after the day's labour was over, in the long hot afternoons, when the lord and lady of the estate sat with their guests at table, smelling lotus-flowers, and feasting on savoury messes of roast kid, and fish from the lakes, and fruit and seed-cakes, the servants sat at the end of the long hall, and played tunes on harps, or stood up and danced and performed juggling tricks, for the entertainment of their master and his friends. The farm-labourers, though they had task-masters set over them with sticks in their hands to correct them when they were idle, seem to have managed to talk a good deal over their work. There are pictures of them stopping in the middle of the ploughing and harvesting to chatter together in groups, or refresh themselves with draughts of water from water-skins hung for coolness in the trees that shaded the pleasant fields. They sang over their work too. Here is a monotonous song, copied from the walls of a tomb, which the threshers of those old times used to sing as they heaped the yellow corn in a great pile on the round bare place at the end of the harvest-field, used as a threshing-floor, and drove a team of oxen, fastened together in a row by a wooden pole tied to their horns, round and round to tread out the grain:—

> "Tread out, O oxen,
>   For yourselves—
>   **Tread** out yourselves,
>   **For** yourselves—tread out
>   The straw for yourselves,
>   **For** men the grain, who are your masters."

It is an old, old song, and its repeated words may well have floated on **the air from some** busy harvest-field to Abraham's ears as **he** journeyed from Zoan to Heliopolis, and must have been very familiar to Joseph when **he was** Potiphar's overseer, **and** stood (as the **pictures** show us the overseer standing) with an ink-horn at his side, **and a** reed-pen and strip of papyrus in his hand to number the baskets of ears of corn that were poured out on the threshing-floor.

Evidence of the light in which an ancient Egyptian lord regarded his duties to his dependants, and to **the** district over which he ruled, is afforded **by** an inscription on a rock-tomb at Beni Hassan. **The owner of** the tomb, a governor **of** the **Twelfth** Dynasty called Ameni, under **the** picture **of** himself painted on the wall of the entrance-chamber, has left written up this account of his own doings :—

"I have caused all the lands near me, north and **south**, to be regularly sown. I merited the thanks of **the king** for the beauty of the cattle in which I paid **my** taxes **to** him. Nothing has ever been stolen out **of any of the** workshops on my land. I worked myself, and made every one round **me work.** I never oppressed a widow **or** an orphan. I never **was** hard on a fisher, or took unfair advantage of a shepherd.

Want was unknown in my time, for I never left anyone to suffer hunger when the harvests were bad. I was generous to all women, widows and wives, and never preferred the powerful to the weak in any judgment I ever pronounced."

In a neighbouring tomb another nobleman of the same period, called Nehora, boasts of the sumptuous manner in which he, with his family, dependants, and servants, kept all the holidays and festivals set aside for rejoicing before the gods.

In a country over which such lords as Ameni and Nehora presided, and where so many festivals were kept, even serfdom may have been a tolerable condition; and, taking everything into consideration, one feels that slaves and masters, women and children, had a busy, gay life of it, and that Egypt, in the early time before the conquests of the great kings of the Theban dynasties had filled it with foreign slaves, was for rich and poor a kindly and happy place to live in.

An Arab visitor, if he were admitted into these country homes, or the houses of the towns of Memphis or Heliopolis, would have remarked with some surprise the greater freedom which Egyptian customs accorded to women, and the higher position which the wife held in the household than she enjoyed in any other part of the world at that period. The early tombs afford evidence that monogamy was the rule among the ancient Egyptians, and that the wife—"the lady of the house," "the lady of the abode"—enjoyed great consideration, and was associated with the husband in the **government** of the **household.** She sits always by his **side, and entertains his** guests with him **at** the table. **She** receives strangers, and walks **out** unveiled, **and** with **her** children—sons and daughters, **a** pleasant family group—joins in the fishing **and** fowling expedition on the lake, or the sail in the boat on the river.

But more forcibly than **by any other** custom of the country, **or** novel **arts which** he might see practised, **a** visitor **to** Egypt in the early times would have been struck with the amount of time **and** interest which **all** these people whom he saw leading such gay lives, and entering with such eagerness into all manner of business and amusement, were all the time giving to the erection and adornment of the place in which their bodies were to **lie** after they were dead. In every household, besides the field-work, **and the** furniture-making, and the boat-building, and the ministering **to the** daily pleasures **of** life, there was another occupation going on, looked after every day, **and** watched with careful, anxious eyes towards its completion. Westward of the great house where the family lived, a second house **was** rising up under the eyes of the lord and lady of **the** place; the best materials were put aside for its **adornment, the** most skilful artificers and painters and **scribes** of their dependants told off to work upon it. **An** Egyptian lord of that time, if a stranger **came to visit him,** especially **if** he were a foreigner of distinction like Abraham or **Joseph,** let us say, would be **very** likely, after **showing off his** dwelling-house and his granaries and his vineyards and his fishponds, to take his guest to see what was being done in this second building, and to address him in some such words as these: "All the rest of the things I have shown you to-day are what I possess just for a little while, and must soon leave to others; but this is really mine, this tomb that I am making ready for myself. It is my everlasting habitation, 'my house of eternity.' Look round and tell me if you think that it is worthy of me, a fit place for a body to sleep quietly in, for a wise soul that has seen the gods to come back to when it wants to claim its own after the long cycles of changes are passed."

To a visitor like Abraham the predominance of this one thought in the midst of so much activity may well have been the feature in Egyptian society that he cared most to inquire into and ponder over. Perhaps this tendency of the Egyptian people to carry with them, through all the busy occupations of their lives, thoughts of the mysterious future that lay beyond, may have been fostered into greater prominence than it attained among other nations by the natural peculiarities of the country in which they lived.

The sunny, fruitful, brilliantly-coloured Nile valley, with its barrier of sterile hills and the silent untravelled desert stretching away westward to regions from which no tidings had ever come to living man, seems to be in itself a symbol of an ancient Egyptian's life, with his thoughts of the after-life round it. The sun setting behind the western hills, turning from the valley of happy life to the wide death region of trackless sand, was every day a more suggestive *memento mori* than the mummy said to be introduced at their feasts. "*Ra*, the sun god," they said, "went down every evening into Amenti the 'vast,' the 'shadowy,' the 'tenderly-coloured,' western land; and his namesake *Phra*, the earth king, with all his servants must, sooner or later, follow where he led. Their souls would go at least, taking the forms of human-headed birds, across the rocks, across the stretch of desert to the unknown land where the god pointed the way. But the bodies the spirit had deserted must be kept safe in 'eternal houses' till, in like manner as Ra returned climbing the yellow eastern hills, and claiming the Nile valley to be brightened again by his rays, the souls should return and resume possession of their old servants."

So they built eternal houses for themselves, and gave much of their riches and much thought to their fitting adornment. Yet in the early times, while the religious rites, which afterwards degenerated into mere ceremonial, retained their power over the minds of the people, the richest lord, even the Pharaoh himself, built and decorated his tomb with a certain awful doubt hanging over him whether his body would ever be allowed to repose there. For a custom prevailed, and in early times was honestly carried out, of calling a solemn tribunal to sit in judgment on every deceased person, and only when the verdict was favourable was the body allowed to take its place in the tomb. The judgment of the dead body on earth was an actual picture of what they believed was going on with respect to the soul in Amenti: only there the presiding judge was the lord Osiris, the god of the land of shades; the accusers and advocates were spiritual beings who had watched over the soul during its earthly life; and the question tried was not the righteousness or wrongfulness of certain acts done in the body, but the condition of the soul itself weighed against perfect truth in the Hall of the Two Truths, into which the soul had been summoned. In quite early times, when the trial on earth was real, and not, as it became afterwards, a mere conventional ceremony, the friends of a deceased person would doubtless consider a favourable verdict pronounced on the dead body a sufficient warrant for concluding that its late companion, the soul, had passed its more tremendous ordeal happily, and would complete the funeral rites with relieved and comforted hearts.

The tombs consisted of several chambers, decorated with pictures descriptive of the life of the deceased on earth and of the funeral ceremonies; at the end was a deep pit where the body, in its painted mummy-case enclosed in a stone sarcophagus, was deposited. The mouth of the pit was closed up, but the upper chambers were left open, and were visited at stated times by the survivors of the deceased's family, who left behind them, on an altar dedicated to the guardian spirits of departed souls, garlands of lotus flowers, offerings of food, and specimens of those mummied figures of the god Osiris in blue pottery, of which numbers may be seen in museums of Egyptian antiquities. Sentences from the sacred litanies of the dead were written on the wooden mummy-cases, on the cloth in which the bodies were wrapped, and occasionally on the walls of the tombs. But we are, fortunately, not wholly dependent on these detached sentences for our knowledge of what were the beliefs of the ancient Egyptians in the first age about the spiritual world.

There are in existence a number of rolls of papyrus which have been taken from mummy-cases, and which on examination have proved to be chapters or complete copies of a very ancient book called "The Book, or Litany of the Dead." It appears to have been one of the forty-two sacred books which the Egyptians attributed to the god Thoth, the "lord of divine words," and which they guarded with extreme reverence, holding them to contain doctrines of so high and awful a nature respecting the gods and the condition of the soul after death, that only members of the priestly order were permitted to read them. Copies of them were carefully kept in the royal libraries and in the colleges of the priests, and were never allowed to fall into profane hands. That some of these very ancient writings should have come down in safety to us, is owing to a fortunate custom the Egyptians had of placing a papyrus roll, inscribed with one or more chapters from the sacred book that specially concerned the condition of the soul in the other world, in the hand of the deceased person before his mummy-case was closed up, and burying it with him. They seem to have regarded the roll as a sort of passport to Amenti, which the dead had need to take with him. A great number of these papyri taken from coffins have found their way into the different museums of Europe, and have been carefully examined by learned men. It was soon discovered that they were all manuscripts of one book, though there were variations in the text, and some of the rolls contained many more chapters than others. The writings claim for themselves the title of "The Book,"—the book of Thoth; and whatever may be said as to their authorship, their great antiquity is proved by the fact that sentences of them are found on very early tombs and sarcophagi, and also by internal evidence of language and archaic form of hieroglyphic writing. The passports placed reverentially in dead hands, that were warm in the time of Joseph and Moses, have been received and read at last in a western world as strange to the bearers of them as Amenti itself could have been. What news from beyond the desert of the dead years do they bring to us!

CHAPTER V.

THE BOOK OF THE DEAD.

THE best preserved copy of the sacred Ritual yet found is now in the museum at Turin; the whole has been translated into English by Dr. Birch, and the principal part into very beautiful French by M. de Rougé, who has given many years of labour to the task of comparing the papyri of different epochs together, to arrive at the most ancient versions of the sacred text. He has come to the conclusion that four of the 164 chapters of which the Turin copy of the ritual is composed, are late additions; the remaining 160 chapters he believes to consist of two parts,—a very ancient text, older than any other writing in the world, and a running commentary, which at a later but still very remote period was inserted between the sentences of the original sacred book by the scribes who copied it. The sentences are generally very much more easy to understand than the commentary, which appears to have been written when a complex mythology had thrust aside the simpler early faith.

Each chapter has a title at the beginning, and at the end a symbolic picture, which frequently is found to throw great light on the obscure meaning of the text. I will translate from M. de Rougé's papers in the *Revue Archéologique*, the substance of some of the chapters, and his descriptions of the little pictures that accompany them. This will give you some idea of the subjects of which this oldest book in the world treats. It is a strange Pilgrim's Progress of five thousand years ago, only here it is the disembodied spirit that begins and concludes the journey, and it is conducted through scenery as fantastic and terrible as any that Dante's imagination conjured up. What poet of five thousand years ago saw or dreamed it, and, struggling with almost insurmountable difficulties of imperfect language and means of writing, dimly pictured it forth so that we can trace its outline still? The first seventeen chapters have a general title, and appear to have originally formed a separate volume of the sacred writings.

The frontispiece shows the funeral procession—the weeping parents and friends, the dead man drawn along in his coffin; a calf bounds before him, emblem of the new life on which he has entered. Step by step the chapters of the old poem follow the deceased in his wondrous progress through the under world.

In the first stage of the journey the departed soul is manifested to the light; he finds himself alive after death, and proceeds to travel through a region which is not the abode of departed spirits, but a shadowy tract lying between the worlds of the living and of the dead. Walking in heavenly paths, he discovers that no one is permitted to work in this under world. He finds himself in the empty regions of the giant

Apap, the king of the desert, of void lifelessness and impotent death. These regions it is desirable that the soul should leave in the day-time, lest, being steeped in a double darkness, he should wander into Ammah, one of the hurtful regions of the shadowy land. Leaving the empty waste in the day-time, he is justified before his enemies and accusers in the under world, and advances towards light; the stains on the soul begin to be wiped out, and kneeling down the deceased bursts into a hymn of praise to Ra, the god of light. "Swallowed up in light," he is now borne onward to the termination of his first trial. Here a picture shows the traveller in four different scenes: in the first he turns on the furthest verge of the border region to look back on his friends in the world of the living, who are still bringing offerings to his tomb; in the second and third, leaving old things, he has joined himself to a band of spirits who adore, first the rising and then the mid-day sun of the new world he is entering on; in the last scene he enters into the ship of God, and is permitted to worship light in its threefold manifestation. From the ship of God he lands on another more advanced region of the land of shades, and forms part of the following of Osiris; he is nourished with the food of the justified; he shines out in the day; he takes every shape he desires. At length he, the living soul, the justified Osiris (the departed soul takes the name of Osiris, and is always spoken of as the Osiris), devoted to the great gods, is admitted into the Palace of Wisdom, and addresses a prayer to Thoth. He prays that Thoth (the wisdom of God) will remember the justification of Osiris, and justify him from all his sins. The justified is crowned, and his mouth is opened; the dead speaks; the new soul-language is opened to him. Many chapters of the Ritual relate to this part of the soul's advance, and a picture represents the soul standing before a spiritual being, who instructs him in sacred words, while he himself is permitted to utter the sentences of the sacred books he has stored up in his memory during his lifetime.

And now that his tongue is opened it becomes a question about the heart of the man. The spirit-heart, enlightened and purified as it is, cannot live again truly till it is in some sort reunited to the old natural heart, which (if he is a justified soul) spiritual beings have taken in charge, and have been keeping warm with life since his decease.

Kneeling down, the spirit-man speaks to his heart, which he holds in his hand. He entreats the four spiritual beings who preside over the funeral rites to protect his heart—not to take it away from him—to let him live again truly. Rising from this invocation, he adores the Scarabæus, the emblem of creative power which alone can invest him with the second life. And now that his heart is restored to him, and the past human life and the wondrous shade-life are linked together so that the flood of memory pours in, a series of combats begins : he traverses a tract peopled with fantastic, horrible creatures (which probably symbolize the sins and sorrows of his past life)—crocodiles, serpents, tortoises, evil things of nameless shape, devourers of heads and hearts, scented with death, and with fingers of steel. He fights his way through them with a lance in his hand, pronouncing sentences from the sacred ritual as he advances, before which **the** horrible phantoms give place. **After this** experience he learns what are **the woes that** may befall a wicked **soul in** the under world. He is instructed not to nourish himself **with** corruption, but to seek to escape the second death, and so to carry himself that he may not **be** turned back from his celestial house long since prepared for him. Here there is a picture **of** the celestial house, and of the soul (represented by a mummied figure) approaching **it from the** right; **to the** left of the house sits a phœnix, the emblem of the completion of a period of time. The pictures accompanying these chapters represent the deceased either as fighting his way through enemies, or as embraced and supported **by** Anubis, one of the presiding deities of the funeral rites. The evil region is symbolized by a sword resting on a block of wood.

And now that he has had **a** glimpse into the terrors that await the wicked, **he** begins to experience the favours that are accorded **to** virtuous souls. Kindly winds speed him on his **way, the** water of life is given him to drink; and **here a** picture shows the **deceased** reposing after long travel in an arm-chair, while the goddess of the blue of heaven pours out for him living water from the top of a sycamore tree, the tree of life. The draught preserves him evermore from being scorched by the nether fires; he walks on triumphant towards **yet** more distinct manifestations of light. Now he approaches **a** chapel, where sits a hawk with outstretched wings, **the** emblem of new life rising out of death; now he worships before two human-headed deities; now he seeks, by the aid of a serpent, to unswathe his lower limbs, and to walk like a man. At length he arrives at a celestial Heliopolis—that is to say, he has completed a period of transformation; the arrival of the phœnix at Heliopolis, or rather the Heliacal rising of the star Sothis observed at Heliopolis, being the event from which the ancient Egyptians dated a new period of time.

In the next more advanced stage of progress the virtuous soul finds he may assume what form he pleases in the under world. He may be a hawk, and carry the staff of dominion; he may become a phœnix; he may fly like a swallow; he may take the shape of the prince of princes; and even while he walks along the dark way assume the form of a god. Here there is a picture of the deceased walking with Osiris himself, who is however partly hidden from him by a dividing disk or screen of light. In this period of the soul's progress a union of the body and soul is spoken of. A human-headed hawk flies to the mummied body, which holds out to it the symbol of life, a hieroglyphic sign something like a cross. The deceased opens the door of a cell, from which the soul flies. The deceased now seeks for greater intellectual enlightenment. He implores the god Thoth to give him his papyrus and reed; he visits the place where Thoth lives, and becomes an enlightened spirit in the under world. He is permitted to sail with the sun over celestial waters, and arrives at the house where Athor (Love) dwells, and sits down in the presence of the great gods. He receives a cup of joy, learns to know the spirits of the East **and of the West, and is** introduced to other spirits of departed men dwelling in various regions of the under world. And now he nears the end **of** his journey; he pauses and **prays** before the sacred door. **He** enters the Hall of **the** Two Truths (or perfect justice), and there he has to make his way through all the sins he has committed in his life before he can look upon the faces of the great gods. The last chapter, of the group of chapters which relate to this part **of** the journey, is headed by the celebrated judgment picture, of which the illustration furnishes a faithful copy. Osiris sits on his **throne** in the Hall of Perfect Justice, holding **in one hand** the symbol of life, in the other the **staff** of dominion. The deceased is introduced **into his** presence by Thmei (Truth) herself. Before Osiris stands an altar of offerings, surmounted by a waterlily, which supports the four presiding spirits of Amenti. Cerberus, the surly guardian of the palace, the "accuser," whose office **it** is to see that none enter unworthily, crouches before Osiris. Seated above in **a** long row, as witnesses called to testify for or against **the** deceased, are the forty-two assessors of the dead. **Each** spirit is the stern watcher against a certain sin, and addressing each in turn the deceased has **to** plead—

"I have made no one weep."

"I have **not** brought evil report **on any one.**"

"I have not neglected God in **my heart.**"

"I have not been indolent."

"I have not robbed."

"I have **not told lies**"

JUDGMENT PICTURE FR(

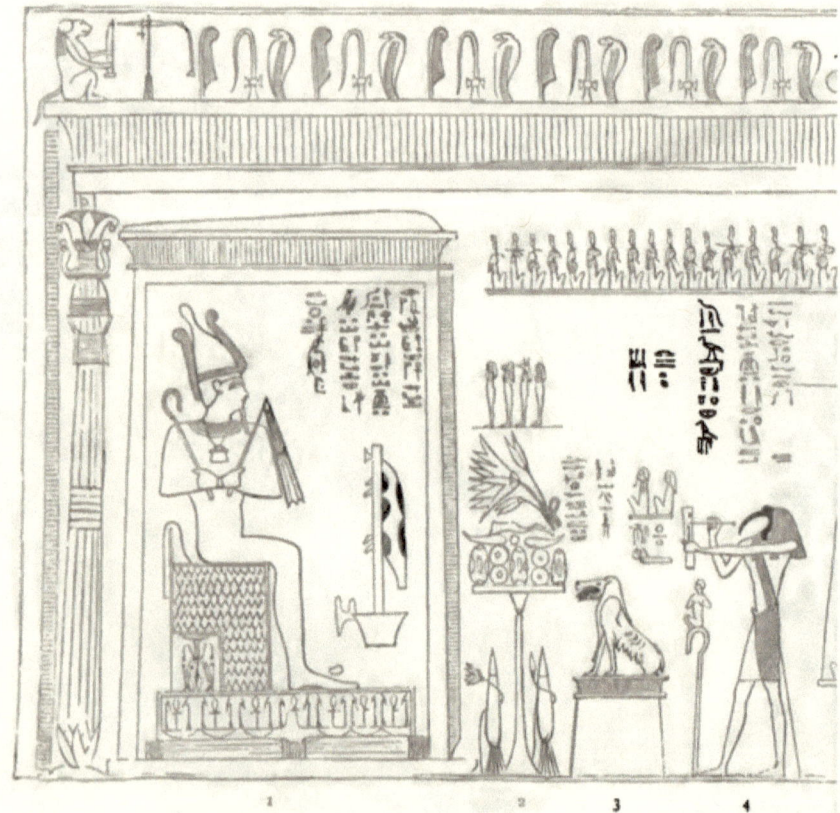

1.—Osiris on his Throne of Judgment.
2.—Table of Offering, surmounted by the four Genii of Amenti, who preside over funeral rites.
3.—Cerberus, guardian of the Hall of Judgment.
4.—Thoth recording the judgment with reed-pen on slip of papyrus.
5.—Symbol of Truth, used as a weight to balance the heart of the deceased.
6.—Anubis, guardian of the dead.

7.—Dog-headed Ape, emblem of Thoth.

8.—Horus, son of Osiris, holding the emblem of life in his hand, watches the weight.

9.—Vase containing the heart of the deceased, protected by Guardian Spirit, who proclaims that the balance is even.

10.—Thmei (Truth) welcoming the deceased into the Hall of Perfect Justice.

11.—The deceased entering the Judgment Hall.

12.—The forty-two Assessors of the dead assisting at the judgment. A figure of the deceased kneels before them.

"I have not multiplied my words more than necessary."

"I have not applauded my own word."

—on through the long catalogue of offences.

Ibis-headed Thoth, the god of intelligence, stands ready with papyrus, scroll, and reed-pen, to record the pleading. Horus, the symbol of the new life, aided by Anubis, the wise-judging friend of the dead, holds and directs a gigantic pair of scales, in which the heart of the deceased is to be weighed. An ape, the symbol of Thoth (intelligence), sits on the beam of the scale, watching intently to see which way the scales incline. In one scale is placed a vase enclosing the heart of the deceased, in the other the symbol of perfect truth. Is he true of heart? If not, the dreaded sentence of the second death will be pronounced upon him.

The judgment happily ended, the deceased invokes four spirits (who are shown in a picture presiding over a lake of fire), whose business it is to wipe out the stains the soul has contracted in its journey through the under world. On their favourable answer to his prayer, he is instructed concerning the nature of the inhabitants of the different regions through which he still has to journey. He prays, and invokes the sun of the upper and of the lower world. He again enters the barque of the sun with his companions. Osiris himself is seated in the celestial boat; a hawk's head shows that the sun is rising (a new life beginning); a phœnix at the prow symbolizes the completion of a period. He sails in company with the princes of the celestial sphere, and at length reaches heaven. A picture shows him marching towards the disk of the sun; he enters his celestial house, and is instructed in the nature of God, and learns all the names of God, and to know the places where Osiris best loves to dwell. Athor and Isis receive him. He stands before Atoum, the essential god; and it is said of him, "He is Toum, the essential man; he is come into his own country; he has won to the end of his journey; the stains of iniquity are purged away from him:" he has become himself Ouati (an eye of fire), a new source of light, co-operating with the great gods in the warfare between light and darkness, good and evil, that goes on eternally.

Prayers to Osiris, and hymns of praise to Ra in his various manifestations—as rising, mid-day, and setting sun—bring the ritual to a conclusion, and occupy many chapters interspersed among those which appear to narrate the soul's progress. The arrangement of the chapters in the Turin papyrus is perhaps not very ancient. Many of them treat of the same subjects, and appear to be repetitions; and many are probably misplaced. The 17th chapter, which ends the first division of the Ritual, entitled "The manifestation of the Soul to Light," contains an epitome of all the teaching on which the later chapters enlarge, and is considered by M. de Rougé to be the most important portion of the ancient book. Interspersed with its account of the soul's life in the under world are sentences put into the mouth of Osiris, and hymns and prayers addressed to the gods, which M. de Rougé believes to contain the real doctrines concerning the nature of the Godhead, and the genesis of the earth, that were received in Egypt by the priests and those who were deemed worthy of initiation into sacred mysteries.

From a careful study of the obscure symbolism under which these doctrines are veiled, and a comparison of the ritual teaching with that set forth in inscriptions and pictures on early tombs and temples, M. de Rougé arrives at the conclusion that the Egyptians believed in one God, self-existent and omnipresent. In the Ritual He is called Atoum, the concealed one, who made "Being" and "not Being" from Himself. He is also called Cheper, and represented by a scarabæus, the symbol of self-existence. This one eternal concealed God from the earliest times had different names in different places. He is Amun at Thebes, Pthah at Memphis. One, there is still a duality in His essence. He is the Father and the Son, the Creator, and that which He produces out of Himself. Under that aspect Atoum appears in the 17th chapter of the Ritual in the double character of Osiris and Ra—Osiris, thought; Ra, appearances; or, as they are symbolized, the sun of the spiritual world, and the sun of the visible world. Osiris precedes the light and the day. He dwells from eternity in the abyss. He himself is eternity, and eternity is unfathomable, brooding night, the teeming womb of all existences. On a day He calls, "Come to *us*," and Ra the visible sun comes to Osiris in the under world, and the visible order of the universe springs into existence. From henceforth Atoum the essential divine exists in its form of "twins." Osiris (spirit) rules in the world of spirits, but to the inhabitants of the upper world He is a dead God, swathed and mummified, hidden from them under the ever-changing forms of that which he has projected from Himself, viz. Ra, and the outward world over which Ra rules.

Yet each man is himself an Osiris. He belongs, as no other outward thing does, to both sides of the divine nature. He lives in Ra's world, but he has that within him which is destined hereafter to take its place in the home of eternal realities.

Mingled with these metaphysical subtleties there was no doubt a large amount of actual worship of the disk of the sun; but in the purest time of the Egyptian faith the sun seems to have been reverenced as a symbol of divinity, not as divine in his material substance.

In his daily setting and rising the ancient Egyptians saw an emblem of perpetual renewal. It was the aspect of nature they best loved to contemplate, and considered most godlike—life growing out of death; fresh beginnings germinating under decay; Isis and Nephthys walking the world hand-in-hand, conducting the soul through many successive livings and dyings till they brought it at length into the presence of the fount of true being, the undivided, changeless Atoum himself.

The highly symbolic form under which these doctrines are set forth in the Ritual was resorted to, no doubt, in the first instance, from the imperfections of language and the nature of the hieroglyphic writing, hardly advanced beyond the picture stage when the sacred books were first indited; every thought had to be expressed by a sign that appealed to the eye rather than the ear. It is easy to see how the use of these symbols gave rise among the uninitiated to polytheistic notions of the Deity. In the lapse of time certain symbols came to be identified with religious ideas, and reverence was transferred from the thought to the sign.

The various attributes of God, put into forms at first to make them intelligible, were regarded by the vulgar as separate gods. Thoth, the wisdom of God; Anubis, the righteousness of God; Kneph, the creative power of God—became distinct personages, and had genealogies invented for them, and were ranged in orders of worth. The aspects and forces of nature found a place, too, in the cosmogony. If Ra the visible sun was twin with Osiris in the Divine Being, then Hapi the great river, the soil of the Nile valley, the wide blue of heaven, the moon, the stars, were parts of Him too, and might be conceived of as distinct existences worthy of worship.

To add to the confusion, the meaning of the old symbols began to be forgotten, and new stories were invented to explain them. The history of the death and burial of Osiris—which from allusions to it in the Ritual appears in early times to have allegorized the work of creation, when Osiris dismembered and concealed himself to produce the visible order of the universe, died that the world might live—in later times was amplified, and had a variety of new meanings given to it. Osiris was said to have been destroyed by Typhon, the evil principle, and restored by the care of Isis, his wife, and sister. It is impossible to say when the change in the meaning of the myths began, or even how far the notion of some violence having been done to Osiris by the powers of evil is justified by the sacred writings, for frequent mention is made in the Ritual of enemies of Osiris.

Still more puzzling and difficult to account for is the worship of animals, which certainly prevailed in Egypt at a very early time. Manetho tells us that the bulls Apis and Mnevis, and the Mendesian goat, were appointed to be gods by a king of the Second Dynasty.

The sacred animals were not reverenced merely as symbols of certain attributes of the Godhead. The bull Apis, at all events, seems to have been regarded as the vehicle through which the god Osiris, the god of the spiritual world, manifested himself to men, and in which he dwelt among them. As soon as an Apis died, it was believed that a re-incarnation of the god took place, under the form of another bull marked by certain traditional signs, and priests were sent all over Egypt to seek for the divine guest in lowly shape that they believed had come to dwell among them. When found, the sacred bull was treated with the greatest reverence through its life, and honoured at its decease with a more pompous funeral and grander sarcophagus than that accorded to the Pharaoh himself.

It was of the bull Apis, the incarnation of Osiris, god of the under world, that the children of Israel made an image when they grew weary of waiting for the return of Moses from Mount Sinai. During their long sojourn in Egypt they had grown familiar with the feelings of the Egyptians about the Apis. They had witnessed the mourning in which the interval between the death of one Apis and the finding of another was passed, and they had taken part in the frantic rejoicings into which the whole nation burst at the news of his discovery. One of the mythological stories that had grown up about Osiris in the later times was, that he had fought with and overcome a giant called Apap, the king of empty places, of wild howling wildernesses, and deserts of sand. They looked round, and saw the dominions of Apap stretched on every side, and their dread of being deserted of any helper grew strong. Who should deliver them from Apap if not Osiris? "Where be our gods to go before us?" they cried, as they pressed round Aaron, and, even with the thunders of Sinai in their ears, forced him to give them as close a likeness as could be procured of the worship they had been used to.

Strange as it is that such debasing forms of worship should co-exist side by side with such spiritual teaching as the "Book of the Dead" discloses, there can be no doubt that such was the case in Egypt for many centuries. Amid all confusions, however, the sacred books remained, and, to those who took the pains to study them, must always have conveyed something, at least, of the old truths. M. de Rougé considers that the belief in one supreme God, and in the immortality of the soul, was never completely lost in Egypt, though it was probably confined to a few of the learned class.

The king whom Abraham visited appears to have been a believer in one God. But if he was a devout and understanding student of the Ritual, there would be a wide gulf between the simple faith of the patriarch in an ever-living personal God, who in this present life revealed Himself in direct communing with the spirits of living men, and the metaphysical Egyptian's conception of a concealed divine essence, who could only be rightly known when the life on earth was over.

Already in Abraham's time, remote as it appears to us, the evil effects of concealing the highest teaching from the mass of the people, under symbolism understood only by the learned, were beginning to show themselves.

To pass from talk with an Egyptian sage on the nature of Atoum into the midst of a crowd of worshippers prostrate in trembling joy at the news of the discovery of a new Apis, or the birth of a sacred cat or crocodile, must have been to a thoughtful foreigner a strange experience. Josephus says that Abraham lived several years at Heliopolis, the town that M. de Rougé believes to have been the chief seat of the ritual worship, and that he conversed with the priests there and taught them many things. If such discourse as Josephus speaks of did take place at Heliopolis 4,000 years ago, it is clear that some of the very same topics that are subjects for argument still must have come into it, and that Abraham and the pantheistic Egyptian priests must have represented schools of thought that have not come to any understanding with each other yet.

CHAPTER VI.

ISRAEL IN EGYPT.

IN thinking over the much and the little that is known of Egyptian history at different periods of time, we are reminded of the aspect of the country in flood-time, as it is described by travellers of ancient times, who, traversing the raised roads, saw on all sides of them a monotonous waste of turbid water, broken here and there by some grand elevation, lifting a temple with its conspicuous sculptures and brilliantly coloured walls, or a city of handsome houses, high and dry above the swamp. So certain groups of well-preserved monuments lift up particular periods of the history to our remembrance high above the waters of oblivion under which the intervening ages have in the long course of time been submerged.

The first period that stands up thus conspicuous and clear, is that illustrated by the tombs of the generation who saw the Pyramids built. Then after a blank time, the length of which we have no certain means of estimating, we have the reigns of three or four of the Twelfth Dynasty kings, whose events we follow in the records left on the walls of the rock tombs at Beni Hassan. The long period of the rule of the Shepherd (or Arab) Kings in Egypt follows, concerning which we have only detached scraps of information coming to light, like a foot or two of high land showing above the level waters; some puzzling sentences about the Shepherd Kings in Manetho's history, a fragment of torn papyrus, one or two tombs of somewhat uncertain date, which just serve to build conjecture upon. That swamp of uncertainty passed, we are landed again among the rich memorials preserved at Thebes and in Nubia of the kings of the eighteenth Theban dynasty,—the great Thothmes and Amunophs, who after finally expelling the Arabs from the country, and uniting the land under the rule of native kings, carried their conquests to the regions beyond the Euphrates, and established the supremacy of Egypt, not only over the east and the south of Africa, but across the sea, in the Grecian islands, and on the coast of Italy. At the end of some hundreds of years of unexampled prosperity, another tide of foreign invasion appears to have swept over the country, which terminated in the elevation to the Theban throne of a race of stranger kings, with whose origin and history we are as yet very imperfectly acquainted. From this eclipse the native line of kings splendidly emerged in the reigns of the great kings of the Ramesside family, Sethi and his son Ramses the Great. There is scarcely a year of their lives whose events are not blazoned on some tomb or obelisk or section of a temple wall. Then gradually from that mountain height of knowledge we slide down to the level of ignorance again.

By comparing together the evidence afforded by these different groups of monuments to the state of the country at the periods to which they belong, we find that we get two tolerably distinct pictures of Egypt. The first is given by the records on the tombs round the Pyramids, and by those of Beni Hassan, and represents the Egypt that Abraham visited. The second is found on the monuments of the great Theban kings, and shows us the country as it was while the children of Israel underwent their captivity there.

Considering that between the closing of the last Beni Hassan tomb, and the building of the first of the Eighteenth Dynasty temples at Thebes, there is an interval of four hundred years, during the greater part of which the country was ruled by foreign kings, we are surprised to find the changes so few, and that they seem to have resulted from the natural development of ancient customs and laws rather than from any new influence. The most important change is a political one. The old landed aristocracy has disappeared, and the king and the priests are now sole possessors of the soil of the country. We have an explanation of this change in the account given in the forty-seventh chapter of Genesis of Joseph's policy during the famine, when he bought up all the estates; in the country except those of the priests, and gave them to the king. It is clear, however, that the power of the old noble families must previously have been broken and their wealth wasted during the long civil war with the Shepherds, or they would not have been reduced to the necessity of selling their lands even by so serious a calamity as a seven-years' famine. Like Ameni and Nehra, they would have had stores of their own from which they could have fed themselves and their dependants for at least a part of the time. But when Egypt rose up after the expulsion of the Arabs to be once more a powerful and united state, the old limited monarchy, with its purely agricultural and peaceful people, had totally passed away. We find the country governed by successive dynasties of despotic warlike emperors carrying on an aggressive policy with respect to foreign nations, and ruling their own subjects by the aid of an influential priestly caste and a large standing army.

Laws and customs are more inflexible and binding than ever, and the impress of one supreme will is visible everywhere. The king is the state, more emphatically than was the case in France in the time of Louis XIV. Everywhere we see him, a gigantic figure, equalling the gods in stature, conquering and ruling, gathering all the riches of the earth into his private treasuries. His subjects, rich and poor alike, appear as pigmies looking up to him and serving him. The great river, the Nile itself, overflows for his pleasure. He is represented on the monuments as binding up water plants, in company with the great river god Hapi, with whom he assumes to be joint proprietor and protector of Egypt. The war gods go out with him to battle, and fight by his side; they are his fathers, his brothers, rather than national deities. His individual honour and prosperity are their object and care; the people have no existence even before the gods, except as they are represented by him. He is Pharaoh, the eye of the earth, as conspicuously as the sun is the eye of heaven.

The evil effects of this despotism were, however, mitigated in Egypt by the extreme reverence for law and custom which characterized the whole nation. If the king filled the largest place in people's thoughts, and arrogated to himself all the glory of the government, it was the secret, all-pervading influence of the learned priestly class that in reality moulded the life of the nation, and enwound kings and people alike in a network of regulations and observances which the boldest Pharaoh had not courage to break through. Hardly any of the daily actions of life were considered too unimportant to be made subjects of regulation by the learned class. They enacted laws about the tunes that were to be played at festivals, and the meats that were to be eaten, and the dances that were to be danced, and the clothes people were to wear. A certain style of drawing was prescribed for the figures of the gods on the temple-walls and the decorations of the tombs, and no alteration was ever allowed to creep in through any artist's superior observation or fancy. One unfortunate result of the restrictions under which all kinds of work were carried on appears to have been, that while all the arts that tended to increase the luxuries of the rich (who made the laws) were fostered into great perfection, no ingenuity seems to have been expended in contrivances to lessen the toil of the labourer. The fields continued to be watered, and the great stones used in building the temples and houses raised, by the most primitive and toilsome methods. The gigantic king and the learned luxurious priests clearly did not care how hard people worked in their service. The whole population of the country was divided into castes or classes, according to their occupations. The king and the priests formed the first class, towering above the others as high as the king is made to stand above other men on the monuments. Next below them came the military class and the farmers who rented land of the priests or the king; below them came merchants, shopkeepers, and artisans of all kinds; and last, the farm-labourers and shepherds, among which lowest class the children of Israel must have ranked, even during the time when they were most favoured by the Egyptian kings.

The extreme uncertainty that hangs over the date of the children of Israel's entrance into Egypt makes it impossible to determine what were the circumstances that led to the change of policy of the Egyptian rulers towards them.

It has, however, been conjectured with much probability that the change was brought about by the civil commotions that occurred at the end of the Eighteenth Dynasty, when the throne of Thebes was usurped by a race of kings of foreign extraction, who introduced changes very distasteful to the populace in the temple-services and in the customs of the court.

After the overthrow of these stranger kings, and the restoration of the native royal family in that branch which founded the Nineteenth Dynasty, a jealousy of foreigners, and a fear of a second usurpation, was likely to be very strongly felt by monarchs and people. The best authorities on Egyptian antiquities have, for this and other reasons, come to the conclusion that the kings of the Nineteenth Dynasty were the oppressors of the children of Israel, and that Ramses Maiamun, the third in succession, was the Pharaoh on the throne when Moses was born. His eldest daughter, who is mentioned on the monuments as enjoying great consideration, and exercising some power in her father's lifetime, was probably the princess in whose household Moses was brought up.

The character of this monarch, as it is revealed to us by the pictures and inscriptions on his great public works at Thebes, and in some papyrus records of his reign that have recently come to light, accords remarkably with the supposition that he was the tyrant from whom emanated the order for the destruction of the Hebrew children.

He seems to have been the first native Egyptian king who set aside that strict observance of settled laws and customs which had hitherto been the safeguard of the people against abuses of despotic power.

A curious account of a conspiracy that took place in the royal harem in his time has been deciphered on a torn leaf of papyrus that has come down to us.

Some of the women of the household, the royal daughters and wives (can Moses' patroness have had anything to do with it?), seem to have been accused of conferring with the king's ministers for private ends of their own. They were brought to a trial before legally constituted authorities, and it is related that the king reversed the judgment of the judges, and, on his sole authority, condemned to death persons on whom they had pronounced a less severe sentence, and that he even went so far as to order the judges themselves to be beheaded, in order to deter others from being indiscreetly merciful.

This little bit of authentic history concerning the royal household may stand beside the traditional stories of the court where Moses grew up, which Josephus and other Jewish writers have preserved. Josephus describes the Pharaoh as having been all through Moses' childhood extremely jealous of his daughter's adopted son, whose future greatness was on several occasions foretold by the magicians of the court. It was also (so says the Talmud[1]) revealed to the king himself in the following beautiful dream. One night Pharaoh dreamed of an aged man who was holding a balance in his right hand. In one scale he placed all the sages and nobles of Egypt, and a little lamb in the other, and it outweighed them all. Pharaoh was amazed at the weight of the lamb, and told his dream on the following morning to his attendants. They were terrified, and one of them said, "This dream forebodes a great affliction which

[1] Midrash, p. 51.

one of the children of Israel will bring upon Egypt. If it please the king, let us issue a royal edict, commanding every male child of Hebrew parents to be slain at its birth." The king did as he was advised.

On another occasion, when the royal princess brought her foundling to her father to show him into what wonderful beauty and intelligence the child had grown, it is related that Moses roused the anger of the king, by snatching his crown from his head, throwing it on the ground, and putting his feet on it. A scribe standing by saw in this action an evil presage for the kingdom of Egypt, and tried to kill the child; but his royal protectress snatched him up in her arms and bore him away in safety.

To turn back again from traditional tales to sober contemporary records. The monuments erected by Ramses the Second are covered with pompous descriptions of the wars which occupied the early and late years of his reign; but though he has been represented as the great conqueror, he does not appear to have added any fresh territories to the empire established by the kings of the Eighteenth Dynasty. The wars of the first years of his reign were principally waged against the petty kings of Canaan and Southern Syria, who had confederated together to throw off the Egyptian yoke, and even against them he was not uniformly successful. In his inability to hold the numerous nations his ancestors had subdued in peaceful subjection, Ramses invented the cruel system, so largely practised by Assyrian conquerors of a later time, of carrying away the entire population of a conquered town or district, and planting them bodily in a distant part of the empire. He caused negro tribes from beyond the cataracts to be dragged from their southern homes and established in Arabian villages, whose inhabitants were transported to the lands from which the negroes had been rooted out, thus isolating both tribes from others of their own race and language.

Many of the wars in the latter part of his reign appear to have been undertaken for the sole purpose of kidnapping slaves, who were afterwards condemned to perpetual toil on the splendid public buildings which in every part of Egypt and Nubia attest Ramses' ambition and indifference to human suffering. It has been calculated that every stone of them must have cost a life.

Under this policy the sunny Nile valley became from south to north, to at least a third of its inhabitants, a dreary house of bondage. In Southern and Middle Egypt bands of Hittites and Amorites, carried off in Ramses' last successful raid into Canaan, chiselled out great monolithic obelisks in the burning stone quarries of Silsilis and Assouan, or painfully dragged along the broad white streets of Thebes the stones for the pyramidal towers of Karnac, or the gigantic seated statues that were to guard the entrance to Ramses' great palace on the western side of the river.

And in the north the children of Israel toiled under their taskmasters, making clay bricks for the building of the strong cities Pithom and Ramses, where the king hoarded his treasures, and working at the great frontier wall designed to defend the cultivated lands from the incursions of the Midianites of the desert.

The poorer classes who were not slaves, and even the farmers who rented lands from the priests and the king, had at this time to suffer exactions that rendered their condition hardly preferable to that of slaves.

In an interesting collection of letters made by a priest who lived in Ramses the Second's reign, there is one describing the condition of the cultivators of the soil such as it was in his day. It seems to show very clearly that there were no longer governors of provinces like Ameni and Nehra, who plumed themselves on the good condition of the crops in their districts, and the freedom of their people from unjust burdens and vexatious interference.

"Only consider," the writer of the letter exclaims to some friend whom he is persuading to "enter the priest's office for a piece of bread," instead of choosing the profession of a farmer; "only consider how wretched the condition of the countryman is who spends his life in tilling the land. Before he begins to cut his corn, insects destroy part of the crop; multitudes of rats get into his field; then come the locusts. Stray cattle trespass and devour the ripe corn; flocks of small birds attack the sheaves. If he does not make haste and house his harvest, robbers carry it all off. His horse dies of over-fatigue in ploughing time. The tax-gatherer arrives at the chief town of the district with a whole army of hungry agents with staves, and negroes armed with palm-rods; 'Give us your corn,' is all their cry, and he has no way of escape from their extortions. By and by the miserable man is seized, bound, and sent off with a gang of other unfortunates to forced work in the canals. His wife is ill-used, his children robbed of their clothes, and all this time his neighbours are occupied with their own troubles."

Another letter of the same series dwells on the privations and dangers to which even a well-born member of the military class was exposed on a war expedition, or when sent to garrison a fortress in one of the conquered provinces, whose inhabitants were always on the brink of breaking out in revolt against the now hateful Egyptian rule. Yet while the bulk of the nation suffered from the exhaustion brought on the country by unnecessary wars and costly public buildings, there was no diminution in the comforts and luxuries indulged in by the rich priestly class, who, being exempt from the burdens of taxation, increased in importance as the other classes decayed.

Among this privileged class Moses' lot was cast during the greater part of his residence in Egypt. The office of educating the younger members of the royal family belonged to the priestly caste. In one of the tombs of the priests it is recorded that its occupant, a learned scribe, was tutor to one of Thothmes the Third's daughters; and there is a pleasant picture on the walls of the tomb, of the priest and priestess seated at a dinner-party in the double chair which husbands and wives shared together when they entertained guests, with the little royal pupil perched on the priest's knee. In some such kindly and learned household Moses, as the adopted son of Pharaoh's favourite daughter, would be placed, and there, in company with other members of Ramses the Second's numerous family of children and grandchildren, he would share the advantages of initiation into the deeper branches of learning and higher thoughts of religion which, together with all the other good things of life, the members of the priestly caste kept to themselves.

As he grew to years of discretion he would be permitted to take part in the official duties which fell to the lot of the younger members of a priestly community. He would have opportunities for observing the good and the evil of the Egyptian system of government and of the priestly teaching, which must have prepared his mind for the great position to which he was afterwards called. Josephus tells a story about his having been sent, when he was quite a young man, into Ethiopia at the head of an army to quell an insurrection, and having performed prodigies of valour, and met with unexampled success. There are many pictures on the monuments of expeditions into Ethiopia, undertaken towards the close of Ramses the Second's reign; and though the incidents recorded do not any way resemble those which Josephus relates, it is not at all improbable that Moses did take part in some of these Ethiopian wars, and was one of the royal sons whom the pictures show as fighting by the side of their father. At all events he must have witnessed the return of the king in triumph to Thebes or Memphis after his southern conquests. He must have seen the long lines of captives following the royal chariot, the heaps of spoil, the tokens that the great king had swept through some peaceful land like a destroying whirlwind, leaving desolation and ruin in his track. He must have watched at Thebes and Memphis, the summer and winter residences of the court, the gradual rising up of the great temples to the gods, on which the spoils won in these expeditions were lavished, and on which the sad-faced captives toiled. The pictures on the temple walls of the great king trampling upon his dwarf-like enemies, the repeated figures on the massive columns at Karnac, of the king received and blessed by ibis-headed and ram-headed deities, must have been designed and painted under his eyes. On occasions of great sacrifices in honour of the king's successes, he must have seen the priests in long succession bearing the sacred arks down fair avenues of columns; between pylons heaven high; past the stately red and pink granite obelisks (shown in the illustration), that Thothmes the Third (Joseph's Pharaoh) and his haughty sister reared to commemorate the triumphs of their reigns; till, at the end of all this magnificence, they came to a small richly-decked sanctuary where lived enshrined some cat or hawk or ibis, in whose dumb form the worshippers were content to see a personification of their god. The strange sight of such worship offered before such an object, must have made a deep impression on the mind of a Hebrew who had heard from his parents of Abraham's God.

The great tomb of Ramses the Second, with its

The Temple at Karnac.—P. 82.

pictures of judgments, its fantastic scenery of the spiritual world, its long series of representations of the trials of the soul after death, must have been in the course of preparation at that time; here, or at some of the many richly-decorated priestly tombs at Memphis, Moses will have come in contact with what there was of sublime and heartfelt in the Egyptian creed. The one grand figure in the Egyptian mythology, the swathed Osiris, with his calm, dead face, staff of life, and knotted scourge of dominion, held in all the funeral scenery the prominent place which the initiated gave him in their thoughts. This highest Egyptian idea of a god—a god of the dead—whose chief office was with the emancipated soul in the land of shades, must have suggested to a thoughtful mind many questions to ponder over. The upper world, in Egypt, was very visibly the king's, to enjoy, to rule, to trample upon—afterwards, in the dim strange land of Amenti, came the reckoning up. There the righteous Osiris, with Thoth his wisdom, and Thmei his truth, took account of men's doings and let his righteous will be seen. May not what Moses heard and saw among the priests in Egypt have something to do with the absence of direct teaching respecting the life beyond the grave which characterizes the Mosaic books? The strongest inducements to a righteous life that could be drawn from a doctrine of future rewards and punishments were presented to the minds of the ancient Egyptians in the ritual teaching. Moses had abundant opportunity of seeing how it had worked; how the duty of aiming at purification was gradually postponed from this life to the next, and the religious training of the soul in the present life confined to mechanical familiarity with observances and sacred words, to which a sort of magical efficacy was attributed. From this religion of the dead and of the shades, Moses was called to the knowledge of a Divine Presence in the world, a Righteous Ruler and Guide, who in this life took cognizance of the thoughts and deeds of men, and regulated their outgoings and incomings by his providence.

We have a curious proof of a change in the feelings of the Egyptians towards their sacred book in a difference in the style of copying the Ritual, which is observed to begin about the time of the Nineteenth Dynasty. In the earliest examples we have of sacred rolls taken from mummy-cases, the writing is very beautiful, and great care has evidently been taken to copy the sacred words accurately. Later, mistakes begin to creep in—the pictures at the heads of the chapters are still beautifully painted, but the writing of the text has been entrusted to a careless hand. It would almost seem as if a knowledge of the meaning of the chapters had been lost, and that the copyist was only required to fill up the allotted space with words. Yet there is a greater disposition than heretofore to ornament the tombs with inscriptions taken from the "Book," and more and more as time passed on the words of Thoth came to be esteemed as incantations and spells, the use of which, without any regard to the teaching contained in them, was capable of producing magical effects.

CHAPTER VII.

EGYPTIAN ROMANCE.

This temper of mind with respect to the sacred book is curiously illustrated by an old Egyptian tale lately translated into French by M. Brugsch, the hero of which is one of the numerous sons of Ramses the Second. It was written by some romance-writer of those old times, in demotic character (Egyptian running-hand), on papyrus, and the copy from which M. Brugsch translates has had a curious history. It was found in the tomb of an Egyptian monk of the 4th century, who, we must suppose, prized the old heathen novel very dearly, since he could not bear to be parted from it even after he was dead. As a picture of Egyptian life and modes of thought in Moses' time, it is worth reading. I render part of it into English from M. Brugsch's translation. Part of the papyrus has unfortunately been torn away, and the first sentences of the story are wanting. We gather from the context that in the opening scene, Setna son of Ramses the Second, a young man devoured by a restless curiosity to dive into sacred mysteries, is in conversation with the spirit of one of his ancestresses. Apparently he has been to make the usual funeral offerings and prayers at the departed priestess's tomb, and the mummied figure, lifting the stone covering of the sarcophagus, turns on her stately painted couch, and begins in a tone of solemn warning to relate the history of her life.

"I am Ahura," she says; "I married my brother, Ptah-neferka, and his name was inscribed on the rolls in the college of Hiero-grammatists (highest order of priests). My husband Ptah-neferka took, as you do, great delight in visiting the tombs at Memphis, and in reading the writing on the altars and on the memorial tablets, for he was a very learned man: and speaking of reading inscriptions, I must tell you that among my husband's friends was a Cher (a kind of priest), a very learned old man called Nesptah. It fell out one day that Ptah-neferka, going to the temple to recite his evening prayers, walked behind the Cher, and paused every now and then to study the writing on the temple walls. On that the Cher laughed. 'Wherefore do you laugh at me, O Cher?' cried my husband; but the Cher went on laughing. 'I am not laughing at you,' he said at last, 'but I cannot help smiling to see you study such writing as this with such interest and pleasure. If you would like to read what I consider a writing—— Ah, well! Only come with me, and I will show you the place where the book that the god Thoth wrote with his own hand is to be found. If you read only two pages of that book, merely what is written on the outside covering, immediately you will have power to charm the heavens, the earth, the abyss, the mountains, the sea (by sea the ancient Egyptians generally meant the Nile). You will have knowledge of all the birds of the air and of all reptiles, and you will see the fish come crowding up from the depth of the sea, drawn by the sweet power of divine words. If you afterwards repeat the second page, it will happen when you have passed into Amenti that you will be able to resume the form you have worn on earth. You will see the god Ra, who rises in the heavens, and the circle of the nine gods, and the moon at her rising.' 'By the life of Pharaoh!' cried Ptah-neferka, 'but this is good news that you bring me. Send me to the place where this wonderful book is to be found, and I will give you whatever you please to ask of me in return for the information.' 'If you are really in earnest in wishing to undertake such an adventure,' replied the priest, 'I will send you to the place, and you shall give me one hundred pieces of silver to lay by for my burying.' Then Ptah-neferka called a young servant, and sent him in haste to his house to fetch one hundred pieces of silver, and paid them on the spot to the Cher, and the Cher resumed his narrative. 'This book that I have been telling you about is to be found in the middle of the river of Coptos. There you will find a casket of iron; inside the iron casket is one of bronze; inside the bronze, one of ebony and ivory; inside the ebony and ivory, one of silver; inside the silver, one of gold; inside the gold, the book. A serpent, a scorpion, and all kinds of venomous reptiles live in the place where the iron casket is, to guard it.'

"Ptah-neferka could not imagine what sort of place in the world this could be. He hastened out of the temple, saying to himself, 'Now, if I can but keep all the wonderful words I have just heard in my mind, I will set out at once to Coptos in search of this book, and make a quick journey of it. If only I could be quite sure that this old priest has not been telling me lies!' He, however, presented himself before the king his father, Mer-neb-ptah, and related to him all he had just heard from the Cher.

"'Well, what do you want me to do about it?' asked the king, when the young prince's story was finished. 'Let a royal barque properly equipped for a voyage be placed at my disposal,' answered Ptah-neferka, 'and give me your royal permission to take my wife Ahura, and our little son Merhu, on a journey to the south. I will find this book and bring it back with me. I promise not to linger on the way.' The king gave his consent. My husband, the child, and I went down to the quay, embarked in the royal boat, and set sail. In due time we arrived at Coptos. The priests of the goddess Isis of Coptos, headed by the high priest, came down to the river to meet us; they were impatient to present themselves before my husband Ptah-neferka. Their wives also came down to welcome me. We repaired first to the temple of Isis of Coptos and Harpocrates, where my husband caused an ox, a goose, and some wine to be brought for a burnt sacrifice and a libation. And this done, we were led into a very beautiful house. There Ptah-neferka remained four days, passing his time gaily with the priests of Isis. I, too, had spent very happy days with the wives of the priests. When the fifth morning dawned, Ptah-neferka sent his servants on to the river with orders to work night and day searching for the casket. At length news came that they had come upon the scorpion and reptiles that surrounded and guarded the iron casket. My husband hastened to the spot, and recited an incantation as he confronted the serpent, the scorpion, and all the reptiles, but he could not make them leave the place. At last he seized a little serpent, and, having a knife in his hand, he killed it. It came to life again, taking its old shape. He seized it a second time, and killed it again. It came to life again in just the same shape. He killed it a third time, and now for a moment the two halves remained apart. Ptah-neferka hastened to throw some grains of sand between them, and after that the serpent could not come again in its old shape. Then he went boldly on and discovered the casket; an iron casket it was that met his eyes first. He possessed himself of it, and broke it open, and there, just as the old priest had told him, was the bronze casket, then the ebony and ivory one, then the silver, then the gold, then the book. It was all as the old priest had told him.

"He drew the book from its golden case, and read some of the writing on the outside, and immediately he found he had power to charm the heavens, the earth, the mountains, the sea. He had knowledge of all birds of the air, of all fish of the sea, of the wild creatures that dwell in mountains.

He was there with them, and had become a part of them all. He read another page of the book. He saw the sun rising in the heavens, and the circle of the nine gods, and the moon at her rising, and all the stars in their courses. He saw the fish drawn by the strength of the charm from the depth of the sea. As for me (Ahura) I, for my part, did nothing all this time. I stood stunned, like one who had already passed into another world; at length I said, 'Ptah-neferka, you must let me see this book, for I fear much that we have found misfortune in finding it.' My husband put the book in my hands, and lo, the charm worked for me too: I had power over the heavens, and the earth, and the mountains, and the seas; I became instantly acquainted with the nature of all living things, and could bring them to me. Then Ptah-neferka took a piece of new papyrus, and copied on it all the words in the mystic roll before him; and when he had filled it entirely, he threw it into some water. He watched the papyrus melt in the water, then he swallowed the draught, and found that he knew all the wonder-working words by heart.

"After this my husband and I returned to Coptos, and spent an entire day in rejoicing before Isis of Coptos and Harpocrates; on the morrow we embarked on the royal barge, and began our homeward journey.

"We left Coptos behind us, and sailed to the north, and there suddenly the god Thoth, who knew all about Ptah-neferka and the sacred book, met us on our way.

"The god Thoth had not tarried. He had gone before Ra, and made a communication. 'Knowest thou,' he said, 'that my law and my hidden science are now possessed by Ptah-neferka, son of king Mer-neb-ptah? He has broken into my most sacred abode. He has robbed me of my casket. He has killed the guardians I appointed to watch it.' Then answered Ra, 'I give him into your hands, him and all the people that belong to him.'

"On this, a power was sent from heaven to hinder Ptah-neferka from ever getting back to Memphis. A spell came over him, and upon all the people near him. An hour had passed, when the little child Merhu ran from under the shadow of the canopy of the royal boat, stumbled, and fell over the side of the ship into the river. He invoked the name of the god Ra as he fell, and called aloud for help; but all were under a spell—all remained inactive; Ptah-neferka alone had presence of mind to recite a charm out of the book; and, obedient to the sacred words, the child's body rose up out of the water and came after the ship. He spoke to my husband of all that had happened, and informed him of the communication that Thoth had made to Ra.

"But the child was dead; we could do nothing but return to Coptos with his body. We re-entered the beautiful house where we had spent our time so pleasantly; we performed all the prescribed rites, and embalmed him with the solemnity befitting the child of a royal house. We buried him in the necropolis of Coptos. Again we set sail for Memphis. Again the power was sent down from heaven to hinder us from entering the city. Again an hour passed; then I left the shadow of the boat, drawn by a force I could not resist. I stumbled as I reached the side, and fell into the water. It all happened just as it had done in the case of the child; no one could stretch out a hand to help me, but my husband read aloud a passage from the book, and my body, obedient to the spell, rose out of the water, re-entered the boat, and I related to my husband how it had fared with me in the hour of death, and what I knew of the displeasure of Thoth against him.

"Then Ptah-neferka debated within himself, saying, 'Shall I go back to Coptos, and live by the tombs of my wife and child? If I return to Memphis, directly I enter the city the king will send for me and say, "Where are my children?" (Ahura his daughter and Merhù his grandson.) I cannot answer, "I took your children to the Thebaid and was the cause of their death, and I remain alive." If I go back to Memphis, how shall I bear my life?' So Ptah-neferka caused strips of byssus-cloth to be brought, and made a girdle, in which he wrapped the sacred book, and bound it round his waist. It made him feel very strong, yet no sooner had he come up from the cabin than he was drawn to the side of the ship. He fell over into the water invoking the god Ra, and supplicating the people on deck to stretch out their hands to help him; but they all stood spell-bound, and could do nothing but cry aloud, 'Oh, the sad misfortune! Oh, the terrible misfortune! Alas, alas!

the good scribe who has not his equal, he will never come back to us!' and they let the royal barge float on, without any one observing the precise spot where Ptah-neferka fell. Arrived at Memphis, they acquainted the king with all that had happened; he hastened down to the boat, and there, to the surprise of every one, the body of Ptah-neferka lay in the cabin of the boat. They took the sacred book from his girdle, and the king caused the dead body of his son to be prepared for its everlasting abode. Till the thirty-fifth day, the adorning of the body went on; till the seventieth, the embalmment; then it was buried in Ptah-neferka's own tomb among the sepulchres.

"I have endured all these sorrows," Ahura continued, "on account of this book, and yet you say, Give it to me. Do not ask such a thing of me. Has not the book cost us all our happy life on earth—all the joys we might have had, my husband and me?"

Setna answered, "Nevertheless, give me the book, Ahura. Let me at least look at it as it lies between you and Ptah-neferka, or I shall snatch it away."

Then Ptah-neferka raised himself, and sat upright in his bed, crying, "Is not this Setna, to whom a dead woman has related all the unhappy history of her life? Beware how you touch the book."

In spite of all these warnings, Setna insisted on having the book of Thoth, and proposed to Ptah-neferka that they should play a game of fifty-two points at draughts, and that the sacred book should be the prize of the winner. Ptah-neferka consented, but so unwillingly, that he tried to cheat in the game when he perceived that his antagonist was getting the better of him. Setna, however, discovered the fraud and won the game. Then Setna called to his brother An-ha-hor-ran, who was with him in the tomb, and begged him to hasten above ground, and tell king Ramses, their father, all that had happened, and get him to lend them the talismans of Pthah, which belonged to him, and his magical books, and hasten back with them to the tomb.

An-ha-hor-ran quickly left the tomb, and told the whole story to the king, who made no difficulty about letting him have the talismans of Pthah, but desired him to take them and the magical books at once to Setna.

An-ha-hor-ran hurried back to the tomb, and touched the body of Setna (who apparently was under some spell that prevented him from taking the book or leaving the tomb) with the talismans of Pthah. Immediately the body of Setna grew light and floated in the air, and he stretched out his hand, and took the book from Ptah-neferka's sarcophagus. He took it and left the tomb, and light preceded him, and darkness followed him.

Ahura cried after him, saying, " Glory to thee, king of light ; glory to thee, king of darkness."

Ptah-neferka said to Ahura, " Let not your heart be sad, I will make him bring back the book. A knife and a staff shall be in his hand, but there shall be a brasier of fire on his head."

The latter pages of the papyrus narrate somewhat confusedly a number of strange adventures and temptations which terminated in Prince Setna's being forced, by a series of misfortunes that befall his family, to return the papyrus. The moral of the story seems to be the danger of prying into forbidden mysteries, and seeking to become wiser than the gods design mortals to be.

It may be called a historical romance of that time, for the people mentioned in it really lived. Mer-neb-ptah was a real king, and Ramses the Second had a son called Setna, who ruled as viceroy in Memphis, and died before his father. The belief in magic, and in the power of written words used as spells, was evidently strong enough, even among educated people who could read stories, for the incidents of the tale to seem quite sufficiently probable to be interesting. The Pharaoh of the Exodus had magicians at his court, and it is evident, from the narrative in Exodus, that he at first looked upon Moses and Aaron merely as more clever magicians than ordinary, who had got hold of some mightier charm than the Egyptian necromancers had as yet been able to possess themselves of.

This story helps us to understand how it was that the wonders wrought by Moses and Aaron, while they were just what would naturally arrest the attention of the Egyptian king, and dispose him to listen to the message they brought, failed to overawe or convince him of Moses' divine mission, and how he went on until nearly the end, hoping to overcome the Hebrew leaders by the counter-enchantments of his own band of wizards.

Perhaps the family of Ramses the Second was

specially addicted to necromancy; the story seems to hint this. The Exodus Pharaoh, who had, we know, a staff of magicians at his court, was the younger brother of Setna mentioned in the story. His name was Men-ptah, or Ptahmen, and he seems to have been the only one of Ramses the Second's numerous sons who survived him. He had no children. On his succession, Moses, as the adopted son of Pharaoh's favourite daughter, might, if he had not elected to throw in his lot with the Hebrew captives, have claimed the position of heir-apparent to the Egyptian throne. There was no Salic law in Egypt, and the king who eventually did succeed Men-ptah claimed the throne by right of his wife, who is supposed to have been a daughter of Ramses the Second.

Moses, however, was living with his father-in-law Jethro among the Midianites of the desert, when Men-ptah became king; and when he did return to Egypt, it was not to assume the position at court to which he was entitled, but "choosing rather to suffer affliction with the people of God," to appear as the leader and champion of the down-trodden slaves whose cry had gone up to God.

Men-ptah's reign seems to have begun disastrously by a revolt in the Thebaid, and an invasion of Lower Egypt from the west by the Libyans, aided by a large body of confederates, Sardinians, Sicilians, Etruscans, and Achæans, who were only repelled after a severe struggle. Driven from the upper and western districts of the country, Men-ptah appears to have fixed his court at Zoan or Avaris, the old capital of the shepherds, and one of the frontier towns lying between the desert and the rich pasture-lands of Goshen. It was a strongly fortified place, with a bridge, defended by towers, spanning the easternmost branch of the Nile on which it was situated; a very convenient fortress for a king threatened on many sides by dangers and revolts to retire to. Here among the pleasant pasture-lands which the old pyramid king had loved so well, Men-ptah must have been living when Moses and Aaron confronted him with their unwelcome demands, and here were wrought the wonders of God in the "field of Zoan." The rich level pasture-meadows, and barley-fields, and rice-grounds, and flax-gardens of the flowery Delta, were swept by storms of hail, and eaten bare by armies of locusts from the desert. The broad Tanitic branch of the Nile, with all the numerous canals fed by it, the countless little rills surrounding every field and vineyard, the fish-ponds and pleasure-lakes in the gardens behind the country houses, had their blue waters troubled, and thickened, and changed to the colour of blood; loathsome creatures filled the pure sunny air, and defiled the marble floors and sculptured chambers of the king's palace-temple; and, more terrible to the ancient Egyptians than any calamity short of death, the sun, the god Ra, the heaven-king himself, hid his face from them, and left them, the votaries of light, a prey to darkness that might be felt. At length came the night when in every house in Zoan, in all the clustering palm-shaded villages far and near, in every white mansion dotted over the wide lands, a great cry arose, for there was not a house in Egypt where there was not one dead.

The hasty command given to the children of Israel to depart from the country, their spoiling of the Egyptians, the change of mind of the weak king, the night pursuit through the desert, the Egyptian discomfiture on the shores of the Red Sea, are precisely the class of events to which we may be sure we shall find no allusion in the boastful inscriptions written or engraved by Egyptian chroniclers. Disastrous reigns like Men-ptah's are almost always a blank as to records, but we know that a period of depression has come by the sudden break in the chain of illustrative monuments that in happy times testify year by year to the successes of the king.

Men-ptah left behind him no complete record of any kind. His name occurs in one or two inscriptions graven on the temple walls and obelisks his great father raised, and he began to excavate a tomb for himself next to his father's, in the Valley of Kings at Thebes, but it was never finished; it contains merely an entrance passage and a single chamber or hall. This circumstance has been held by some writers to prove that Men-ptah was drowned with his army in the passage of the Red Sea, but the Bible narrative nowhere affirms the death of the king. The revolt which took place in the upper country in the beginning of Men-ptah's reign would account sufficiently for the abandonment of works begun by him at Thebes. It is quite possible that after witnessing the triumph of his enemies, he may himself have escaped with a small remnant of his followers to Zoan, and tyrannized and vacillated through a few more years of a disastrous reign.

CHAPTER VIII.

THE KINGDOMS OF CANAAN.

THE period of the Exodus of the children of Israel from Egypt, which marks the beginning of the slow decay of the Egyptian empire, was for the northern nations, whose influence on the destiny of the Israelites succeeded to that of Egypt, the commencement of their gradual rise into prominence. For many centuries before this time the history of the kingdoms of the East is chiefly concerned with the successive rising and falling of two rival races—the Hamite race in Egypt and Chaldea, to whom the first mission to settle and civilize the world had been given, and the wandering Arab tribes who surged round their settlements like waves of a desolating sea round a cultivated coast. The Shemites, from whom afterwards sprang some of the highest forms of civilization come before us at first as destroyers, or at all events arresters of progress, and the periods in early history when their power predominated are marked by no buildings or records that can throw light on their history. They seem to have come and gone, leaving no trace behind them.

The ancient Cushite kingdom of **Chaldea,** of which Ur and Erech and Babel were the chief cities, fell under the sway of Arab kings, and sank into insignificance about three hundred years after the time of its greatest prosperity under Chedorlaomer; and at a somewhat later period, four hundred years' obscurity, followed by a disastrous civil war, was brought on Egypt by the irruption into that country of successive tribes of Arabs from the desert and from Palestine.

After the expulsion of the Arabs, the empire of Egypt was for a time firmly established throughout the East. In its records—chiefly long rolls of conquered towns which the Thothmes and Amunophs of the Eighteenth Dynasty have left on their temple walls—the names appear of all the cities afterwards famous in the East; of Gaza, Tyre, Damascus, Carchemish, Nineveh, and Babylon.

But it does not appear to have been the policy of Egyptian conquerors to dethrone the native rulers of the countries they overran, or to interfere with the government or customs of the country. They contented themselves with exacting a certain yearly tribute; with leaving garrisons in a few frontier towns, important for their position as affording access into the country; and occasionally, by way of punishing a revolt or long-continued neglect of tribute, the sons of the reigning king and of his chief nobles were carried away to be educated at the court of Egypt, and serve as hostages for future good behaviour. These young princes and nobles, on their return to their homes, doubtless brought with them much of the

Egyptian culture, and through this influence all the nations of the then known world had something of the character of Egyptian civilization and art impressed on them in the first stages of their progress.

Whenever a period of internal calamity came upon Egypt, the people of the conquered countries, Assyrians, Syrians, and Canaanites, took the opportunity of intermitting the tribute and asserting their independence, and during some centuries the accession of a powerful king at Thebes was always followed by the incursion of a vast Egyptian army into Asia, and the speedy subjection of the revolted tributaries. Ramses the Second, once erroneously supposed to have been the greatest of Egyptian conquerors, is the first well-known Theban king from whose list of tributaries the names of the Mesopotamian cities drop out. His warlike efforts were principally directed against the Canaanites, who in his reign engaged in a protracted struggle for freedom.

The disturbed reign of the weak Men-ptah (the Pharaoh of the Exodus) afforded an interval of freedom from foreign incursions to the inhabitants of Palestine. It was after the country had been in the enjoyment of tranquillity for some years that the Israelitish spies sent by Moses visited it, and were at once ravished by the sight of its beauty, its countless watercourses, its sunny vine-clad hill-sides, its deep fertile valleys, its groves of oaks and sycamores, so different from anything they had ever seen before; and terrified by the aspect of its inhabitants, the many men and tall, whose massive stone fortresses crowned every hill.

The faint-hearted refusal of the children of Israel to encounter these formidable foes, notwithstanding the signal deliverance that had been already vouchsafed to them, was punished by the divine command given to Moses to turn back from the confines of the Holy Land, and remain in the desert forty years, till a new generation, more worthy of the triumphs designed for them, should have grown up.

Meanwhile the old oppressors of Israel were made to fight their battles for them, and prepare the way for their entrance into the land of promise. The Hornet, under which name the king of Egypt is designated, because the hieroglyphic sign for his title as king of the Lower country was a hornet, " was sent before " to drive out the Hittite, and the Hivite, and the Canaanite.

The last of the many incursions made by the kings of the Ramesside Dynasty into Palestine took place during the Israelites' forty years of wandering in the desert, and was conducted by Ramses the Third, the last of the long series of Theban conquerors and builders who, after the period of anarchy that followed the death of Men-ptah, succeeded once more in establishing a branch of the ancient royal line on the Theban throne. Like all the other powerful rulers of his house, Ramses the Third employed the spoils gained by his conquests in the erection of great buildings, and on the walls of his splendid palace-temple at Medeenet Haboo we have a series of pictures and inscriptions recording his conquests in Palestine, which show us the state of the country just before the Israelites entered it.

We see pictures of fenced cities with "high walls, gates, and bars," such as are described in Deuteronomy, and representations of large armies coming out to oppose the Egyptian king, "with chariots and horses very many," and we find from the inscriptions that these armies were the confederate forces of independent tribes with petty kings at their head, such as were the king of Hazor, and the king of Madon, and the king of Shimron, and the king of Achshaph, and the kings of the mountains and the valleys, that went forth to fight Israel at the waters of Merom. Egyptians and Canaanites fight and struggle, and do homage and triumph, quite unconscious of the near approach of the new claimants to the territory, before whom victors and vanquished will have alike to give place.

After the settlement of the children of Israel in Palestine, the names of the Canaanitish tribes over whom the Egyptians had so often recorded their conquests do not again recur on the monuments. The Egyptian annals tell us nothing further of incursions into Palestine till Shishak of the Twenty-second Dynasty records his conquest over Rehoboam king of Judah, and causes his Jewish features, surmounting the shield and figure of a bound captive, to be carved on the walls of Karnac.

The southern lowlanders were exterminated or driven away into Phœnicia; the hardy Hittites and Amorites expelled from their stone fortresses on the hills; the Gibeonites reduced to be hewers of wood and drawers of water; the Moabites and Amalekites were driven away towards Arabia.

The history of the old Palestinian people, shadowy even with the help of such light as Egyptian pictures throw upon it, here abruptly terminates, and we should have remained in almost total ignorance of their characteristics, religion, and customs, at a loss to understand the denunciations against them with which the sacred writings abound, and the fear of their influence over the Israelites which caused so stern a doom to be pronounced upon them, had there not existed another branch of the same Canaanitish race, speaking the language, following the rites, and sharing the national characteristics of those the Israelites superseded, who played a more conspicuous part in the world's history, and left behind them some records and monuments which make them known to later ages.

It is difficult to connect the thought of the Sidonians and Tyrians, the great merchants and colonizers of the ancient world, with the degraded Canaanitish people whose names are used in the Bible as epithets of reproach. Yet the identity is very firmly established by recent researches among Phœnician remains, and by the testimony of language and tradition; and our surprise is lessened when we take into consideration that on Egyptian monuments the Canaanites are uniformly represented, from quite early times, as a highly civilized people, pre-eminent in the arts for which the Phœnicians were famed, and living under the same mixed form of monarchic and federal government which subsisted among the maritime cities of Phœnicia for many centuries.

It is probable that the Sidonians (descendants of Sidon, eldest son of Canaan), who betook themselves to the strip of coast lying between the mountain range of Lebanon and the sea, owed the prosperity which distinguished them from the other branches of the Canaanitish race to the nature of the country they chose for their habitation.

Shut in by mountains to the north and west, which prevented them from spreading landwards, and having before them a coast broken by sunny promontories and safe harbours, and flanked here and there by islands standing out into the sea, the design of turning the wide stretch of waters into a territory, and reaping harvests of riches from its waves which the narrow land denied them, naturally presented itself early to their minds.

There was a tradition among the Phœnicians mentioned by Herodotus, that in some very far back time their ancestors had come from the shores of the Persian Gulf, and had brought the knowledge of boat-building with other arts from those Cushite cities by the sea where the first germs of Asiatic civilization sprang up. But if not the first navigators, the Sidonians were for many centuries the only people who had courage to undertake long voyages and brave the perils of unknown coasts. The Egyptians, clever boat-builders as they were, confined their navigation chiefly to their own beautiful river, for they held the sea to be a foreign and accursed element—the domain of the evil god Set; and considered it a sin against their own native gods to venture upon it.

CHAPTER IX.

THE FISHERIES.

THE name of the most ancient of the Phœnician settlements, Sidon, signifies "The Fisheries," and shows the humble origin from which their greatness rose. A few families of peaceful men settling themselves round a promontory favourable for carrying on their trade of fishers; hollowing out frail boats from the trunks of palm-trees; creeping up and down the coast, further and further away, till they came to know all its sheltering nooks and dangerous projections; founding fresh settlements, here on a rock standing out a mile into the sea, there on a sunny stretch of coast wooded down to the beach with the fine palm-trees, from which the strip of country where they had settled themselves was afterwards called Phœnicia by the Greeks; improving in the construction of their craft, till at length a longer voyage than has been yet undertaken is planned by some adventurous spirits, and the first band of maritime explorers trust themselves on the bosom of the sea, and on some soft starlit summer evening row out of sight of the old landmarks, and of the friends grouped on the shore to bid them farewell, and drop down towards the unknown.

The return of the first adventurers with tidings of their having reached new lands beyond the sea, after nights and nights of rowing, and of their having found there strange inhabitants and productions of nature different from those of their own country, would give a new impulse to the activity that seems to have belonged to all the Canaanitish tribes, and started the Phœnicians on the career of commercial enterprise which gradually changed their little fishing villages into splendid cities, gathering all the riches of the world into their ports.

We have not any records of the doings of these earliest heroes of travel; their adventures belong to a time too remote for rumours from it to have reached down to us, even in the guise of such mythical tales as those under which the Greeks veiled the histories of the founders of their commerce. We can only guess what they must have suffered and braved, by the testimony which relics of early Sidonian settlements in remote parts of the world afford, of the distances to which they penetrated, and by our knowledge of the difficulties under which such journeys must have been made in the then state of the world. We know that at the very early time when Egypt was governed by Shepherd Kings, the little strip of coast on the north-west of Palestine behind Lebanon had already made itself the commercial centre of the known world, and that all intercourse between distant nations, and all the interchange of commodities between different regions, which the pictures of tribute on Egyptian monuments show to have been very considerable, was carried on by its inhabitants.

In very early times the Sidonian ships appear to have ventured the passage of the Hellespont and the Bosphorus, braving the dangers of the Straits which the Greeks fabled to be guarded by two enormous revolving rocks of ice, called the "Crashers," that met at intervals with a loud noise like thunder, and crushed unwary ships between them. They skirted the coast of the Euxine, the "inhospitable" sea, as far as Colchis, whence they brought away the rich mineral treasures in which the country abounded, worth all the dangers of the quest, as furnishing materials for their principal manufactures; the bronze shields inlaid with gold, and the delicately-carved silver and gold and bronze drinking-vessels, for which the Sidonians were celebrated.

Homer mentions the gold-edged silver bowl which Menelaus had received from Hephæstus king of Sidon, and gave to Telemachus, and a silver cup of Sidonian workmanship which Achilles offered as a prize to be contended for at the funeral games of Patroclus:

> "A silver urn, that full six measures held,
> By none in weight or workmanship excell'd;
> Sidonian artists taught the frame to shine,
> Elaborate with artifice divine,
> Whence Tyrian sailors did the prize transport,
> And gave to Shoas at the Lemnian port."

Several centuries afterwards the Greeks, following

in the track of the Sidonians, wrested from them the monopoly of the rich traffic of the Euxine Sea—a feat which the Greek poets have celebrated in the fable of the quest of the Golden Fleece by Jason and the Argonauts.

The shoals and rocks and whirlpools of the Archipelago and the Ægean Sea, which furnished the Greek mariners with materials for so many fearful tales, had fewer perils for the Sidonian ships, because they had at a very early period planted settlements on the principal islands, and fitted up harbours for the shelter and repair of vessels distressed by storms. With this aid they were able to pursue their voyages past the southern point of the Peloponnesus to the shores of Italy and Sicily, and even up the Tyrrhene Sea to the Gulf of Lyons, where they had a settlement which afterwards grew into the colony of Tarshish, so often alluded to by the Hebrew prophets. By means of this intercourse, and of the stations for commerce which the Sidonians established wherever they went, the first beginnings of civilization were spread through Europe. The half-savage people of Greece and Italy were still using the rude flint tools of the stone age, and living little better than the beasts of their own woods, when the Sidonians came to them, and taught them to exchange the raw produce of their countries for bronze utensils and tools wrought in Phœnician workshops, and linen and embroidered stuffs from Egypt. The great extent to which commerce was carried on between Greece and Phœnicia in early times is shown by the fact that the Greek names for all articles of luxury are derived from the Phœnician, that is to say the Hebrew tongue, for the Phœnicians spoke a language differing very slightly from that of the Jews.

But it was not only by means of their ships that the Sidonians spread themselves and their wares all over the world; they had an elaborate system of land-carriage, and performed journeys that seem almost incredible now. From their settlements at Tarshish, in the neighbourhood of the Gulf of Lyons, they sent caravans that traversed the dense solitary forests of Central Europe, and reached the shores of the Baltic Sea, whence they brought yellow amber, only to be found in that part of the world, and then highly prized for making ornaments and caskets.

An equally difficult journey took them to the furthest coast of Gaul in quest of tin from Cornwall, which was brought across the Straits by the natives, and conveyed by the tedious land route to Tarshish many centuries before the Tyrian ships ventured to pass the Pillars of Hercules. In the early times, when bronze (an amalgam of copper and tin) was employed for all the purposes to which we apply iron, tin was a more really valuable metal than silver or gold; and as it was only found in countries far removed from the earliest seats of civilization, the longest journeys of ancient times were undertaken in search of it, and more than any other circumstance, the need of tin led to the spread of civilization in the first ages of the world.

Europe, however, owes the Phœnicians a greater gift than even the substitution of bronze for flint weapons, and linen clothes for undressed leather; the letters of the alphabet were, as M. Renan expresses it, one of their exports, and of all the good things they brought into the West the one for which we owe them the deepest gratitude. We have seen how in very early times the Egyptians and Chaldeans took the great step of changing the rude pictures and symbols of things and ideas, of which the first attempts at writing consisted, into signs expressing sounds, and so spelling words; but though that great discovery came to them, they failed to carry it out to a perfect alphabetic system. They continued to mix up the old and new methods of writing together, sometimes using signs as true letters, and putting a group together to spell a word; sometimes making a single sign stand for a syllable; sometimes using it as a picture or symbol of the thing they were writing about. The Sidonians, the first merchants in the world, having occasion to keep accurate accounts, and send written directions to people living at great distances, were the first to feel the inconvenience of this uncertain method of writing. Their intercourse with Egypt had made them acquainted with the hieroglyphic system, and the fortunate thought came to them of choosing a few signs from the immense number in use, and making each one uniformly signify a single sound. Twenty-two was the number of hieroglyphic signs first chosen, and to this, the first true alphabet ever invented, all the alphabets now in use, and all that have ever been used in Europe, can be traced back.

Wherever the Phœnicians went they took their alphabet with them, scattering the twenty-two precious seeds in the fruitful Grecian soil first, as Cadmus sowed the dragon's teeth, and a more wondrous harvest than Cadmus's sprang up,—all the beautiful and graceful shapes that live in poetry and history, all the heroes that Homer sang and Herodotus wrote about, who, but for the Sidonian invention, could never have come down to us.

The prosperity of Sidon seems to have continued unbroken by any disaster all through the long period of Egyptian supremacy in the East. There is a papyrus in the British Museum, translated by M. Chabas, which contains an account of a pleasure journey through Phœnicia, made by a general of Ramses the Second's time, as he was on his way home from a successful campaign against the northern Hittites. It is interesting because it is perhaps the very first book of travels ever written; at all events, it is the most ancient we can read now. The traveller evidently feels himself as much at home on Phœnician ground as if he had already arrived in Egypt. He passes from city to city; from the northernmost Gebal, whose renown as a holy city he mentions, to Tyre. He describes Tyre as "the city in the sea," and records the abundance of fish with which its inhabitants were supplied, and the fact that all their fresh water had to be brought to them in boats from the mainland.

The next historical mention of Tyre is in the 19th chapter of Joshua, where it is spoken of as a strong city, which the children of Ephraim, to whom the seacoast up to the confines of Tyre is assigned, are not permitted to attack. The Phœnicians do not appear to have done anything to help their kinsmen, the southern Canaanites, in their deadly struggle with the Hebrews. They stood entirely aloof in the contest, indifferent to the fate of the other tribes of their race so long as their own territory was not invaded. Their narrow strip of country became, however, the refuge for all the fugitives from the hills and valleys of Judea that escaped the swords of Joshua's soldiers; and to provide for so large an influx of new subjects the Sidonians sent out at that time two large bodies of emigrants, and planted their first important colonies. One party, under the conduct of a leader known in history under the name of Cadmus (the Eastern), went to Greece, and founded Thebes; the other sailed to the coast of Africa, possessed themselves of a large tract in the north-west, and grew into a powerful people.

The first blow to the prosperity of Sidon came from the Philistines, the great foes of the children of Israel, who rose into importance in the south-west of Palestine as the power of the Egyptian kings, to whom they had hitherto been tributary, declined. The causes which so increased the military strength of this people as to enable them, about three hundred years after the settlement of the Israelites, to assume an aggressive attitude towards their neighbours, are not at present known. All we clearly know is, that while no allusion is made to them in the history of the conquest of Canaan by the Israelites, nor in the partition of the country among the twelve tribes, they are found, three hundred years afterwards, not only to have wrested the seacoast from the tribe of Dan, to whom it had been assigned, and to have pushed the Danites from the busy harbours and fair lowland cornfields of their inheritance, but to have penetrated into the interior of the country and forced the allied tribes to pay them tribute.

The first outburst of this spirit of conquest was directed northward. The proud cities on the northern coast, with their accumulated treasures of centuries of successful commerce, offered a far more attractive prey than the villages and fields of Israel.

About B.C. 1209 a fleet of Philistinian ships, sent out from Askelon, attacked Sidon, took it by assault, and razed the ancient city, so long the queen of the sea, to the ground. Satisfied with this triumph and the rich spoil they bore away with them, the Philistines do not appear to have made any attempt to settle in Phœnicia as they did in Judea.

The Phœnicians, warned by the disaster that had befallen the proudest of their cities, began after that time to enter into closer bonds of union for mutual defence than had ever existed before. Like all the Canaanitish nations, the Phœnicians had a tendency to split up into small communities. Each of the sea cities, though inhabited by a people speaking the same language and following the same pursuits, had an independent king and government, even a god to itself—a Baal or lord devoted specially to its interests. After the fall of Sidon a sort of federal union was entered into by the cities, which to a certain extent obviated the evils to which their division of interests had given rise. Each city sent its king, or a deputation of its principal nobles, to a stated place of meeting at a certain time of year, and an assembly empowered to decide all questions of mutual defence and policy towards foreign nations was constituted.

Sidon was rebuilt shortly after its destruction by the Philistines, but it never quite regained its former greatness. Tyre became the chief city of Phœnicia, and was the place where for a long time the meeting of kings was held. Its strong position, situated on a rock in the sea, secured it from any sudden attack like that under which Sidon had fallen; and from the time of its becoming the head of the confederacy it continued to increase in importance till its riches and the extent of its commerce far exceeded those of the elder capital in its most prosperous days. Almost all the denunciations of the Hebrew prophets against the luxuries and sins of the maritime cities were addressed to Tyre; the name of the younger city being always put first—"Tyre and Sidon"—whenever the two capitals were spoken of together; partly on account of its superior importance, as head of the confederacy, and partly because its near neighbourhood to the kingdom of Israel made the example of its splendour and its vices more hurtful to the Jewish people.

More than one description of Tyre by travellers of ancient times, who visited it in the days of its prosperity, has come down to us, but none of them gives so vivid an impression of what its greatness and beauty must have been as we gather from the expressions of admiration into which the prophet Ezekiel breaks out in the midst of his prophecies of its coming overthrow.

"Thou wast perfect in all thy ways from the day when thou wast created till iniquity was found in thee!" he exclaims, pausing in his denunciations to cast a regretful glance back at some happier and better time, before the "wisdom of its kings and rulers" had been dimmed by pride and jealousy, and its "beauty defiled" by the "iniquity of traffic." "Thou sealest up the sum, full of wisdom, and perfect in beauty." "Thou hast been in Eden, the garden of God; every precious stone was thy covering, the sardius, topaz, and the diamond, the beryl, the onyx, and the jasper, the emerald, the carbuncle, the sapphire, and gold." "O thou that art situate in the midst of the sea, a merchant of the people for many isles!" "Thy builders have perfected thy beauty. They have made all thy shipboards of fir-trees of Senir: they have taken cedars of Lebanon to make masts for thee." "Fine linen with broidered work from Egypt: blue and purple from the isles of Elishah was that which covered thee."

The descriptions of heathen writers dwell much on the same points of excellence—the strong position of the city in the midst of the sea, the stately shipping, the beauty of the stones of its buildings, and the variety of merchandise accumulated in its stores. The Egyptian poet Nonnus, who visited Tyre long after its days of dominion were over, wrote a poem in its praise which, though somewhat vague in the description it gives of the glories of the place, will still serve to set some of the features of the Venice of the old world, the first bride of the sea, before our eyes. The poet, whose words I render into English from the French translation of the Comte de Marcellus, describes the god Dionysus as having lately left "the tufted forests on the slope of Arabia," and passed through Phœnicia, the land of Cadmus.

"Arrived at Tyre, the god is enchanted with the exquisitely coloured stuffs displayed in all the shops before the eyes of loungers in the streets: clothes of various hues from Assyria, white muslins from Babylonian looms, webs coloured from the Tyrian shell, and glowing with the sea's own purple lustre. The very dogs on the shore he sees crunching the fish enclosed in the precious shell, and dyeing their white faces with the liquid lustre designed for imparting the splendour of the purple to the robes of kings, the only mortals the sea condescends to clothe. He congratulates himself again and again on seeing this wonderful city, which Neptune has not wholly encircled with his wet girdle, but which assumes the shape of the moon in its third quarter. Tyre sleeps on the waters, divided on the land, but knit together by the sea. It resembles in shape a virgin floating on the waves, her hands stretched out toward two seas, her feet pressed against her native shore, while her wet spouse Neptune swims round her, girdles her with his indissoluble chain, and encircles her neck with his tumultuous arms. Dionysus praises Tyre, the only city in the world where herdsmen can sit on the shore playing their flutes in company with boatmen; where goatherds consort with fishers dragging their nets over the wet sand; where the plough on the hillside traces a furrow to match one made by gleaming oars through the waters below; where sailors meet woodcutters, and converse together in groves sloping down to the shore; where the ripple of waves, the lowing of heifers, the creak of cordage, the whisper of leaves, at one moment delight the ear; where masts and living forest trees, fishers' nets and sheep-folds, white sails and gleaming helmets, combine to bring a scene of perfect enchantment before the eye."

"Was ever an island before joined on to a continent? Never before was such beauty seen! The largest trees bend their branches, murmuring to the crests of the waves, and naiads and hamadryads whisper together. Sweet airs from Lebanon blow across the Tyrian sands and over the cultivated fields that skirt the shore, bringing rich harvests to the farmer, and a happy voyage to the merchant. Oh happiest city in the world, mirror of earth, type of heaven, thou holdest the triple reins of the sea in thine hands, and bindest the fickle ocean to thyself! So spoke Dionysus, and turning, surveyed the city with curious eye. Long streets, whose buildings rivalled the changeful brilliancy of metals in colouring, stretched out before him. He saw the house of his ancestor, Agenor, the palace of Cadmus, the work-room whence Europa was snatched away. Then he paused to contemplate the deep wells that supply the city with a limpid water, which, after having dipped down almost to the centre of the earth, here springs up to the light."

These deep wells of water, which excited so much admiration in the god, and the artificial mole joining the island on to the continent, of which he speaks so enthusiastically, did not exist in the city's most prosperous days. Both were relics of seasons of adversity; for the wells were first dug to supply the citizens with water during the long blockade of thirteen years which ended in the sack of the city by the Assyrians under Nebuchadnezzar, and the mole was constructed by Alexander the Great when he laid siege to the place. In Tyre's happiest days, the city consisted of three parts, divided, as the islands of Venice are divided, by bright sheets of water, along which square-sailed ships and barges were constantly passing to and fro. One division of the city stretched out on the mainland, and consisted principally of streets of private houses, flanked by magnificent gardens and groves of palm, citron, and orange trees. It was called by Greek writers Palætyrus, Old Tyre, but it was probably built later than the busy maritime portion of the city, which quite filled up a rocky island, standing about a mile out in the sea. The great harbour was on one side of the island, and in its neighbourhood the work-rooms, the store-shops, and the abodes of those engaged in mercantile affairs were congregated; walls of immense height surrounded the rock, and to a strong citadel within the walls the king and all the principal inhabitants retired, as to an almost impregnable fortress, whenever any danger threatened the state.

CHAPTER X.

THE HIGH PLACES OF BAAL.

A THIRD division of the city of Tyre stood on another much smaller rocky island, and consisted of the Temple of the Tyrian god Baal-Melkarth, and of the houses of the priests, and other sacred buildings connected with the temple service. It was a sort of holy island, to which not only Phœnicians, but strangers from different parts of the world made pilgrimages. Herodotus heard of the glory of the Tyrian temple, and made a voyage to Tyre expressly to visit it. He found it, he says, richly adorned with a number of offerings, among which were two pillars, one of pure gold, the other of emerald, "shining with great brilliancy at night."

It was dedicated to Baal, the sun or fire god, under the title Melkarth, king of the city. The building itself was probably not of any great size. In common with all Phœnician and Syrian temples it would consist of two parts: an outer court, where Herodotus must have seen the pillars of gold and emerald, or more probably stained glass,—for, like the Venetians, the Tyrians were the cleverest artificers in glass of their time,—and the sanctuary, where were kept the sacred symbols, and the arks on which the symbols were placed when brought out for worship. The Tyrian sanctuary contained a very large cone-shaped emerald, whose lustre was supposed to symbolize the strength and brilliancy of the fire-god.

The religion of the Phœnicians was the same as that of all the Canaanitish people, and, with some slight variations, of the Philistines and of the wandering tribes—Moabites, Midianites, and Amalekites—who hovered round the confines of Palestine, always ready to take advantage of the times of Israel's weakness to rush in and oppress the land.

From seeing the worship of Baal followed by all the nations round them, the Israelites were continually tempted to fall away from the pure service of Jehovah to take part in its degrading rites. It is the form of idolatry which in the sacred narrative is constantly put in opposition to the true religion. Was Jehovah God? Was Baal God? The prophets and reformers from Gideon to Elijah were continually putting this problem before the people, who continued for centuries to waver in their allegiance; sometimes following Jehovah, and then again bowing down to the gods of the nations round them.

To understand the full force of the contrast between the service of Jehovah and the worship of Baal, we must consider who Baal was, and what the Canaanites meant by their worship of him.

The word Baal means lord or king, in the sense rather of owner than of ruler. The Canaanites do not appear to have been in the habit of representing their god Baal under the form of any graven image. In the shrines of his temples he was usually represented by an emblem of stone, a cone-shaped marble, or an aërolite fallen from heaven, or as at Tyre, by a precious stone; these stones they called Beityls (Bethels, houses of God), because they believed that somehow or other the power of the god had got into the stone. Creative power seems to have been the attribute they personified and reverenced in Baal—power alone, disunited from any conception of righteousness or goodness in the wielder of it; and thus contemplating the Creator under no moral or spiritual aspect, they became unable to separate Him in their thoughts from His works. Baal, the lord, became Baalim, lords, and was worshipped at different places under different names, till each town and village found a principle of division instead of a principle of union in the national religion, and worshipped its own separate divinity within its own walls, Baal-Sidon, Baal-Melkarth.

Besides these local divisions, fresh names and personifications were invented for the god as new aspects of nature came to be considered.

He was first and chiefly Baal-Samin, the sun-god, the lord of the heavens, the begetter and nourisher of all life. But he was something besides this, something nearer and more dreadful,—he was Molech; the bright heat of the sun come down to the earth as fire to consume or aid—a god whose fierce destroying nature must be propitiated with cruel rites, by priests cutting and wounding themselves with knives, and children dragged through the fire.

In a gentler mood he was Baal-Thammuz or Adonis, lord of the spring sun, and of the abundant verdure and tender fresh flowers that spring up under his rays; lord of the dawn too, and of youthful beauty, also of change and death. His worship was a mixture of funeral ceremonies and birth songs, of weeping and rejoicing: for as the spring verdure was seen to wither under the summer sun and come back to reclothe the earth next year; and the dews and shadows of the dawn were eaten up by the fires of mid-day to reappear in the evening; so Thammuz was fabled to be continually slain and continually reborn to gladden mankind.

The principal seat of the worship of Thammuz was at Gebal, a city lying about sixty miles north of Tyre on the coast, near which flowed a river said to be reddened every autumn with the blood of the slain god; but he seems to have had votaries all over Phœnicia. Devotion to him was a special temptation of the maidens of Israel, whose weeping for Thammuz formed part of Ezekiel's vision of the sins that had brought destruction on his nation.

A somewhat similar conception of the vivifying and destroying power of the sun's rays gave rise to another and less graceful personification of Baal. As president over the decomposition and subsequent reconstruction under new forms of organized matter, he was Baal-zebub, the lord of flies. In this character he was principally worshipped at Ekron, a town of the Philistines. Among the Jews in later times the name came to be a title of contempt and derision, and was applied to the evil one: "Beelzebub the prince of the devils" (Matt. xii. 24).

Like all worshippers of the powers of nature, the Phœnicians and Canaanites recognised a feminine receptive element in nature, which they personified and worshipped side by side with the vivifying and destructive forces. The chief of the feminine deities was Ashtoreth or Astarte—in some cities the moon goddess, in others connected with the planet Venus. In the Bible the name is put always in the plural; for as there were many Baalim, so were there many different forms of Ashtoreth worshipped in conjunction with them, but everywhere with the same corrupt rites that caused this goddess to be spoken of as the abomination of the Sidonians.

The Ashtaroth were symbolized by trees or pillars of wood, in the same way that the Baalim were represented under the form of columns of stone. These symbolic trees, called Asherah (a word frequently translated "grove" in the Bible), were sometimes kept inside the temples, and sometimes planted round the altars of Baal. It was a grove of symbolic trees or pillars of Ashtoreth surrounding an altar of Baal that Gideon and ten of his servants cut down in the night at the command of the angel of the Lord; and of the same nature was the grove that the pious king Josiah brought out of the temple and destroyed when he banished the worship of Baal and Ashtoreth from Jerusalem.

Natural groves were, however, considered to be sacred to the goddess, and were much resorted to by her worshippers; for though the Phœnicians are said by Berosus to have been the first people who built temples for the residence of their gods, they seem to have conducted a great part of their worship in the open air. Every deep well, every fountain, every fruitful field, was looked upon as the residence of a god. The planets were "The Strong Ones," and worshipped as the special protectors of mariners; the mountains were "The High Ones," the faces of the gods; trees, apart from their connexion with Astarte, were reverenced as sacred. The Bible tells how the contagion of this idolatry, connected as it was with licentious rites and revelry, spread to the people of Israel and Judah, and how they defiled the land by making "every high hill" and all the "tops of the mountains," every thick oak and green grove, all the "pleasant places," scenes of debasing idol-worship. The rites practised by the Phœnicians and Canaanites are said to have been more corrupting than those of any other idolatrous worship. Pre-eminent for cruelty was the service rendered to the special deity of Tyre, Baal-Melkarth, identical with Molech and Chemosh, the fire-god. We learn something of the manner in which the Tyrian priests approached and addressed their god from the description in the eighteenth chapter of the First Book of Kings; of the conduct of the four hundred and fifty priests of Baal who assembled on Mount Carmel to answer the challenge of the prophet Elijah. It was the Tyrian Baal-

Melkarth, the sun-god descended to earth in the form of fire, whose worship Jezebel, the daughter of the Tyrian king, had introduced into Samaria, and Elijah's challenge to her priests to prove their power by calling down their god from heaven touched them in the most vital part of their belief. It was the pride of Tyre to worship the "power" under the form in which it approached men most nearly. Had they not got it manifest among them, burning night and day in the heart of their glowing emerald in the shrine at Melkarth? If fire would not come down at their call, the Tyrians were deserted by their special god.

We are told how they prepared the sacrifice, and with what despairing energy they called from morn till evening, "O Baal, hear us," and leaped on the altar; and how in answer to Elijah's mockery they cried aloud, and cut themselves after their manner with knives and lancets till the blood gushed out upon them; and how there was neither voice, nor any to answer, nor any that regarded.

But scenes of frantic invocations, enforced with self-torture, were not the most terrific that were acted before the altars of the Tyrian Baal. In times of danger, or on special occasions, such as the sending out of a new colony, it was customary to propitiate his favours by offering sacrifices of children, sometimes to the number of two or three hundred at a time, whom their parents gave up to be burned alive, or dragged through the fires on his altars.

It is strange that the descendants of Abraham,

acquainted with the history of the special instruction he had received from God on the subject of human sacrifices when he was withheld from offering up Isaac, should ever have fallen away from their faith in a heavenly Father so far as to take part in dark and fearful rites like these. Yet the denunciations of the prophets, and the enactments of the Law, show that the practice of offering children to Molech must have been common among the Jews for several centuries. At their first settlement in the Holy Land they learned to worship the fire-god from the Ammonites and Moabites, and at a later period their connexion with the Tyrians gave a fresh impulse to this form of idolatry.

According to Jewish tradition, idolatrous services in honour of the fire-god were celebrated before a great brazen image, set up without the gates of Jerusalem, and surrounded by seven chapels. The figure was hollow within, and had "the face of a calf, and hands stretched out like the man who holds out his hand to receive something of his neighbour." A fire was kindled within the hollow image, and the child about to be sacrificed was placed on the outstretched hands, and burned or scorched to death by the flames rising up from beneath. The place was called "Tophet," because they used to make a noise with drums (*tophim*), that the father might not hear the cry of his child and have pity on him; and also "Hinnom," because the babe wailed (*menahem*), and the noise of his wailing went up. Thus "they sacrificed their sons and their daughters to devils and shed innocent blood, the blood of their sons and their daughters, whom they sacrificed unto the idols of Canaan;"[1] and built high places of "Tophet" to burn their sons and their daughters in the fire.[2]

The brazen image used for burnt-offerings by the Carthaginians, who brought the worship of the fire-god from Tyre, seems to have been precisely similar to the idol at Jerusalem. Diodorus Siculus says that during Agathodes' siege of Carthage, the Carthaginians sacrificed two hundred children in one day to Baal-Melkarth, placing the infants on the outstretched hands of the brazen idol, that dropped them into a blazing furnace beneath. W. Lenormant is of opinion that the Grecian stories of the Cretan man of brass Talos, and of the Minotaur that devoured children, are founded on recollections of brazen images of Molech, which the Tyrians had set up on those spots during the early occupations of the islands of the Ægean.

So corrupt a religion must naturally have had a debasing influence on the character of the people who followed it, and we find the Phœnicians unfavourably spoken of even by heathen writers. They are said to have been cruel, perfidious, and selfish, each separate city greedy only of gain for itself, and incapable of any generous care for the good of the country as a whole. The Bible history furnishes us with two examples of Phœnician character: the wicked Jezebel, Elijah's enemy, and her daughter Athaliah, the remorseless murderess of all the royal family of Judah.

[1] Ps. cvi. 37.   [2] Jer. vii. 31.

For several centuries after Tyre became the chief city of the Phœnician confederacy, there appears to have been very little intercourse between the Tyrians and Israelites. The Phœnicians, as far as we know, did not enter into any new war with the Philistines after that one in which Sidon was captured; and though they must have seen with satisfaction the successes of the Israelites over their ancient rivals and enemies, they never appear to have taken any part in the long struggle which for many centuries made the border-line between Philistia and Judea a scene of constant warfare.

CHAPTER XI.

HIRAM, KING OF TYRE.

WHEN at length the victory was gained for the Israelites, when the splendid triumphs of David had broken the power of the Philistines, and secured the strong fort of Jebus for the capital of the new empire he was founding, the people of Tyre sent the first overtures of friendship. Hiram the Second was at that time king of Tyre. The Bible tells us that he was "ever a lover of David," and that one sentence about him makes him stand out before us as a real personage, as no other Tyrian monarch does. We think of him while he was young, following with enthusiasm the steps of David's adventurous career, rejoicing in his escapes and successes; and at length, when he was himself king of Tyre, and David had gained one great wish of his heart, and possessed himself of the stronghold of Zion, sending him an embassy to congratulate him on his triumph, and to offer him presents of oaks and cedars from the forest of Lebanon, and carpenters and masons from Tyre to instruct his people, who had hitherto chiefly resided in tents, in the art of house-building. Though the express command of

God deferred the building of the Temple till a more peaceful reign than David's had dawned, the alliance with Hiram enabled David to make those preparations for the great work which solaced him for not being permitted to begin it himself.

Only by the aid of the Tyrian traders, whose ships went out into all parts of the world, could he have got together the immense stores of cedar-wood and precious stones, "glistening stones and onyx stones, and marbles and metals of every kind in abundance," that he left at his death ready for Solomon to begin the building of the Temple.

But while Hiram was sending cedars and marbles and skilled workmen to David and Solomon, he did not neglect the adornment of his own island city. He was a great builder on his own account, and did more than any other prince to give to Tyre that "perfection of beauty" of which the prophet Ezekiel speaks.

He rebuilt with very great magnificence the temple of Baal at Melkarth, and made it what it was when Herodotus visited it; he constructed an artificial mole to connect the islet where the temple stood with the rock of Tyre, and surrounded the whole with the massive walls that enabled the city to withstand so many sieges. He also built a very magnificent palace for himself within the city walls.

We may form some idea of what Hiram's palace was like by reading the description in the Second Book of Kings, and in Josephus's Antiquities, of Solomon's "house of the forest of Lebanon," which being the work of artists sent to Jerusalem by Hiram was probably constructed after Tyrian models. Josephus tells us that Solomon's palace was a very spacious building, constructed to contain a great multitude. It was surrounded by open courts, and was approached through porches of great beauty—" the porch of pillars and the porch of judgment"—covered with cedar from one side of the floor to the other. The roof was supported by cedar pillars, and the walls built of precious marbles arranged in rows; the fourth row being adorned with sculptures, "whereby were represented trees and all sorts of plants, with the shades that arose from their branches and leaves that hung down from them. Those trees and plants covered the stone that was beneath them, and their leaves were wrought so prodigiously thin and subtle that you would think they were in motion; but the other part up to the roof was plastered over, and as it were embroidered with colour and pictures."

Hiram's affection for David descended to his son Solomon. As soon as he heard of Solomon's accession to the throne, he sent an embassy to congratulate him and take part in the ceremony of his coronation. The Jewish king acknowledged the attention by sending a letter in his own handwriting to his brother monarch.

This letter, and a copy of Hiram's reply to it, were kept among the Tyrian records for several hundred years, and were still in existence at Tyre in Josephus's time, who gives a somewhat longer version of them than is found in the Book of Kings:

SOLOMON TO KING HIRAM.

"Know thou that my father would have built a temple to God, but was hindered by wars and continual expeditions, for he did not leave off to overthrow his enemies till they were all subject to tribute; but I give thanks to God for the peace I at present enjoy: and on that account I am at leisure, and design to build a house to God; for God foretold to my father that such a house should be built by me. Wherefore I desire thee to send some of thy subjects with mine to Lebanon, to cut down timber, for the Sidonians are more skilful than our people in cutting of wood. As for wages to the hewers of wood, I will pay whatsoever price thou shalt demand."

HIRAM TO KING SOLOMON.

"It is fit to bless God that He hath committed thy father's government to thee, who art a wise man and endowed with all virtues. As for me, I rejoice in the condition thou art in, and will be subservient to thee in all that thou sendest to me about: for when by my subjects I have cut down many and large trees of cedar and cypress wood, I will send them to sea, and order my subjects to make floats of them, and to sail to what place soever of thy country thou shalt desire, and leave them there, after which thy subjects may carry them to Jerusalem: but do thou take care to procure us corn for this timber, which we stand in need of, because we inhabit an island."

In accordance with Hiram's proposition, Solomon fixed on the seaport of Joppa, which was only seventy-four miles from Tyre and thirty-two from Jerusalem, as the spot to which the Tyrian sailors were to bring the floats and deliver them into the hands of his subjects. Strabo says it was reported in his time that the towers of Jerusalem could be seen from the high hill on which Joppa stood. It is hardly probable that the towers could actually be seen, yet that such an idea should exist enables us to realize the shortness of the distance between Jerusalem and Joppa, and the ease with which communication between Tyre and Solomon's capital might be carried on. Ancient writers tell us that after the first exchange of letters a very constant intercourse subsisted between the two kings. Solomon is said to have paid Hiram a visit at Tyre, and to have worshipped in the great temple of Baal at Melkarth—curious, no doubt, to compare the works which Hiram was carrying on there with his own temple and the cedar house then growing up at Jerusalem under the hands of Tyrian artists. When the two kings were apart they kept up their friendship by a frequent interchange of letters containing riddles and dark sayings, each king having promised to pay a forfeit for every riddle he could not solve. For a long time the victory was uniformly on Solomon's side; neither Hiram nor any of his sages could fathom the problems he sent, while Solomon never failed to return ready answers to all theirs. At length Hiram found a very clever Tyrian youth called Abdemon, who not only furnished the right replies to

Solomon's questions, but supplied him with queries which occasionally puzzled the Jewish sage himself.

Arabian writers have preserved many riddles and dark sayings attributed to Solomon, some of which no doubt have a strong likeness to the questions that Hiram and the Tyrian wise men pondered over. Here are some questions with which, according to Arab tradition, Solomon puzzled the sages of various nations, while he was himself still a young man. "Tell me what is everything, and what is nothing? Who is something, and who is less than nothing?" Solomon supplied the answers when the wise men, after pondering over them from morn to evening, confessed their inability to reply. "God, the Creator, is everything, but the world, the creation, is nothing; the believer is something, but the hypocrite is less than nothing." On another occasion he asked, "Which is the vilest thing, and which the most beautiful? What the most certain, and what the most uncertain?" and again was called on to supply the solution of the enigmas. "The vilest thing is a believer who apostatizes, the most beautiful a sinner who repents; the most certain thing is death and the last judgment, the most uncertain life and the fate of the soul at the resurrection."

The close alliance of Solomon, the most powerful monarch in the East, with the Tyrians appears to have given a fresh impulse to the trade of their city, and to have directed the enterprises of its merchants into somewhat new channels. The navigation of the Ægean Sea and the Archipelago was no longer as free to the Tyrian ships as it had been in the earlier times. The Greeks had some time before carried off the Golden Fleece, that is to say, the rich trade of Colchis, and the other regions lying along the coasts of Asia Minor; and now, while Hiram was reigning in Tyre and Solomon at Jerusalem, the armed galleys of the heroes of the Trojan war were passing to and fro between Asia and Europe, and turning the Archipelago into a Grecian highway. Finding themselves confronted by such formidable rivals in the nearer seas, the Phœnicians became anxious to open out new routes through which their commerce might be carried on unmolested, and gladly furnished ships and sailors for the expeditions to the far East which Solomon planned, and which he sent out year by year from a port in the Red Sea which his father-in-law the king of Egypt had ceded to him.

Hitherto the precious productions of remote Eastern countries had found their way to Phœnicia in small quantities by long perilous land journeys; now the united navies of the two enterprising monarchs, Hiram and Solomon, penetrated to what must have seemed to them the very home of riches—Ophir, now identified with the region of extensive gold mines on the coast of Malacca. Spices, precious stones, ivory, great plenty of almug-trees (sandal-wood), apes, and peacocks were brought away from thence and from the southern coast of Hindostan with the gold, and served to increase the luxury and splendour of Hiram's capital as well as that of his ally.

Fresh activity was also given, through the Jewish

alliance, to the ancient trade with Sheba, whose queen perhaps first heard of Solomon's wisdom from the visits of Tyrian ships passing along the coast of Southern Arabia, where Sheba is supposed to be situated, on their way to Ophir.

"The merchants of Sheba occupied in thy fairs," Ezekiel said, speaking of the trade between Southern Arabia and Tyre, as it had continued to his day; "they were thy merchants in all sorts of things, in blue clothes, and broidered work, and in chests of rich apparel, bound with cords and made of cedar." Voyages were also undertaken by the Jewish and Tyrian vessels in company: to Tarshish, the ancient Sidonian colony, and to still more remote Western lands; to Spain, whose silver mines then yielded so abundantly, "that silver was not anything accounted of in the days of Solomon;" and thence to our own Cornish coast, from whence the Tyrians about this time began to carry away tin in their ships, instead of having it conveyed by the overland route through Gaul to Tarshish.

As a seal to their long friendship Hiram gave his daughter in marriage to Solomon, and Solomon ceded to him a portion of Galilee lying on the borders of Tyre, which Hiram coveted because of its fruitfulness in corn. The district was still called the coasts (or boundaries) of Tyre and Sidon when our Lord visited it and healed the daughter of the Canaanitish woman who sought Him there. Hiram's daughter was one of the strange women who had such a fatal influence over Solomon, and turned away his heart from the

God of Israel in his old age. For her sake he introduced the worship of Ashtoreth the Phœnician moon-goddess, the "abomination of the Sidonians," into the Holy City itself; and for her use and that of his other Canaanitish wives he erected three altars—to Ashtoreth, to Molech, and to Chemosh (another name for Baal)—on the three heights of Olivet that overlooked the gardens of the cedar palace, which caused a portion of the hill of olive gardens to be called "the Mount of Offence" down to the times when our Lord frequented it.

Hiram died many years before Solomon. He is the only one of all the Tyrian kings whose name is connected with any monument that remains to this day. Amid the utter desolation that reigns over the site of the first Bride of the Sea, there stands a weather-beaten sarcophagus, raised on three pillars of stone, which is still known by the name of Hiram's tomb.

The prosperity to which Hiram had raised the Tyrian state declined after his death. His son was murdered in a popular tumult in the same year that the disruption of Solomon's empire was brought about by the rebellion of Jeroboam.

More than fifty years of civil disturbance and constant change of government followed for Tyre, during which its neighbour the kingdom of Israel was also torn by continual civil wars and changes of dynasty. When the two states once more, about the same time, obtained a settled government—the Israelites under the house of Omri, and the Tyrians under the rule of a king of priestly race, Ethbaal high priest of Ashtoreth, who is said to have reached the throne by the murder of his brother—a close alliance again sprang up between them. This time the connexion was altogether disastrous to Israel, for it led to the marriage of Ahab king of Israel with the daughter of Ethbaal, who was that wicked queen Jezebel with whose evil life and tragical death the Bible narrative has made us acquainted.

A pre-eminence in crime seems to have been an inheritance in the house of the fratricidal high priest of Ashtoreth. His daughter, the witch Jezebel, who had evil strength to defy the greatest of the Hebrew prophets, Elijah, has, by her crimes, caused her very name to become an epithet of reproach. The same character of ruthless cruelty reappears in Jezebel's daughter Athaliah, the murderess of all the royal house of Ahaziah; and two generations later the same family produced another monster of iniquity in Pygmalion king of Tyre, whose murder of his brother-in-law and attempt to seize his sister Dido's inheritance caused a revolution in the Tyrian state, which was followed by the departure of a large number of its chief nobility and citizens, under the leadership of Dido, the foundress of Carthage. It seems strange that the kings and citizens of Tyre, living within thirty miles of Samaria—so near that the news of every great event occurring there must have been brought to them very soon after it took place—should have heard of such catastrophes as the slaughter of Baal's prophets (probably most of them Tyrian citizens) at the brook Kishon, and the tragical murder of Jezebel in the palace of Jezreel, without being roused to avenge the death of their co-religionists and the princess of their royal house by proclaiming war upon the kingdom of Israel. Their non-intervention, even under such extreme provocation, is, however, consistent with the national character of the Tyrians, and the selfish course of policy they invariably pursued, which led them in all circumstances to sacrifice everything to the preservation of their trade, and never suffer themselves to be drawn into warfare except to protect its interests. Their traffic with Israel and Judah was even more important to them than that of any other nation, for the populous city of Tyre depended on the corn-lands of Samaria for food, for the artificers in its great workshops, and for the sailors who manned its numerous fleets.

The grudge owed by the Tyrians to the people of Israel and Judah for their severities against the votaries of Baal, which must have been intensified whenever a faithful king purged the country of the idolatries imported from Tyre, though it never led to an open rupture between the nations, rankled in the minds of the Tyrians, and showed itself in a disposition, apparent through all the subsequent course of their history, to render covert help to the enemies of Israel, and to rejoice whenever misfortune befell her. They made themselves, Ezekiel tells us, "a pricking briar" and a "grieving thorn" to the chosen people. The prophets Joel and Amos denounce the Tyrians and Sidonians for having helped the Edomites against Jerusalem, and for buying Hebrew captives from their enemies to sell to the Grecians. Ezekiel dwells on the jealousy of Tyre against Jerusalem, and her ungenerous triumph when Judah was laid low. "Son of man, because that Tyrus hath said against Jerusalem, Aha, she is broken that was the gates of the people: she is turned unto me: I shall be replenished, now she is laid waste: therefore thus saith the Lord God; Behold, I am against thee, O Tyrus, and will cause many nations to come up against thee, as the sea causeth his waves to come up."

The triumph of the Phœnicians over the Hebrews was always short-lived, for the successes of the Assyrians and Babylonians in Palestine, over which they in their short-sighted jealousy rejoiced, in every case brought misfortunes to them equal to those inflicted on their rivals.

CHAPTER XII.

"BEHOLD, I AM AGAINST THEE, O TYRUS."

THE first great blow to Phœnician prosperity was inflicted by Sargon king of Assyria, who, after conquering Samaria and carrying off the Ten Tribes, invaded Phœnicia and laid a heavy tribute on all the coast cities. Tyre alone resisted, and sustained a siege of five years, from which the Assyrian king retired without gaining any advantage. The Phœnician confederacy was, however, broken up, and the chief maritime cities on the coast were incorporated in the Assyrian empire. On the next occasion when an Assyrian army passed the Lebanon, the fleets of Sidon and Gebal were employed against Tyre, and the hitherto impregnable city fell before the attack of its old tributaries. Crippled in power, and deprived of most of its foreign settlements, Tyre still continued to flourish as the chief trading city in the world; its importance as a centre of commerce increased by the decay of the neighbouring ports. More than a hundred years after its conquest by Sennacherib, when the Assyrian power in the East had been superseded by that of Nebuchadnezzar king of Babylon,

Ezekiel describes the wealth of Tyre, and the manifold ramifications of its trade, stretching to every part of the then known world; and predicts, as speedily to come, a greater disaster than has yet befallen it.

"By thy great wisdom and by thy traffic hast thou increased thy riches, and thine heart is lifted up because of thy riches: therefore thus saith the Lord God; Because thou hast set thy heart as the heart of God; behold, I will bring strangers upon thee, the terrible of the nations: and they shall draw their swords against the beauty of thy wisdom, and shall defile thy brightness, and bring thee down to the pit, and thou shalt die the deaths of them that are slain in the midst of the seas." "Because that Tyrus hath said against Jerusalem, Aha, she is broken, that was the gates of the people . . . Behold, I will bring upon Tyrus Nebuchadrezzar king of Babylon, a king of kings, from the north, with horses, and chariots, and companies, and much people . . . They shall make a spoil of thy riches, and a prey of thy merchandise: they shall break down thy walls, and destroy thy pleasant houses; and shall lay thy stones and thy timber and thy dust in the midst of the water. And I will cause the noise of thy songs to cease; and the sound of thy harps shall be no more heard. And I will make thee like the top of a rock: thou shalt be a place to spread nets upon; thou shalt be built no more: for I the Lord have spoken it, saith the Lord God."

The Tyrians who said "Aha," in triumph over

the downfall of Jerusalem, added **the sin of treachery towards allies** to that of selfish exultation over the destruction of an ancient rival; for they had themselves **taken an active part in** the insurrection that brought **the terrible** vengeance of the Babylonian king on the city of **Jerusalem.**

They had been foremost **of** all the Palestinian nations in following the policy, so strongly denounced **by the** Jewish prophets, **of** supporting the kings of **Egypt in** their attempts **to** re-establish the ancient **supremacy** of the Pharaohs in Palestine against the **Assyrians; and when** on the decline **of Assyria,** Pharaoh-Necho entered Palestine, defeated **king Josiah** at Megiddo, and conquered Syria, they hastened to place themselves under his protection, and showed the greatest **exultation in** throwing off a yoke that had **long been oppressive to them.** The growing power **of Nebuchadnezzar did not** detach them from their faith in **Egypt. The kings of Tyre** and Sidon were two of **the monarchs to whom** the prophet Jeremiah sent **bonds and yokes, by the** hands of the ambassadors they had sent to **Jerusalem to** persuade **king** Zedekiah to rebel **against** Nebuchadnezzar, **with** the message, **"Thus saith the Lord of hosts, the God of Israel; Say** unto you masters, **I have made the earth by my great** power **and by my outstretched arm, and have given it unto whom** it seemed meet to **me. And now have I given it into the** hand of Nebu**chadnezzar king of** Babylon, **my servant;** and it **shall come to pass that the nations that will not** serve **the same Nebuchadnezzar will I punish, until** I have consumed them by his hand; but the nations that bring their neck under the yoke of the king of Babylon, and serve him, will I let remain in their own land, saith the Lord God, and they shall dwell in it and till it."

In spite of this warning, however, the Tyrians continued to urge resistance against Babylon on all their neighbours; yet when Nebuchadnezzar, "the terrible of the nations," proceeded to punish Jerusalem, they appear to have stood aside, not taking any part in the warfare—hoping perhaps, when the angry monarch's vengeance had been slaked on nearer foes, they might make terms for themselves by the surrender of a portion of their accumulated riches.

During the terrible sixteen months of the siege of Jerusalem in Zedekiah's reign, while their late allies underwent the extremities of suffering, the Tyrians looked on with indifferent, even with unfriendly eyes; and when at last the tidings came that Jerusalem had fallen, the sullen, long-brooded-over enmity, which neither community of interest nor alliance against a common enemy had softened, burst forth in unseemly exultation. "Aha," they said, " she is broken that was the gates of the people."

Their triumph was, however, soon swallowed up in mourning for themselves. The northern cities of Phœnicia submitted peacefully to the severe terms Nebuchadnezzar imposed on them; but Tyre, trusting to her fleet, her high walls, and her strong position in the midst of the sea, determined to resist. Nebuchadnezzar laid siege to the city, and finding that he could not take it by assault he retired to Babylon, leaving a portion of his army to blockade the island fortress, to which the king, another Ethbaal, and the chief part of the people retired. For thirteen years the blockade dragged on, the inhabitants defending themselves with great courage. It was then that the deep well was dug in the island to supply the besieged with water, which in after years so much excited the admiration of the Egyptian writer whose poem in praise of Tyre we have quoted. But though secure of water, as time passed on the stores of food failed, and the garrison suffered the extremity of want— "Every head grew bald" with care and misery, and every "shoulder was peeled" with the hard toil of carrying baskets of stones to repair the breaches in the walls—toil in which the noblest of the city, the merchant princes, and the delicate daughters of Tyre, whose luxury had been a proverb, partook with the lowest.

At the end of the thirteen years Nebuchadnezzar, weary of the length of time which had been spent on the enterprise, came back himself to Tyre with a great army, and after a vigorous attack took the place by storm, and gave it up to be pillaged by his soldiers.

Then the words of Ezekiel began to be fulfilled: "He shall enter into thy gates; with the hoofs of his horses shall he tread down all thy streets. He shall slay thy people with the sword. He shall destroy thy pleasant houses: and lay thy stones and thy timber in the dust. The noise of thy songs shall cease: and the sound of thy harps shall be no more heard .... Then all the princes of the sea shall come down from their thrones, and lay away their robes, and shall clothe themselves with trembling; they shall sit on the ground, and tremble at every moment, and be astonished at thee. And say, How art thou destroyed, that wast inhabited of seafaring men, the renowned city, that was strong in the sea!"

The full measure of the doom pronounced against the city did not come upon it till more than a thousand years after the time when it had been revealed to the prophetic vision of Ezekiel. Tyre rose from its ruins, and subsisted as an important seaport for many centuries after its destruction by Nebuchadnezzar; but it never again attained the dignity of an independent state. It shared in all the changes of rule that befell the neighbouring nations; flourishing under some of the governments into which it was incorporated, and again falling into decay.

It is only in, comparatively speaking, late times that travellers, visiting the site of the ancient city and looking on its ruins, have found that no words could so adequately describe the scene around them as those which the prophet had used in anticipation, when "the rock, the place for spreading nets," on which their eyes rest, was the richest and most beautiful city of the ancient world.

A traveller who visited Tyre in 1784 thus describes Sour, the modern village that occupies its site: "Sour is situated on a peninsula, which projects from the shore into the sea in the form of a mallet with an oval head. This head is a solid rock covered with brown earth, which forms a small plain about one hundred paces long. The isthmus that joins this plain to the continent is of pure sand. This difference of soil renders the ancient insular state of the plain, before Alexander joined it to the shore by a mole, very visible. The village is situated at the junction of this isthmus with the ancient island, of which it does not cover one-third. The whole village only contains fifty or sixty poor families, which live obscurely on the produce of their little ground and a trifling fishery. The houses they occupy are no longer edifices of three or four stories high, but wretched huts ready to crumble to pieces. Instead of that ancient commerce, so active and extensive, Sour is reduced to a miserable village; has no other trade than the exportation of a few sacks of corn, nor any merchant but a single Greek factor, who scarcely makes sufficient to maintain his family."[1]

"What city is like Tyrus, like the destroyed in the midst of the sea? ... The merchants among the people shall hiss at thee; thou shalt be a terror, and never shalt be any more" (Ezek. xxvii. 32, 36).

[1] Volney's Travels, p. 210.

CHAPTER XIII.

THE ASSYRIAN.

" BEHOLD, the Assyrian was a cedar in Lebanon with fair branches, and with a shadowing shroud. The waters made him great, the deep set him up on high with her rivers running about his plants, and sent out her little rivers unto all the trees of the field. The cedars in the garden of God could not hide him: the fir trees were not like his boughs, and the chesnut trees were not like his branches. I have made him fair by the multitude of his branches: so that all the trees of Eden, that were in the garden of God, envied him."

Under this figure of the trees of the garden of God, which is carried on through several chapters of Ezekiel's prophecy, we see sketched out the history of all the nations of the East in the first ages, as Daniel's vision of the image and of the four beasts sketches the rise and fall of the empires of later times.

Ezekiel sees in his vision the ancient garden of God, Eden—the country watered by mighty rivers, that enclosed first paradise and afterwards the district that was the nursery-ground of all the nations of mankind. There the young trees (the different races of men), the great cedars and the little cedars, the chesnuts and the firs, with their unlike foliage, grew up side by side till the time for their planting out came. Tyre was there a stately tree ("thou hast been in Eden, in the garden of God," Ezekiel says of Tyre in another place), and Damascus and the other Syrian cities the little cedars that tried to hide the young giant cedar of Assyria on its first planting out; and Egypt and Israel were there, great chesnuts and firs towering up into diverse branch and foliage. Then Ezekiel describes the growth of the trees transplanted to their places in the world outside the garden, and notes how, beyond all others, the roots of the Assyrian tree spread and spread; how its plants (its beautiful cities) were made great by waters, the deep Tigris river, and all the little tributary rivers that fenced them round; and how its branches stretched far and wide, and thickened and deepened into a shadowing shroud; till at length it became a great upas growth, under which all the other trees that had been with it in the garden of God languished and withered away. Then he tells how the great tree was cut down and left upon the mountains, and in the valleys, its branches broken and its boughs bent low by its rivers; and how all the people of the earth came out from under its shadow and left it alone.

Almost all nations have traditions, more or less distinct, of a time before the time when they began to live in the place where they are found, when their authentic history begins. An emigration from one place, and a settlement in another, is generally the starting-point for their stories, and behind that a loving, transforming memory of some first home, some Eden of God, or golden age, glows with a faint light. Many conjectures have been hazarded respecting the position of the spot which was the first home of the human race. Mr. Rawlinson believes it to have been that portion of the alluvial plain of Chaldea bordering on the Persian Gulf, where the remains of the first cities of the world—Ur and Babel and Erech—have been found. The planting out of the Assyrian tree from this spot is recorded in the tenth chapter of Genesis. "The beginning of his (Nimrod's) kingdom was Babel, and Erech, and Calneh, and Accad, in the land of Shinar. Out of that land went Asshur, and builded Nineveh."

At some time—it is impossible to fix the date—a spirit of enterprise seized on the Shemite tribes living among the Chaldeans and mixed people who formed the population of the first settled habitations of the world, and prompted them to move northwards to find fresh houses for themselves. Terah led, as we have seen, one band of emigrants from Ur to Haran, and separated the Hebrew people from the rest of mankind; a second band of mixed Cushites and Shemites made their way from the shores of the Persian Gulf to the slip of sea-coast behind Lebanon, and founded the great trading cities of Phœnicia; while a third party, probably larger than either of the other two, ascending the Tigris, began to found cities on its banks, and grew gradually, first into an independent, and then into a powerful people.

The great tree was planted out, and its roots were strengthened and its offshoots nourished by the fostering waters near which it was placed; but, like all mighty things, its growth was for some time slow and noiseless. The Phœnician fishing villages had grown into renowned cities, and their settlements had multiplied and spread into all parts of the world, while Nineveh was still an unimportant place, only mentioned with other towns, in lists of conquered cities, on Egyptian monuments. The children of Israel passed through their long captivity in Egypt, and conquered Canaan, and came out victorious from their long struggle with the Philistines before the Assyrians had made any permanent conquests beyond the district on each side of the Tigris, which may be called Assyria Proper.

In the times of the later judges, however, a warlike monarch, Tiglath-Pileser the First ascended the throne of Assyria, and by his conquests laid the foundation for the greatness of the empire. He stands out distinctly before us from among a number of scarcely known kings that come before and after him, because a clay cylinder of his time, on which is graven in very minute characters an account of all that he did during the first five years of his reign, has come down to us, and has been translated into English by Sir H. Rawlinson. It is interesting for the light it throws on the state of the countries bordering on Assyria Proper in Tiglath-Pileser the First's reign, and for the constant mention of the gods worshipped in Assyria, to whose intervention the successes recorded are already referred. The king tells his own story, and speaks in the first person throughout the document. The style in which he relates his adventures is much more lively and picturesque than that which prevails in the inscriptions of later monarchs. We will give a few sentences in which his more distant journeys are described.

The record begins with an enumeration of titles:—
"Tiglath-Pileser, the mighty king; king of legions of people; king of all lands watered by the Euphrates; king of kings; lord of lords; the arbitrator, the venerable, the majestic.

"In the beginning of my reign 20,000 men of the Muskayans and their five kings, whom no king of Assyria had ever ventured to meet in battle, went and seized the country of Comukha.... In the service of my god Assur I assembled my chariots and warriors; I passed through the difficult region of Kasiyara;.... I fought with the 20,000 men and the five kings, and defeated them, and cut off their heads; their moveables, their wealth, and their valuables, I plundered to a countless amount."

"Then I went on to the land of Comukha. I conquered the whole country; I burned their cities with fire; I destroyed and ruined; .... I travelled over the rough mountains and difficult wildernesses in carts made of iron;.... I smote the fighting men like wild beasts in the middle of their forests; their dead bodies choked up the Tigris, the roaring waters carried them down.

"In the course of fighting, king Kaliteru fell into my power. I took from him his wives and his children, the delight of his heart. I seized his treasures; three times sixty iron vessels, five copper trays, together with the gold and silver gods of the people, and their beds and furniture. I plundered everywhere, and then burned the city and the palace with fire."

"By the constant help of my god Assur I reached the land of Kharia.... As the steep mountains stood up like metal posts, I placed my chariots on waggons, and thus traversed the hills.... I fought the tribes in an inaccessible region.... The ranks of the slain were piled up in heaps on the peaks of the mountains; dead bodies choked up the ravines. I traversed difficult mountain-chains and distant hills, which none of our kings had ever previously reached; the easy parts in my chariot, and the difficult parts in waggons of iron.... The people took away their gods and fled like birds to a valley among rugged hills."

"Twenty-three kings of the countries of Nairi came to fight with me. I swept away their far-spreading troops as with the tempest of Vul. I took their great castles; I converted their cities into heaps and mounds. .... I poured out their wealth before my lord the sun-god, and condemned them to do homage to my great god to their last day.... I overthrew Khurac (their capital) like a heap of corn. I defeated their entire army, and caught their heavy-armed troops in a forest as in a trap. Three great castles of theirs, which were fiery red with burned brick, and vaulted all over, I dug up and reduced to heaps and desolations. I gave six thousand of their soldiers to my own for slaves.

"There fell into my hands altogether, between the commencement of my reign and my fifth year, forty-two countries and their kings from beyond the river Zab to the Euphrates, and from the country of the Khatti [the northern Hittites] to the upper ocean of the setting sun. I brought them under one government. I placed them under the Magian religion."

The upper region of the setting sun probably means the Caspian Sea. The district thus described includes an area of about four hundred miles each way—not larger than France. The fact of so small a country being divided into forty-two separate states, each with its independent king, shows the political weakness of the countries adjoining Assyria at that time, and explains Tiglath-Pileser's easy victories, and the speed with which he overruns one petty kingdom after another. Much the same state of things seems to have prevailed in Syria and in the mountainous regions west of the Tigris as Joshua found in Canaan. The people were split up into tribes, who usually lived in a state of chronic hostility to each other, and every fortified place had a petty king at its head. When danger threatened they made hasty leagues for mutual defence, "four kings" or "five kings" bringing their soldiers and their chariots to some appointed spot to fight the invaders; but jealousies of old standing prevented any real co-operation, and on the first symptom of ill fortune the league split up, and the little army melted away, each chieftain hurrying off to protect his own castle.

As a sequel to the history of his conquests, Tiglath-

Pileser relates his valorous exploits in the hunting-excursions which were his relaxations in the intervals between his campaigns. "I have omitted to mention many hunting expeditions," he says, "which were not connected with any warlike achievements. In pursuing after game I traversed easy tracts in my chariots, difficult ones on foot. The gods Hercules and Nergal gave their keen arms and weighty weapons into my hands. I killed ten large wild buffaloes on the banks of the Khabur; four others I brought home to my capital city Assur. By the help of my guardian god Nebo I laid low eight hundred lions. All the beasts of the field and the birds of heaven I made victims of my shafts."

The egotism of the narrative is somewhat lessened by the constant reference to aid rendered by the gods of the country and of the royal house in whose service Tiglath-Pileser professes to have undertaken all his expeditions. Their names are enumerated on the cylinder, and we find that, with one or two exceptions, they are the same gods worshipped by the Chaldeans when Terah lived among them, the gods whom Abraham left behind him when he crossed the Euphrates. These are the titles Tiglath Pileser gives them, and the prayer to them with which he opens his record of victories:—"Assur, the great lord, the giver of sceptres and thrones; Bel, the lord king of the circle of the constellations; Sin (or Hurki the moon-god), the leader, the powerful, the conspicuous; Shamas [the sun-god], the establisher, the vanquisher of enemies, the dissolver of cold;

Ishtar, the eldest, the queen of victory; ye gods, who rule over heaven and earth, who made the depth and the height, O majestic beings, enlarge the royalty of Tiglath-Pileser, and place him in the love of your hearts."

At the end of his annals Tiglath-Pileser intimates that his prayer has been heard, for that Assur and Nin have exalted him to the utmost wishes of his heart. He has acknowledged them in all his deeds, he professes, and by this means has obtained a prosperous and long life. In return for so much favour he set himself to the task of repairing the altars of the gods which in former reigns have fallen into decay.

"In the beginning of my reign," he says, "the great gods Anu and Vul invited me to repair their shrines; so I made bricks and raised a lofty mound of earth, and laid the foundations of the temples on it. I built it up fresh from its foundation to its roof. I built lofty towers in honour of their noble godships, and rejoiced their hearts. I fashioned everything carefully, inside as well as out, and beautified the entire building. As I have laboured on this excellent house for the residence of Vul and Anu, and have finished it successfully to the delight of their noble godships, may they preserve me in power, may they bring the rain, the joy of the earth, on the cultivated land and on the desert in my time. May they preserve me victorious in battle, and keep the lands I have subdued faithful to my children. I have graven the history of my victories on my clay cylinders, and placed them in the temple, to stay there till the last days. In after times, if the temple falls into decay, may the prince who comes after me repair it and my tablets. Whoever shall injure my cylinders, moisten them with water, or scorch them with fire, or assign them a position in the holy place where they cannot be seen or understood, or erase the writing and inscribe his own name there instead of mine, may the great gods assign his name to perdition, may he be cursed with an irrevocable curse, may Vul (the wind-god) tear up the produce of his land, may famine afflict his country, may he not be called happy one day, may his name and his race perish from out of the land."

Tiglath-Pileser's anxiety about his clay cylinders reads curiously now, when we think of the vicissitudes which have befallen the one on which he has recorded it. Through hundreds of years its delicately traced minute writing has escaped being erased, or scorched by fire, or moistened by water; and after lying long in a place where it could neither be seen nor understood, it has been rescued from its obscurity by a strange series of events, and set up once more under the daylight of strange skies, to be an object of wonder and interest to a race of men of whom the old king had never heard.

Later on in his reign, Tiglath-Pileser engaged in warfare with the Babylonians; when, after some successes, he met with a serious reverse that must somewhat have disturbed his happy confidence in his exclusive possession of Divine favour.

With something of the same superstitious feeling

to which the children of Israel about the same time gave way, when they carried the Ark of the Covenant before them to battle against the Philistines, Tiglath-Pileser carried images of his great gods with him in his campaign against Babylon. The Babylonish king succeeded in capturing and carrying off the images, as the Philistines captured the Ark, and the Assyrians had to retreat to their own land, leaving these precious trophies of victory behind in the hands of their enemies. That the loss was felt as a serious misfortune and deep humiliation by the nation is evident from the tone of triumph in which an Assyrian king, who took Babylon four hundred years afterwards, records his recovery of these images and his restoration of them to their own temples.

Tiglath-Pileser died while Samuel was righteously and peacefully ruling Israel. His successors for the next two hundred years are little known. The power of Assyria waned, while the kingdom of Israel was rising into importance, and was for a time entirely eclipsed by the glories of the empire established by David, and maintained by his son Solomon.

Only once is there any appearance of the Assyrian kings having made an attempt to withstand the advance of the new power, whose rapid growth might well have awakened their jealousy. In the tenth chapter of the Second Book of Samuel, which relates the league of the Ammonites and the Syrians against David, and their defeat by David's great captain, Joab, an allusion is made to "Syrians from beyond the river," whom the confederate Ammonites and Syrians summoned to their aid when they found themselves unequal to cope with the Israelites. These Syrians from beyond the river (the Euphrates) must have been either Assyrians, or troops of some tributary nation, sent by the Assyrian king, to help the confederates in their attempt to crush the new monarchy that had suddenly become formidable to its neighbours.

After the signal defeat of the Ammonites and their allies by David in person, the Assyrians withdrew finally from the contest; "fearing," as the sacred historian tells us, "to help the children of Ammon against the Israelites any more."

In the 83d Psalm, "David's complaint to God of his enemies' conspiracies," the names of the nations who joined in this confederacy are enumerated; the verse, "Assur also is joined with them," is thought to refer to the Assyrians, who were the descendants and worshippers of Assur (or Ashur), Assur being also at that time the name of their chief city.

It was not till after the breaking up of Solomon's empire that a king again sat on the Assyrian throne who felt himself powerful enough to carry his arms into the countries Tiglath-Pileser had overrun.

His name was Assurizirpal (the god Assur protects his son). In his time the arts of building and architecture made a great advance in Assyria. The temples and palaces of the earlier kings, those which Tiglath-Pileser prided himself so much on restoring, do not appear to have differed greatly from the massive, unornamented, brick structures that Urukh and Ilgi reared in the earliest known cities of Asia.

THE ASSYRIAN.

From Assurizirpal's reign date the marble slabs, sculptured with battle and hunting scenes, and strange figures of eagle-headed and fish-tailed divinities, that form the distinguishing feature of Assyrian architecture in its best times. His sculptured palace, the first of the kind, was situated at Calah, now called Nimroud, the spot once thought to be Nineveh itself, from whose gigantic mounds of ruins Mr. Layard brought so many treasures of ancient art to England. The slabs that once lined Assurizirpal's great halls and galleries came with others, and, ranged along the walls of the British Museum now, make the name of the "well-protected son of Assur," his high-featured face, his marches through forests of tall palm-trees, his passage of rivers swarming with fish, his encounters with his enemies, his chariots, his scaling-ladders, his presentation of offerings to eagle-headed gods, very familiar to English eyes.

Assurizirpal's marbles are distinguished from those of later kings by having inscriptions cut across the middle of the bas-reliefs. These disfiguring lines tell, in much the same style as that of the clay cylinders of Tiglath-Pileser, the story of the different years of Assurizirpal's life—how he overran the mountainous country lying to the north-east of the Tigris; how he took two hundred and fifty strong walled cities, and made their kings prisoners, and flayed some of them and hung others up on their town walls; how he marched against a town in central Nairi, whose people had rebelled against him; how they grew frightened at his approach, and hastened to submit their city and their king to his mercy; how he showed his mercy by sending the king in chains to Nineveh to be dealt with at his leisure, and by crucifying and hanging and cutting off the ears and noses of the chief inhabitants of the place. Well might the author of the seventy-fourth Psalm, writing while kings of similar character were ruling in all the heathen countries around, complain that the "dark places of the earth" were full of "the habitations of cruelty."

The most interesting of the many wars was that of the ninth year of Assurizirpal's reign, waged in Syria, when the king, after taking Carchemish, and defeating the Northern Hittites—whose chiefs, he tells us, came out and kissed his sceptre—crossed the Lebanon and received the submission of the Phœnician cities, Tyre (where Ethbaal, the father of Jezebel, was then reigning), Sidon, and Aradus. This was the first threatening of danger from the far East that had reached the Palestinian peoples—the little cloud no bigger than a man's hand that was hereafter to overshadow all their sky. The maritime cities appear to have been content to buy off an attack by bringing an ample tribute. Assurizirpal boasts of having seen the great sea of Phœnicia, and of having sacrificed to his gods on the tops of its high mountains, and brought away from Tyre the wood of the country for his new buildings at Calah—probably cedars of Lebanon, such as Solomon had received from Hiram for the building of the Temple a hundred and fifty years before.

Like Tiglath-Pileser, Assurizirpal was a keen sportsman as well as an indefatigable warrior. He breaks off in the history of his battles and sieges to recount how he "slew fifty large wild bulls on the left bank of the Euphrates," and how on another occasion he took captive "twenty live ostriches and killed as many more." The twenty live ostriches, with other strange animals that fell in his way on his expeditions into foreign countries, he sent home to Calah. He seems to have had a menagerie of wild beasts in his pleasure-grounds there, for he records having received a present of elephants from the Tyrians, who must have brought them from India or Africa, and says that he placed them in his park, where they throve and bred.

He does not say quite as much as Tiglath-Pileser about the gods, but besides his own great palace temple he built several temple-towers that were more richly ornamented within and without than any edifices of the kind in former reigns. At the foot of one of them a shrine has been discovered, which contains a bas-relief of the monarch himself surmounted by sacred emblems, and having in front of it an altar of sacrifice. This seems to indicate that either during their lifetime or after their death the Assyrian kings received divine honours from their subjects. Sir Henry Rawlinson and Mr. Layard are of opinion that the splendid Assyrian palaces which Assurizirpal set the example of building, were designed not merely as residences for the king, but as temples for public worship. Their peculiar construction, the number of sacred emblems used in their decoration, and the length of the great halls which occupy the chief part of the space enclosed, appear to show that they were planned with a view to the accommodation of ceremonials of a stately and solemn kind; while, on the other hand, the mixture of secular subjects in the bas-reliefs and the prominence of the king's figure everywhere, would lead to the conclusion that if any sort of worship was carried on in them it must have been the worship of the monarch himself, who, in Assyria even more than in Egypt, was evidently looked upon as the representative, if not an incarnation, of the Divine power. This was the idolatry in which the old worship of powers in heaven and earth and air at last culminated; a servile bowing down before the coarsest form of power that could be set up for adoration—the despotic will of a fellow-man.

CHAPTER XIV.

AN ASSYRIAN PALACE.

THE Assyrian palace temples, which all more or less resembled in their style of architecture the first sculptured one of Assurizirpal, were built on high square platforms, the piling up of which to an immense elevation formed a suitable task for the crowds of miserable captives that the warlike kings who reared the palaces brought back from their foreign expeditions. These artificial hills were usually situated close to the city walls, frequently at the corner of the town, so that two sides of the palace, towering high above the city walls, looked towards the open country. These two sides were defended either by wide moats lying without the walls, or, as was the case with Assurizirpal's palace, by having the river on which the city was built flowing past them.

The country fronts of the palaces were broken by no doorways, as the palace was only entered from the city side; but the pleasantest of the apartments, perhaps those set aside for the private house of the king, must have been situated there. The building did not cover the entire area of the high platform;

there was room on it for one or more open courts, perhaps laid out as gardens, and ornamented with pavilions and sculptures, round which the buildings were ranged. The walls, of immense thickness, were built of crude brick, faced within and without with stone slabs ranged in double rows, and sculptured in bas-relief. Small slabs, covered with writing explanatory of the pictures, divided the bas-reliefs. Above the stone pictures and the writing, to the top of the wall, a space of about three feet was filled up by courses of enamelled bricks of brilliant colours, arranged in patterns which, outside and inside, must have contrasted beautifully with the shadowed pale yellow or cool grey of the sculptured stone beneath. These high, solid walls were not pierced by any windows. The light which illuminated the minute writing and the processions of strange figures, and that glinted back from the bright-coloured tiles that lined the long halls they enclosed, must have slanted down either through openings in the roof, or through interstices between the tops of the walls and the roofing. Mr. Ferguson is disposed to think that double rows of short cedar columns were placed on all the walls—partition walls and outside walls alike—and that these, with other tall wooden pillars placed at equal distances apart in the halls, supported a flat wooden roof. Light and air could thus freely enter between the columns, while the overpowering heat of the sun might be moderated by a system of shutters, or silken curtains arranged between the rows of short columns on the outside walls.

Mr. Rawlinson thinks that the lighting was effected through openings in the wooden roof, which might also have been protected in inclement weather by carpets drawn across, or coloured awnings. Under either system it is difficult to believe that the wooden roof could have been solid enough to support an upper story; but its flat surface of sweet-smelling cedar wood must have been a delightful walking place, and was no doubt strong enough to hold up some little chambers or secret pavilions, to which those who were weary of gazing on the fantastic sculptured scenery within, and wished to refresh themselves by looking abroad, might come up. There would be a magnificent prospect for them, and the choice of contrasted scenes. A promenader on the roof of an Assyrian palace, if he chose the country side for his walk, would see, looking down the sheer depth of city and palace wall, a still moat covered with water-lilies; or, if it were Assurizirpal's palace he was walking on, the rapid waters of the Tigris (the arrow-river) darting past far below his feet. Beyond the river fortifications would lie the king's and queen's pleasure gardens; and further away the enclosed park, where the lion cubs the king had brought from his last hunting expedition and the Tyrian presents of elephants were kept, and where gentler specimens of foreign zoology were perhaps permitted to roam about freely.

If he tired of the country prospect, and chose either of the other sides of the great elevated quadrangle for his walk, he would have the whole of the busy city lying at his feet, and might watch the citizens and courtiers passing through the lion-guarded gates, up the hundred steps of the platform to the grand entrance of the palace, to pay their respects to the king in his hall of state; or note the exits and entrances of the servants and other *habitués* of the palace by the numerous smaller doorways, all flanked with gigantic stone sphinxes, that opened on to the enclosed courts.

Unfortunately there are no pictures on any of the sculptures of Assyrian private houses, so that we can form no idea what would be the appearance of the streets of the great cities. The houses of the chief nobles, however, would no doubt imitate the palace on a small scale, and the dwellings of the poorer class would probably be crowded together towards the centre of the town, as the outskirts seem invariably to have been chosen for the royal residences. There would certainly be a sufficient space left in the neighbourhood of the palace for the magnificent approaches to it to be seen to advantage. The first gateway was at the foot of the elevation on which the palace stood. Passing between the massive man-headed bulls that guarded it, a visitor to the king would cross a paved yard, and ascend a wide shallow flight of stone steps, till he reached a terrace, also paved with slabs of stone carved in elegant patterns, such as we should now call arabesques. Here he would find a second still grander gateway, with supports of winged lion or bull headed monsters, and under its deep shadow he would pause for a time before attempting to mount a second high flight of steps blazing white in the hot sun; for here, in some small unroofed buildings that abutted on the gateway, part of the morning business of the court would be going on. A judge would be hearing some causes not important enough to be brought before the king; or the chief eunuch would be granting petitions or receiving offerings. Groups of courtiers, in their passage to and from the presence, would stand or sit under the portico, gossiping concerning the royal temper for the day; and suddenly all would shrink aside, for there would emerge from the palace portal the grand vizier or the chief of the cupbearers, with his attendant slaves holding a canopy over his head, fresh from his morning audience, who, hurrying on with an air of life-and-death importance to speed some royal errand, would, Haman-like, cast a rapid glance round to see if there were any Mordecai in the gate who did not rise up to do him honour.

The upper terrace on which the palace stood being gained at last, the visitor, if he were a stranger from a foreign land, might well feel in glancing back as the queen of Sheba felt when she saw the ascent that Solomon had built to the temple of the Lord, and had no more spirit in her for wonder and envy. The palace, with the intense light of the sun falling upon it, would not fail to strike him with even greater awe of its beauty and grandeur. Gigantic winged and man-headed bulls standing back to back, the wings meeting in an arch behind, seemed to support the building with their mighty strength, while their stolid wise faces overlooked the approaching crowds. Eagle and lion headed sphinxes crouched before the doors. Giants with lions tucked under their arms held up the portals on their heads. The lower part of the building, faced with stone sculptured in high relief, was all bright lights and deep fantastic-shaped shadows; and above the sculptures, contrasting with their black and white, a belt of vivid colour running round the top of the entire building pleased and satisfied the eye.

Once within the palace, having passed between the stolid bulls, and left the giants behind in the sunshine, the effect would be of coming into a pleasant dimness, a daintily tinted gloom like that of a thick wood. The light, streaming down from the top of the building through carefully-arranged awnings or curtains of coloured silk, would lend an agreeable colour to the endless procession of stone figures along the vast narrow halls and galleries, and would soften the outlines of the grotesque stone guardians of the doorways that led from one apartment to another. If our visitor chanced to come in at the hot, still noontide, when the monarch and his attendants were taking their mid-day repose; and if, like the Cher of the Egyptian story, he took delight in reading inscriptions, what a feast of amusement he would have had, walking from hall to hall, looking up at the pictures and reading the explanations of them chiselled out beneath. The whole house he would soon find was the history of one man's life—every room a chapter. Building and decorating these great palaces was the Assyrian's way of writing history. Assurizirpal began it, and the kings that came after him carried out and perfected his design. The great throne-rooms were their chronicles of the acts of the king, and the long galleries and little square rooms at the back of the halls were the poems they wrote to celebrate their hunting exploits, or the hymns they sang in praise of their gods.

The room into which our visitor would pass at once, if it were Assurizirpal's palace he entered, would be a chapter of the chronicles of the king. As he walks down the long hall on his way to the ivory throne, placed on a raised daïs at the further end, he may look up and read what the monarch seated on the throne has been doing for all the past years of his reign upwards. There, in the corner on the right wall, the king is setting out on his first expedition against his enemies: here he besieges and takes a city: there his army fords a deep river, and fights a battle with a numerous host on its opposite bank. A step or two onwards and the king is returning in his chariot victorious to his capital; minstrels playing stringed instruments precede him, soldiers bearing heads of the slain follow. Again he is on the march: in the upper compartment of the hall a castle is besieged, arrows fly about, women tear their hair on the top of the wall, slain warriors fall headlong; below, the castle is taken, the dead bodies of its late owners lie in heaps outside, the soldiers of the victorious army cook and feast within. It is the same story to the end of the wall and all round the room,—sieges and battles and marches, with here and there a hunting scene interposed.

Let the visitor pass through that great doorway guarded by winged bulls to the left of the throne, he will find himself in another hall as vast as the one he has left. But here the scenery is changed; the figures are all colossal and uniform. Carved on the central slab of the room stands the king with the sun and moon and stars hung round his neck, and all about him up and down the great room are eagle-headed deities standing looking at each other, with a symbolic tree, the tree of life, between them. This room is not a chapter of the chronicle, it is a psalm to the god, or hymn of victory. The psalm-room has a door, lion-guarded at one corner, which opens upon a third great room more beautifully ornamented than either of the others. It is an allegory or fairy tale here. The king sits on his throne, and winged figures, with fir-cones and baskets in their hands and garlands of flowers on their heads, approach him, or the king stands upright and the flower-crowned giants guard him. The third hall opens into a fourth, from which numerous doorways lead into small rooms that were probably sleeping apartments or store closets.

Both the hall of the sacred tree and the hall of the flower-giants have splendid doorways leading into an open court, through which the visitor, hopeless of finding his way among endless suites of dimly-lighted rooms, at length emerges into bright daylight again. The inner façades of the building are even more richly sculptured than the outer ones facing the town. He has only examined one side of the quadrangle, and three more remain. There are similar great halls in all of them—all sculptured, all written within and without with histories of the king. A wonderful illuminated book, full of splendid pages of history and theology and poetry, but costly in the lives of the war-captives, who raised the great stones that are its leaves—and not so durable a record, after all, as those which certain sweet singers of Israel, and one blind old man in Greece, built up in the same age, of ordered words that can never be forgotten.

CHAPTER XV.

A CHAPTER OF HISTORY.

ASSURIZIRPAL reigned twenty-five years, and died after having, according to his own account, reduced under his authority all lands from the rising of the sun to the going down thereof. He was succeeded by his son Shalmaneser, who seems in every particular, during a long lifetime, to have followed in his father's steps, making warlike expeditions in every year of his reign, and filling up the intervals of his time by building a second sculptured palace at Calah on the model of his father's.

Most of the expeditions were made into the same territories and against the same people that Assurizirpal boasts of having already subdued. Shalmaneser sweeps over the lands, north, south, and west of his capital, with the same rapidity that had marked his father's conquests, and boasts of the desolation he had left behind him. "I slew his fighting men, and carried away his spoil." "I overthrew, and beat to pieces, and consumed with fire towns without number." These, or sentences like these, are the summary he usually gives of his year's work.

In the east only, among the nations that had once formed part of Solomon's empire, did he meet with resistance effectual to check his progress for a while. Jerusalem, and the tribes that had remained faithful to the old royal family, were for the present safe from attack, having between them and the encroaching Assyrian power two strong kingdoms still unsubdued : the kingdom of Israel, which may be looked on as the inmost barrier between Judea and the Assyrians; and the kingdom of Damascus, which, at the beginning of Shalmaneser's reign, was the advance-guard of independence against which the wave of invasion for a time broke and was driven back.

Both these kingdoms, at the time when Shalmaneser turned his arms against them, were governed by powerful kings, who, ignorant of the common danger that threatened them, had been carrying on continual warfare with each other. Ahab, the son-in-law of Ethbaal king of Tyre, sat on the throne of Samaria. The king of Syria was that haughty Benhadad who had experienced such singular reverses of fortune in his dealings with his rival;—at one time, at the head of thirty-two vassal kings, contemptuously announcing to Ahab his determination to send messengers to Samaria, and search his palace and the houses of his nobles, and take away all that seemed good to him— gold, and silver, and wines, and children the goodliest ; —at another time, his vast army defeated by the little band of the princes of Israel, reduced to throw himself abjectly on the mercy of the Israelitish king, and send suppliants girded with sackcloth, and with ropes round their necks, to say to Ahab, " Thy servant Benhadad saith, I pray thee, let me live." The mistaken generosity of Ahab in setting him free, to be again the oppressor of Israel, was rebuked by a prophet of the Lord; yet, though it involved the defeat of the armies of Judah and Israel before Ramoth-Gilead and the death of Ahab, it may have been overruled for the good of Israel, as we find Benhadad, at a somewhat later time, taking the lead among the other princes of Palestine in withstanding Shalmaneser, and by his successes keeping back the encroachment of Assyria on Palestine for at least a few years.

The thirty-two vassal kings, who are mentioned as bringing their chariots and their horses to Benhadad's aid when he undertook the expedition against Samaria that so signally failed, no doubt formed part of his following when he took the field against Shalmaneser, but he was also joined by a confederacy of independent princes. Among them were the kings of the Northern Hittites, of Hamath, and of the Phœnician cities Tyre, Sidon, and Aradus, who had equal reason to dread the march of an Assyrian army southwards. Ahab himself seems to have composed his differences with Benhadad for a time, and to have sent a contingent to the confederate army, for his name has been made out in Shalmaneser's list of the princes who opposed his entrance into Syria. A battle was fought between the allies and the Assyrians, in which, according to the Assyrian account, the former were defeated. But as Shalmaneser, from his own history of the campaign, appears to have retired immediately after the battle without receiving submission, and to have abstained from fresh attacks on the allies for several years, it is evident that he had found himself opposed by a stronger force than he was able to overcome.

Five years afterwards he again brought a large army into Southern Syria, and proceeded to lay siege to some of the towns of the king of Hamath; but Benhadad, quickly collecting his forces, came to the assistance of his ally, and once more, in a pitched battle, obliged Shalmaneser to retreat to his own capital without carrying any trophies of conquest with him.

The traits of character displayed by Benhadad in his quarrels with Ahab—his boastfulness on the eve of battle, which prompted the king of Israel's message, "Let not him that girdeth on his harness boast himself as he that putteth it off;" and his want of vigilance when, drinking himself drunk at noonday in a pavilion with his thirty-two vassals, he allowed his army to be overpowerd by his despised enemy—do not prepare us for the display of such courage and good generalship as is conspicuous in the successful stand made by the Syrian army against Shalmaneser.

We are disposed to conjecture that in these campaigns Benhadad must have had some one by his side possessed of higher qualities than he could lay claim to; and we remember the mention in the Book of Kings of a mighty man of valour, Naaman, captain of the host of the king of Syria, who was "a great man with his master and honourable, because by him the Lord had given deliverance to Syria." The story gathered from the clay cylinders of Shalmaneser of his two unsuccessful attempts to enter Syria and beat its cities to pieces, perhaps explains what was the signal deliverance here alluded to, and makes us understand more fully why the life of Naaman the leper was so valuable to his master the king that he was willing for his sake to ask a favour of his old rival and enemy the king of Israel, and send him a letter from his own hand, and a present, on such slender hope of his favourite servant's recovery as could be founded on the suggestion of a little captive maid of Israel.

After Shalmaneser's second repulse, he allowed three more years to elapse before he again attempted to attack the confederate kings. It must have been during these three years that Benhadad's war with Jehoram took place, and the long siege of Samaria, in which the Israelites suffered such terrible extremities of famine, and which ended by the miraculous discomfiture of the Assyrian army, when, panic-struck at "the noise of horses, and the noise of chariots, and the noise of a great host which the Lord made them hear," they fled without pause to Jordan, strewing all the way with the garments and weapons they threw from them in their mad terror.

The shame and depression caused by this ignominious discomfiture must have been still brooding over the Syrian king and his war captains, when he was once more summoned to his northern frontier to join his former allies, the Hittites and Hamathites, in opposing the march of a still larger army than had yet come up against them. "Multitudes that could not be counted" Shalmaneser says he brought with him when he made his third attempt; and though the allies assembled in great force, they were this time utterly overpowered and driven in disorder from the field, leaving their chariots and implements of war behind them. The Hittites and Hamathites submitted without further struggle, and gave up their kings to the mercy of the conqueror; the Phœnicians made a hasty retreat to their coast towns behind the Lebanon; and Benhadad, with the remnant of his army, crossed the strip of desert that divided the land of the Northern Hittites from the oasis in the desert that formed the nucleus of his territory, and retired to Damascus to await the destruction that must inevitably come.

While he lay in his ancient city sick with sorrow, a traveller from the land of Israel set out for Damascus to fulfil a commission that had long since been laid upon him. The countries were still at war, and of all the men of Israel Elisha the Shunammite might with most reason have feared to trust himself alone in the Syrian capital, for he had long been regarded by Benhadad as a more formidable foe than the mightiest man of valour in Samaria. "Elisha, the prophet that is in Israel, telleth the king of Israel all that thou sayest in thy bedchamber," the servants of Benhadad assured him when his heart was sore at the failure, not once or twice, of his best-laid schemes against Israel; and he began to suspect treachery in his own council-chamber. Yet Elisha set forth fearlessly, firm in the persuasion that had upheld him at Dothan, when the king of Syria sent an army to take his life, that "they that be with us are more than they that be with them."

He journeyed through the passes of the Lebanon and across the intervening slip of desert, till he reached the rich green plain at the foot of Mount Hermon watered by the two mighty rivers Abana and Pharpar, whose beauty above all rivers Naaman had vaunted.

The ancient city over which Abraham had once reigned as king, with its straight white streets stretching out amid rose-gardens and groves of citron, orange, and pomegranate, would meet his eyes after three days' journey. But he does not appear to have entered within its gates. He paused somewhere in the neighbourhood,—tradition says at a place called Hobah, where his exiled servant Gehazi was then dwelling in penitence. Though he had never before visited Damascus, he was immediately recognised; perhaps by some servant who had accompanied Naaman to Samaria; perhaps by one of the soldiers who had been smitten with temporary blindness at Dothan, whose lives he had persuaded Jehoram to spare. Soon the news of his arrival was carried to the bed-chamber of the sick king. "The man of God is come hither," some one of his attendants said to Benhadad, and the words brought a sudden spark of hope to the heart of the dying man.

Perhaps he thought of the wonderful cure wrought

on Naaman, and of many another mighty deed of Elisha's that had reached his ears. Here was one who at least could tell his fate. So he called his prime minister Hazael (Naaman was evidently dead at this time, slain probably in the last disastrous battle with Shalmaneser), and instructed him to take a present in his hand—forty camels' burdens of every good thing of Damascus—and go to meet the man of God, and say to him, "Thy son Benhadad king of Syria hath sent me to thee, saying, Shall I recover from this disease?" The arrogant Benhadad could be "the servant of Ahab" and "the son of Elisha" when he was in trouble and wanted anything of them. Elisha's answer to the question Hazael put to him was a somewhat ambiguous one: The king should recover from his disease, or at least his disease was one from which he might recover, and yet the Lord had shown Elisha that he should die.

But it was not to gratify Benhadad's impatient desire to look into the future that Elisha had undertaken his dangerous journey; he had come on a more important errand. His master Elijah had, years before, laid it on him to appoint a king of Syria; and here, without seeking of his, was the very man to whom his message was due come out to meet him. Elisha looked stedfastly in Hazael's face, and saw not only who he was, but all that there was in him —all the deeds of his life, folded up still in the future, but of which the possibilities were there within. As he looked and read, the words he had come to speak failed him, and the man of God wept. "Why weepest thou, my lord?" Hazael asked; and Elisha answered, "Because I know the evil that thou wilt do to the children of Israel; their strongholds wilt thou set on fire, and their young men wilt thou slay with the sword."

Hazael's reply, "But what is thy servant, a dog, that he should do this great thing?" does not express any unwillingness or horror at the thought of the deeds Elisha foresaw for him, but merely incredulity that he, a mere servant, a dog, should have power to work such havoc on his country's enemies. Elisha's answer was given with resigned sad brevity: "The Lord hath showed me that thou shalt be king over Syria."

Then, having delivered the message confided to him, the prophet departed, and Hazael returned to his master. The next day the sick king was murdered in his palace, and the treacherous Hazael reigned in his stead. As Elisha had foreseen, his reign was in every particular disastrous to Israel; he was sufficiently powerful to oppress his immediate neighbours, and yet did not succeed, as Benhadad had done, in preserving his own territories and the adjacent country from the invasion of the Assyrians.

The next war season after Benhadad's death, Shalmaneser again entered Syria. Hazael, though deserted by Benhadad's former allies, made an effort to arrest his progress by posting an army in the mountain chain between his country and Cœli Syria, but he was outnumbered and driven back with great loss.

On the next occasion when Shalmaneser, who

seems to have made marauding excursions into Syria at regular intervals, appeared in the country, Hazael submitted without striking a blow, and permitted his towns, one after the other, to be plundered by the invaders. The kings of the Phœnician cities who had allied themselves with Benhadad heard with dismay of the presence of the dreaded Assyrian army so near their borders, and hastened to avert the punishment with which they were threatened, by sending embassies to offer tribute and make submission to Shalmaneser at Damascus. Among the suppliants came Jehu king of Israel. Though he had taken no part in the former struggle, his homage was claimed by Shalmaneser as the conquered vassal of Hazael, for those were "the days in which the Lord began to cut Israel short; and Hazael smote them in all their coasts, and oppressed Israel." An evidence of this oppression is to be found on a black marble obelisk, sculptured on its four sides with cuneiform writing and processions of conquered people, which Shalmaneser set up as a trophy of his conquest of Syria at the gate of his palace at Calah.

The obelisk has been brought to England, and is now in the British Museum. Conspicuous among the suppliants represented on it, we see the prostrate figure of Jehu son of Omri, as the Assyrian inscription calls him, doing homage as a tributary of the conquered Hazael for his city Beth-Khumri, the "House of Omri," by which name Samaria is always designated in Assyrian records. Behind him comes a procession of Israelites bearing tribute, thick bars of gold and silver, closed vessels, and manufactured articles which are too imperfectly represented on the obelisk to be identified.

The two kings succeeding Shalmaneser, though equally powerful and warlike, have left few records of interest behind them. After their death a succession of kings of a different character occupied the throne of Assyria for a considerable period ; a luxurious, slothful race, of whom the monuments tell us nothing.

It was while one of these *rois fainéants* was reigning in Nineveh that the visit of Jonah to the Assyrian capital took place. We have only to think of the cruel deeds related of themselves by Assyrian kings to understand Jonah's attempt to escape the task which the Divine command laid upon him. He seems to have been a man of fearful and yet impetuous nature; his name signifies "a dove," and tradition declares him to have been the son of that gentle, despairing widow of Zarephath, who was so ready to gather two sticks and make one more cake for herself and her son and die, as soon as her stores failed her; and who, in spite of the miracle wrought in her behalf, could not restrain herself from reproaching the prophet when her son fell sick. "What have I to do with thee, O thou man of God ? Art thou come to call my sin to remembrance, and slay my son ?" The same disposition to hasty despondency, and the same quick, strong feelings, appear to have belonged to the son. When he at length prepared to fulfil his mission, the temptation to fear might well again assail him, as he came in sight of the fenced cities, whose high walls, and temple towers, and palaces reared on artificial hills, seemed to tower up to heaven itself.

From the immense dimensions assigned to Nineveh by ancient writers, it is conjectured that the name of the capital was applied not solely to the city originally called Nineveh, but to a circle of towns in close proximity, whose buildings in process of time had approached each other so nearly that they virtually formed one vast city, where groups of palaces, fortresses, and private houses were divided by extensive pleasure-grounds, parks, and gardens. Thus "the exceeding great city of three days' journey," stretching forty miles from end to end, which Jonah entered, included the magnificent group of buildings at Calah which Assurizirpal and Shalmaneser had reared. The great winged man-headed bulls, emblems of the king's strength and vengeance, frowned down upon him as he commenced his progress; the black obelisk, with its humiliating picture of the Israelitish king grovelling in the dust before an Assyrian conqueror, confronted him as he went on. Everywhere some trophy of victory, or boastful record of vengeance wreaked on enemies of Assyria, met his eyes as he lifted up his voice and cried aloud: "Yet forty days, and Nineveh shall be overthrown."

The succession of indolent kings in Nineveh was terminated by a revolution which set aside the ancient royal family, and placed a ruler on the throne, who is said by ancient writers to have been a man of low origin, a vine-dresser in the king's gardens.

His name was Tiglath-Pileser the Second, and he had no sooner got the power into his own hands than he took active measures to restore the kingdom to the same position among surrounding nations it had held in Shalmaneser's time. Again every autumn saw a vast army emerge from the gates of Nineveh, and taking each year a new direction sweep across the country like a desolating whirlwind, burning towns, depopulating villages, cutting down palm-trees, destroying all that could not be carried away. If Jonah were still alive, he may have been tempted to say again, "It is better to die than to live," for as early as the fourth year of his reign Tiglath-Pileser turned his arms eastward, and terrible were the calamities that during a succession of campaigns he inflicted upon Israel.

While the lazy Assyrian kings had remained shut up in their capitals, the Israelites under Jeroboam the Second had enjoyed a time of great prosperity, almost rivalling the glorious period of the empire under David and Solomon. Jeroboam had conquered Damascus, Israel's former rival and oppressor, and had established his authority over a great part of Syria; but under this fair appearance of prosperity lay the germs of approaching decay. Jeroboam did evil in the sight of the Lord; and the nobles and people, corrupted by his example, fell into a state of utter demoralization.

Rumour of the sins and idolatries practised in the capital reached the shepherd-prophet Amos in his upland home beyond Jordan, and brought him from his sheepfolds and the pruning of his sycamore fig-trees to Samaria, to denounce the vices that were eating out the strength of the nation, and preparing it for destruction. The avarice of the rich had become so great that they grudged the pittance of bread their exactions had left to the poor, and remorselessly sold their debtors to Tyrian slave-drivers for a piece of silver, or a pair of embroidered shoes, while they lavished their unjust gains in festivals to Baal and Ashtoreth. In punishment for these iniquities Amos foretold that an adversary should shortly come up against the land, who would bring down its strength and spoil its palaces.

The years of anarchy in Samaria that followed the death of Jeroboam the Second afforded an opportunity for conquest, which so active an adversary as Tiglath-Pileser was not likely to neglect. The first attack came from a prince named Pul, who appears to have reigned for a short time in conjunction with Tiglath-Pileser. He was induced to depart from before Samaria by the payment of a large sum of money, but the sacrifice bought a very short respite. A few years after his departure Tiglath-Pileser came in person, and overran the entire country, exacting large sums of money as tribute wherever he came. The two kings who suffered most from his exactions, Rezin king of Damascus and Pekah king of Israel, joined in a league for mutual defence as soon as Tiglath-Pileser and his army had returned to Nineveh. Being unable to persuade Ahaz king of Judah to add his forces to theirs, they made war on Jerusalem, intending to dethrone Ahaz and place a prince of their own choosing on the throne.

Ahaz, encouraged and supported by the counsels of the prophet Isaiah, made a successful defence, and obliged the two kings to retreat from his capital; but when the pressing danger was over, he allowed the confidence in the continued protection of the Lord, with which Isaiah had for a time inspired him, to be shaken, and took the impolitic and unpatriotic course of applying to the Assyrian king for aid against his neighbours.

Tiglath-Pileser responded to the appeal of Ahaz by a third invasion of Syria and Palestine, which occupied several years, and brought heavy calamities on all the countries overrun by his soldiers.

King Rezin was defeated and slain, Damascus was destroyed, and all its inhabitants carried away captive and planted in a distant region of Assyria. Then the vast army spread southward, surging through the passes of the Lebanon, and pouring like a destroying flood over the pastures of Gilead. "The land of Zebulun and the land of Naphtali were grievously afflicted." "There was a voice of howling of shepherds, for their glory was spoiled; a voice of the roaring of young lions, for the pride of Judah was spoiled." As the prophet Isaiah had foretold, the land east of the Jordan "was shorn bare as with a razor;" "where a thousand vines and a thousand silverlings had grown there was thorns and briars, and the land was briars."

Nothing could be more complete than the destruction wrought by an Assyrian army. The pictures on the bas-reliefs of the palaces have scenes which show the soldiers engaged in the work of ruin; here three or four men are cutting down a fine palm-tree, from mere love of destroying; there we see a long file of captives with their hands tied behind them, leaving the smoking ruins of their native village, while the victors urge them on their way with blows and insults. The rich, fruitful land between Jordan and the desert, which Joshua had assigned to the tribes of Reuben and Gad and the half-tribe Manasseh, were devastated in this fashion by Tiglath-Pileser's army; the inhabitants —men, women, and children—carried off and planted in distant parts of Assyria, never more to return to their breezy upland pastures, and oaken glades, and sycamore gardens. Samaria, and the country immediately surrounding it, for the present escaped destruction, on the promise of paying a large yearly tribute. Ahaz hardly fared better than the rival against whom he had invoked Assyrian aid. Tiglath-Pileser sent for him to Damascus, and obliged him not only to do homage for his territory, as the servant henceforth of the king of Assyria, but to pay so large a tribute that Ahaz was obliged not only to empty the king's treasury, but to strip the house of the Lord of the gold and silver ornaments with which Solomon had adorned it.

On the death of Tiglath-Pileser the kingdoms of Israel, Syria, and Phœnicia made desperate attempts to throw off the Assyrian yoke.

A powerful Ethiopian king had possessed himself

of the throne of the Pharaohs, and by uniting Ethiopia and Egypt in one kingdom, had raised the African monarchy into a position to become the rival of Assyria for dominion in the East. To this energetic new ruler the people of Palestine and Phœnicia looked eagerly for deliverance from the oppressions and cruelties of the Assyrians. Unfortunately for them Shalmaneser the Second, the son of Tiglath-Pileser, was nowise inferior to his father in capacity and energy.

The history of his reign is that of a continual succession of attempts on the part of the eastern dependencies of his empire to throw off his yoke and attach themselves to Egypt, and of the rapid marches which always brought him and his army to punish the disaffected province before any succour from Egypt could reach them. Hoshea king of Israel brought continual fresh calamities on his country by the pertinacity with which, after every failure, he returned to the project of allying himself with Egypt so as to make an effectual stand against Assyria. Again and again tempted by promises of aid from So, the Egyptian king, he remitted the yearly tribute exacted from him by Shalmaneser; again and again Shalmaneser's army, like a devastating torrent, overflowed the land: "Their arrows sharp, their bows bent, their horses' hooves like flint, and their chariots like a whirlwind." At length, after a third offence, Hoshea was deposed by the Assyrian king, and shut up in prison. The small remnant of territory which remained to Israel after Tiglath-Pileser's conquests was speedily subdued; but the people of Samaria defended their beautiful city, the last stronghold of the country, with the courage of despair.

Shalmaneser was obliged to change the siege into a blockade, and content himself by leaving detachments of troops on the hills round Samaria, while he returned to Assyria to attend to more pressing enterprises in other parts of his empire. The blockade, apparently not very vigorously conducted, lingered on for three years, and before it came to a conclusion Shalmaneser died, leaving only a young son to succeed him. The chief general of the Assyrian troops, a man of obscure birth but great talents, took advantage of the youth and incapacity of the heir to seize the sceptre, and had himself proclaimed king at Nineveh, taking the name Sargon ("I am the established ruler"), by which he is designated in all the numerous records of his triumphant reign.

One of Sargon's earliest exploits was to march down into Palestine and put an end to the siege of Samaria. In a long inscription recounting the events of his reign, from the first to the fifteenth year, Sargon says: "This is what I have done: I defeated the king Elam; I besieged, took, and captured the town of Samaria, and carried into captivity the 27,280 persons who lived in it; I put aside the old established rulers of the land, and put my lieutenants in their place."

Thus the punishment (often predicted) which their long-continued idolatry had deserved, was at length completed. "The Lord rejected all the seed of Israel, and afflicted them, and delivered them into the hand of the spoilers until He had cast them out of His sight."

It is difficult to believe that an entire people could be taken forcibly out of its own country and planted in a fresh place, as a tree might be taken up and replanted, but the Assyrian annals supply details that show how truly and completely this was done in several instances. The inhabitants of the lands they conquered seem to have been regarded by Tiglath-Pileser and Sargon as draughtsmen on a board, that might be lifted up and moved about, and made to take each other's place, just as their removal could best advance the war-game that was being played with them. These kings refer to the system of deportation with pride in their annals. In the long inscription that begins with an account of the taking of Samaria, Sargon says: "In my anger I marched against Azoth with my warriors that always follow my steps. Its king fled to Egypt, and was never heard of more. I took his capital; I carried away his gods captive, his wives, his sons, his daughters, his treasures, every single thing that was in his palace, and all the inhabitants of his country; then I built up again the towns I had destroyed, and peopled them with captives I had taken in the land of the rising sun."

Many pictures on the bas-reliefs represent these sad emigrations in progress. The men formed into bands, and, connected together by chains, were marched off under the guard of Assyrian soldiers; the women followed, sometimes on foot, leading their little children by the hand, but more frequently seated in rude carts, each carrying on her shoulder a small bundle of necessaries which she had been allowed to snatch from the ruins of her home. As the exiles moved away from the smoking embers of their once flourishing town or village, they had the mortification of seeing all the spoil that had been collected out of it—their cherished household goods, their clothes and furniture, the great cooking-pot of Tyrian ware, the millstone at which they had sat grinding their meal—gathered into a great heap to be counted and valued, and, after the king's share had been deducted, divided among their new masters, the rapacious Assyrian soldiery.

The Israelitish captives were placed, some in Gozan, and some in deserted cities of the Medes and Babylonians, whose inhabitants, like themselves, had been carried off; others were taken to the capital, and helped to raise the mounds on which Sargon built his great palace, and perhaps to carve the bas-reliefs where he records his triumphs over their country. The city of Samaria and the districts round were not left empty. Sargon, who frequently boasts of having "changed the abodes of his subjects," sent detachments of conquered tribes—Babylonians, Cutheans, and Arabians—to till the vineyards, reap the cornfields, and rebuilt the pleasant stone houses from which the children of Israel had been torn away.

In the city of Samaria itself he placed the remnants of two Arab tribes who incurred his displeasure, and were punished by him soon after his conquest of Palestine. "The tribes of Thamudi and Adidi," he says in his annals, "of whose country my empire had not yet heard, I chastised, and the remnant of them I carried off and placed in the city of Samaria."

A tradition of the sudden destruction and total disappearance of these two tribes long existed among the Arabs, and has served as the foundation for many strange and picturesque stories. The tribe of Thamud (evidently the Thamudi mentioned in Sargon's inscription), according to Arabian tradition, displeased God by their idolatries, and their refusal to repent on the preaching of a prophet who worked before their eyes the miracle of bringing a live camel out of a rock. In punishment of their contumacy they were all struck dead by an earthquake and a terrible noise from heaven, which some say was the voice of the archangel Gabriel, crying, "Die all of you!"

The tribe of Ad (Sargon's Adidi) also fell into idolatry, and on their refusing to listen to the voice of the prophet Hud, God sent a hot, suffocating wind, which blew seven nights and eight days, and entering at their nostrils, passed through their bodies, and destroyed them all.

The Arabs still show in the Hejaz the deserted houses of the Thamudites cut out of the rock, and the crack from which the miraculous camel issued.

Better still, their imaginations love to dwell on traditions of a beautiful city built by the last king of Ad, which, with the exquisite gardens surrounding it, is said to exist still somewhere in the desert, though it is very rarely allowed to become visible to mortal eyes. Now and then—once perhaps in five hundred years or so—a benighted traveller, or camel-driver in search of a stray camel, lies down to sleep in the desert, with sand, as he imagines, all round him, and waking at early dawn, finds himself in the exquisite rose-garden of Irem, with the gate of the ancient city of Ad, "set with a variety of jewels and jacinths," shining before his eyes. All day he is permitted to wander through the silent streets, and to enter the deserted palaces constructed of gold, with lofty chambers, whose folding doors are set with rubies and chrysolites, and their floors overlaid with pearls, musk, ambergris, and saffron; but when he has once left the city he can never find the entrance to it again, though he return with his friends again and again to the precise spot where he lay down to sleep.

The story told respecting this wonderful city is, that a king of Ad built it for the purpose of causing himself to be regarded by his subjects as a god, and that his pride brought on himself and his people a swift and signal punishment.

Sargon's short sentence, "I destroyed the tribes of Thamudi and Adidi, and placed the remnant of them in the city of Samaria," is the plain, naked truth, which Arab imagination has decked with these shining garments of fancy. The Samaritans, in after times so hated and despised by the Jews, were the descendants of these mixed people whom Sargon imported into the country which the Ten Tribes had formerly occupied.

After the conquest of Samaria, Sargon marched southward, and gained a great victory over an allied army of Philistines and Egyptians that had assembled to withstand him. This seems to have been the first time that Egyptian and Assyrian troops had met in battle since the days of the Thothmes and Amunophs, when the Egyptians had been the invading force, and gained the easy victories that from this time forth fell to the Assyrian arms. Sargon records his victory in proud terms. "Hanon king of Gaza, and Sebek sultan of Egypt, met me at Raphia. They came into my presence; I defeated them. Sebek fled away, and Hanon I took prisoner with my own hand, and I imposed tribute on the Pharaoh of Egypt."

In whatever direction he turned his arms the same success attended him. He made two other expeditions against Egypt in the course of his reign, in one of which he penetrated into Ethiopia, and received the homage of a king dwelling beyond the Nubian Desert. "The king of Meroe lives in a desert country," he says; "from the most remote time it has never been known that an ancestor of his came to offer homage to an ancestor of mine, but the immense fear and dread with which my majesty inspired him, obliged him to acknowledge the might of the Assyrian gods, and to bow down before me."

In Chaldea he gained a great victory over the king of Babylon, Merodach-Baladan, who had rebelled against him; he drove him from his kingdom, and placed a dependant of his own in his place.

The entire subjugation of Babylonia was followed by some years of tranquillity, which Sargon spent in directing the building of a new capital and a splendid palace, which he called by his own name, Dur-Sargina.

Sargon's Palace Wall.—P. 197.

This was the city that anciently stood on the site now called Khorsabad, where M. Botta began the work of investigation into Assyrian ruins. Sargon's palace was the first of the buried palaces that was restored to the daylight, and it has been more thoroughly explored than any other. It does not differ materially in plan or ornament from the ancient model. It is only such a palace as Assurizirpal built, repeated two or three times over, and with all its parts on a grander scale; yet more gigantic bulls and lions; innumerable long narrow halls, with square rooms behind them, ranged round four courts instead of one; higher and wider platforms, approached by grander flights of steps; longer and more boastful accounts of the king's doings graven on the miles and miles of walls. The illustration is a copy of one of the many bas-reliefs graven on Sargon's miles of palace wall, and will give a good idea of the scenery with which the Assyrian kings, from Assurizirpal downwards, surrounded themselves in their palaces. It shows Sargon's army attacking a town situated at the foot of a mountain, whence a river flows. The besieged, who appear to be unarmed and almost naked, defend themselves with arrows. They have erected a kind of fort on the river; it consists of two towers connected by a wall, and commands the causeways by which the Assyrians are bringing up their battering-rams close to the town wall. The besiegers rush on to the attack and scale the walls, discharging arrows from their bows.

This is what Sargon says himself in his famous inscription about his city and palace. "At the foot of the Mousri hills I have built, according to the will of the gods and the wish of my own heart, a town which I have called **Dur-Sargina**. The gods who reign eternally in Mesopotamia have blessed the wondrous splendours and the proud streets of my city. In this city I have erected a palace curtained with seal-skins, inlaid with sandal-wood, cedar, and ebony—an incomparable palace indeed—for my royal seat. I have written it all over with praises of the gods. I have made a spiral staircase in it on the model of one I saw in a great temple in Syria. Inside my palace there are heaps of gold and silver, vases of precious metals, rich dyes of all kinds, abundance of iron, the products of a thousand mines; saffron-coloured stuffs, cloths of blue and purple dye, pearls, sandal-wood; in short, every kind of booty."

The walls of one of the halls in this palace are sculptured with pictures, which tell the story of the cost of human suffering at which this booty of every description had been got together. Mr. Layard calls it "the hall of punishment," for every slab shows the king in the act of torturing, or causing to be tortured, the captives he had taken in his various predatory wars. One he stabs through the head with a spear, another he drags along by a rope attached to a ring inserted in his lip, a third he orders to be flayed alive in his presence. One wonders whether Sargon's heart was really so hard that there never came a time in his later days, after the excitement of war was over, when this hall became what it ought to have been—a hall of punishment to himself, holding up continually the record of his cruel deeds before his eyes.

CHAPTER XVI.

SENNACHERIB, KING OF ASSYRIA.

SARGON reigned seventeen years, and was succeeded by his son Sennacherib, the Assyrian monarch whose name and character are best known to us because of his close connexion with Jewish history.

He too has left a minute account of the events of the first sixteen years of his reign, engraved on a clay cylinder which, fortunately for us, has been preserved to our time.

The first years of his reign were spent in suppressing revolts in the Babylonian and northern provinces, which, according to custom, broke out on the accession of a new king. The tributaries of the Assyrian empire, always groaning under the extortions of their rulers, were ready, on the smallest gleam of hope, to make a fresh struggle for liberty. Every reign had to begin with a new series of campaigns, and each king had an opportunity of acquiring, at comparatively small cost, the fame of a great conqueror, and an excuse for enriching his capital with spoil.

By the fifth year of his reign Sennacherib had restored tranquillity to the nearer districts of the empire, and was at liberty to turn his attention to disorders which, while he was occupied with home affairs, had grown to a great height in the eastern provinces. A powerful king had risen in the city of Sidon, who had managed to place the ancient capital once more at the head of the Phœnician confederacy, and to inspire the other kings of the coast-cities with sufficient confidence in each other to make a united struggle against Assyria possible. Egypt, under the rule of another Ethiopian king, had recovered the depression which had followed the defeat sustained at Raphia, and was once more in a condition to hold out hopes of assistance to such of the nations of Palestine as were disposed to prefer dependence on Egypt to vassalage to Assyria.

There was consequently hardly a town in Philistia, Judea, or Phœnicia which was not divided into two parties: a war party whose trust was in Egypt, and who were always on the look-out for a favourable occasion of coming to an open rupture with Assyria; and a peace party, composed usually of older men, whose experience of the calamities that resulted from an Assyrian invasion disposed them to prefer the yearly exactions to which they had become accustomed to the miseries of an unequal struggle.

In one of the Philistine towns, Ekron, whose neighbourhood to the Egyptian frontier gave them the certainty of obtaining speedy succour if attacked, the Egyptian party had prevailed so far as to dethrone the king of the place, Padi, who was in the Assyrian interest, and to send him as prisoner to the safe-keeping of Hezekiah king of Jerusalem. They hoped that the Jewish king would seek favour with the Egyptians by putting the Assyrian ally to death, but Hezekiah's heart relented towards the captive placed in his power; and though he had too much sympathy with the Ekronites in their struggle against Assyria to set their king at liberty, he spared Padi's life, and contented himself by keeping him in close custody in Jerusalem.

Such was the state of affairs in Phœnicia and Palestine when Sennacherib turned his arms in that direction. His annals relate, very circumstantially, though perhaps with some exaggerations of his own successes, what befell in the campaign that ensued.

"I marched towards Syria; the reputation of my great might fell on Luliya king of the Sidonians, and he fled away to the isles in the middle of the sea, and left his country. All the great towns, citadels, holy places, and temples were filled with dread at the glory of Assur my master and surrendered to me. All the kings of Phœnicia came and brought tribute and acknowledged my empire. . . .

"The inhabitants of Ekron had betrayed their king Padi, who was full of friendship for Assyria, and delivered him up to Hezekiah king of Judah.

"The horses, the chariots, the archers of the kings of Egypt and Ethiopia, innumerable multitudes joined themselves together, and came out against me. Their general drew up in order of battle before the town of Altaku.

"Strong in the might of the god Assur, my

master, I fought them, and put them to flight. I took the chariot-drivers alive, and captured the princes of Egypt with my own hand. Then I marched on to Ekron. I degraded the chiefs who had rebelled against me, and killed them, and stuck their dead bodies on stakes all round the town. Those who had been faithful to their king and done nothing against me, I forgave. I sent for Padi from Jerusalem and reinstated him on his throne, and settled the tribute he was to pay me in acknowledgment of my supremacy."

Meanwhile the news of this victory and of the fall of Ekron fell like a thunderbolt on the people of Jerusalem. The city was far from being in a state of defence. In many places the walls had been suffered to fall into decay, and the citizens, in alarm for the security of the Temple itself, hastened to pull down the houses near the walls in order to build up the fortifications with their stones. Hezekiah and his mighty men sat in council together, concerting measures for turning the course of the waters, so that the streams that supplied the city should be out of the reach of a besieging army.

The whole city, the prophet Isaiah tells us, was "full of stirs and tumults." In the streets were labourers and soldiers toiling at the repair of the walls, while all who were not so occupied rushed to the house-tops to watch anxiously for the cloud of dust on the south-western horizon, or the gleam of distant armour that would show the dreaded invaders were upon them.

Sounds of bitter weeping, and crying to the mountains to cover them, were broken with discordant notes of insane revelry, such as always breaks out among the thoughtless and dissolute portions of a community in times of great national calamity. "In that day," says Isaiah, "did the Lord of hosts call to weeping, and to girding with sackcloth; and behold joy and gladness, eating flesh, and drinking wine. Let us eat and drink; for to-morrow we die."

For some time Hezekiah maintained a dignified attitude towards Sennacherib, neither sending an embassy to excuse his complicity in the offence of the Ekronites, nor returning any answer to the Assyrian king's demand on him to deliver up Padi. Astonished at his obstinacy, Sennacherib broke up his camp before Ekron, and marched towards Jerusalem, destroying and burning all before him. "Hezekiah of Judah," he says in his inscription, "would not submit to me. He had forty-four strong walled towns, and an immense number of villages scattered about, against which I fought, breaking down their pride and fierceness. By fire, by massacres, by battles and sieges, I overthrew them, and filled them with my soldiers. I took from them, and carried off as spoil, 200,150 people, small and great, men and women, with countless horses, asses, mules, camels, oxen, and sheep.

"Hezekiah himself I shut up in Jerusalem his capital city, like a bird in a cage, building towers round the city to hem him in, and raising banks of earth against the gates to prevent his escape.

"Then a great fear of my might fell on this Hezekiah of Judah. He dismissed the sentinels and the troops he had assembled for the defence of the city, and sent an embassy to me with 30 talents of gold and 800 talents of silver, and with precious metals, rubies, pearls, great carbuncles, seal-skins, all the stores in his treasury, as a present to me, to show his submission."

The actual appearance of the Assyrian army in the valleys round Jerusalem, and of the horsemen set in array against the gates, seems indeed to have wrought a sudden change in Hezekiah's policy. He saw the hopelessness of attempting to defend the city against a power so overwhelming, and yielding to the counsel of his chief minister Shebna, he sent an embassy, saying, "I have offended (in the matter of accepting the custody of Padi). Return from me; that which thou puttest upon me I will bear." Sennacherib accepted the terms offered, and withdrew his army; but to make up the required sum Hezekiah was forced not only to give up all the contents of his treasury, but to strip off the plates of gold and silver with which some parts of the walls and porticoes of the Temple were overlaid.

Sennacherib returned in triumph to Nineveh with the spoils of his eastern campaign, but the next war season brought another revolt, this time in the southern districts of the empire; and while he was occupied in these distant quarters, the people of Palestine had leisure to recover from the panic into which the actual presence of the Assyrian army had thrown them.

The Egyptian party at Jerusalem again took the lead. The minister Shebna, who had counselled submission to Assyria, was dismissed; and just at the moment when the reaction from abject fear had set in, overtures of alliance were received from the king of Egypt which seemed to open to the Jewish king a reasonable prospect of regaining his lost independence.

Against the proposed alliance with Egypt, however, the prophet Isaiah was commissioned to pronounce the most emphatic warnings.

The position which the prophet held between the contending parties in the council of king Hezekiah was a difficult and perilous one. At one moment he had to denounce the pusillanimity of those who, like Shebna in time of peril, counselled abject submission to Assyria; and again, when the mood of the people changed, to warn them against dependence on Egypt—equally a national sin, since it showed the unwillingness of the people to believe the assurances of Divine protection which Isaiah intermingled with his remonstrances against foreign alliances.

Sennacherib seems to have understood that the Egyptian king was the moving spring of the revolt in the south-eastern provinces; for though the first symptom of rebellion was probably Hezekiah's refusal to pay his yearly tribute, Sennacherib did not make him the principal object of attack, but marched his army through Palestine by the coast road to the extreme verge of the Holy Land, and laid siege to two towns,

Libnah and Lachish, then subject to Egypt. The courage of the Jewish king and his people was severely tried when they found themselves thus cut off from every hope of assistance from the ally on whom they had so rashly depended. The warning words of the prophet Isaiah were forcibly brought to mind. The might of Egypt, as he had predicted, had indeed proved a "shadow;" it had vanished away, leaving them exposed to the hot fire of the vengeance of their powerful enemy. But with the acknowledgment of the truth of the prophet's warning there came to the more faithful portion of the nation trust in the promises that had accompanied the warnings. "The Lord of hosts shall come down to fight for Mount Zion, and for the hill thereof. As birds flying, so will the Lord of hosts defend Jerusalem; and passing over He will preserve it."

So, "in quietness and in confidence," Hezekiah remained passive while Sennacherib's army was in his neighbourhood—making no offers of submission, and sending no tribute to appease the tyrant's anger, but occupying himself with preparations for a siege, completing the repairs of the walls, getting together stores of armour, and speaking eloquent words of encouragement to the war-captains, and the people, assembled in the city gates to hear him: "Be strong and courageous," he urged them; "be not afraid for the king of Assyria, nor for all the multitude that is with him, for there be more with us than with them." "With him is an army of flesh, but with us is the Lord our God, to help us and to fight our battles."

It would seem from what followed that some report of the substance of Hezekiah's address to his people reached Sennacherib's ears, and prompted the message which, while he was still occupied with the siege of Lachish, he sent to Jerusalem by the hands of the two chief ministers of his court—the Rabshakeh or cup-bearer, and the Rabsaris or chief eunuch, backed by a large detachment of his army.

Arrived in the neighbourhood of the Jewish capital the ambassadors pitched their tents on the north of the city, in a spot long afterwards known as the camp of the Assyrians, and haughtily desired king Hezekiah to come out and speak with them. The Jewish king, instead of attending personally, sent his prime minister and two other members of his council to treat with the servants of the Assyrian monarch. The interview took place in the open field, in the presence of the attendants on both sides, and of crowds of people, who climbed the city walls and thronged round to hear what passed.

The Rabshakeh, the chief of the cup-bearers, was the principal speaker, and his words were addressed, not so much to the Jewish ministers, as to the people around, whom he wished to impress with a sense of the invincibility of his master, and the folly of trusting to such hopes of deliverance as their king Hezekiah had held out to them. He raised his voice to a high pitch and spoke in the Hebrew tongue. "The great king wished to know," he asked in a scornful tone, "on whom the Jewish nation trusted that they dared rebel against him? Was it on Egypt, the bent reed,[1] that, leant on, pierced the hand that trusted to it? Did they look for deliverance to their Lord God, whose high places and altars their king Hezekiah had taken away?" The chief cup-bearer here evidently wishes to rouse the superstitious fears of the people by reminding them of the general destruction which Hezekiah had commanded of altars and high places where Jehovah had been worshipped with illegal rites. He cannot understand how they can hope for deliverance from a God whose choice places of residence they have desecrated. "The offended God has, he declares, spoken to Sennacherib, and sent him to destroy the land."

The Jewish ministers, alarmed perhaps lest these words should impress that party of the people who still clung to the old disorderly form of worship, here remonstrated with the Assyrian ambassador on the impropriety of his conduct in addressing the bystanders instead of them, and begged him to speak in the Syrian language, which they understand; but the Rabshakeh, growing still more violent, openly asserted that he had not come to treat with the rulers, but to command the submission of the people.

Standing up so as to be seen by the whole assembly, and raising his voice still louder, he cried: "Hear the words of the great king! Let not Hezekiah deceive you, for he shall not be able to deliver you out of my hands, neither let Hezekiah make you trust in the Lord, saying, The Lord will surely

---

[1] This is evidently an allusion to the hieroglyphic sign of the title of the king of Upper Egypt, which is a bent reed.

deliver us. Hath any of the gods of the nations delivered at all his land out of the hand of the king of Assyria? Where are the gods of Hamath and of Arpad, of Sepharvaim, Hena, and Ivah? Have they delivered Samaria out of my hand? Who are they among all the gods of the countries that have delivered their country out of my hand, that the Lord should deliver Jerusalem?"

The people received the harangue in silence, and the cup-bearer, disappointed in his expectation of raising a tumult in the city, retired with his attendants, broke up his camp, and returned towards Lachish to report what he had seen and heard to his master.

The Jewish councillors, who during the Rabshakeh's harangue had rent their clothes with horror at the blasphemy they had been compelled to hear, re-entered the city, and told the king the result of their mission. His grief and indignation were not less than theirs; he rent his clothes, put on sackcloth, and went to the Temple, despatching at the same time the two ministers, in the guise in which they had returned from the Assyrian camp, to the prophet Isaiah, to make him acquainted with the insulting words that had been spoken of the God of Israel, and to entreat his counsel and prayers. A day of trouble and rebuke and blasphemy had come upon them, and yet said Hezekiah in his message to the prophet, "It may be that the Lord will hear all the words of Rabshakeh, whom the king of Assyria has sent to reproach the living God, and will reprove the words; wherefore lift up thy prayers for the remnant that are left."

Isaiah's answer was full of comfort for the messengers and the king, who, prostrate on his face in the temple of the Lord, awaited their return. "Be not afraid of the words thou hast heard, with which the king of Assyria has blasphemed me. Behold, I will send a blast upon him; and he shall hear a rumour, and shall return into his own land."

While these scenes were passing at Jerusalem—while the Hebrew king, clad in sackcloth, wept and prayed before the altar, and the prophet saw the veil lifted from the future, and spoke with joyful confidence of the deliverance that was to come—Sennacherib brought the siege of Lachish to a successful conclusion, and proceeded to invest another city called Libnah. On the walls of the palace Sennacherib built at Nineveh there was a series of pictures representing the events of the siege of Lachish, which are invested with great interest when we remember that it was from this place, and while these events were passing, that the Rabshakeh and his party set out for Jerusalem. Lachish is represented as a place of considerable extent, strongly fortified. The neighbouring country is richly cultivated; vines and fig-trees overhang the wall; there is a view of mountains in the distance. The town is evidently strongly garrisoned, for even after one of the gates has been forced and the besiegers are pouring in, the towers are stoutly defended by archers; and the citizens, men and women, crowd to the house-tops and hurl flaming brands down on the scaling-ladders the Assyrian soldiers are planting against the walls.

At a safe distance sits Sennacherib, watching the operations of his army from his throne of state; two or three attendants hold a silk canopy over him to protect his head from the rays of the sun, his feet repose luxuriously on an embroidered footstool; and while thus seated, carefully guarded from fatigue or danger, his eyes rest complacently on a group of executioners who are already dealing with some prisoners brought from the town. Two are stretched on the ground, being flayed alive; others are about to be impaled; several more, stripped of all their clothes, and with ropes round their necks, approach the throne to sue for their lives.

The destruction of Lachish had been completed, and Sennacherib in similar fashion was watching the attack of his army on Libnah, when the embassy returned and reported the reception they had met with at Jerusalem.

Sennacherib listened to his ambassadors' description of the calmness of the Jewish king and his people with amazement, in which something of respect must have mingled, for he took the trouble of sending a letter, apparently written with his own hand, to remonstrate with Hezekiah on his insane confidence, —a boastful, insulting letter, which yet shows how strongly the defiance of Hezekiah had moved him. It asked again the question previously put by the mouth of the chief cup-bearer: "In whom did Hezekiah trust? Had the gods of the nations whom his father had destroyed been able to defend them?"

It was the custom of Assyrian conquerors to carry

away the idols of the nations they subdued and place them in the temple of their great god Assur, as vanquished gods, slaves to their god, in like fashion as the men of the nation were slaves to the Assyrian king. The gods of Gozan and Haran and Rezeph had been so used, and stood as trophies of victory before Assur in Nineveh; what power had the Hebrew God to save His votaries more than these?

This was the letter which Hezekiah took into the Temple and spread before the Lord, with the prayer recorded in the nineteenth chapter of Second Kings, beginning, "Lord, bow down thine ear and hear; open, Lord, thine eyes and see." In answer to his supplication the prophet sent a message to assure him that the Lord God of Israel had heard the words he had prayed against Sennacherib. The king of Assyria was but an instrument in the hands of the Lord to work His will among the nations, and now that his rage and tumult had gone up into the ears of the Lord, He would "put a hook in his nose, and a bridle in his lips, and turn him back by the way by which he came."

The scene and circumstances of the destruction of the Assyrian army are involved in some obscurity. It appears that, after the fall of Libnah, Sennacherib hastened forwards across the desert towards Egypt. He was anxious to meet and engage the forces of the governor of Lower Egypt—a tributary prince named Sethos—before Tirhakah, the king of Ethiopia, and head king of the whole country, could arrive with the powerful army he had assembled in the upper country for the defence of the Delta.

At the end of a day's march Sennacherib found himself within sight of the enemy, who had drawn up before Pelusium, and ordered his camp to be pitched for the night. To him that day had been like any other day of march onward towards victory: perhaps he may have given a thought to the letter he had sent to Hezekiah, which would then be arriving at Jerusalem. He may have speculated for a moment how it would be received; but if he could have looked across the space and seen the letter spread out, and heard Hezekiah's appeal and Isaiah's answer, he would certainly not have discerned any reason for slackening his speed that day, or reckoning less securely on the triumph the next morning was to bring him. All seemed to prosper with him as he lay down to sleep under the sumptuous royal tent; Tirhakah was still far away, and the weakly-armed band of Sethos lay before him an easy prey. "And it came to pass that night, that the angel of the Lord went out, and smote in the camp of the Assyrians an hundred fourscore and five thousand: and when they arose early in the morning, behold, they were all dead corpses."

"So Sennacherib king of Assyria departed, and went and returned, and dwelt at Nineveh," hurrying back "by the way he came," the easy open route along the sea-coast of Palestine, which would offer no obstacle to the retreat of the small remnant of the army and the frightened king, as all the fortified towns had been already subdued and garrisoned with Assyrian soldiers.

So signal a deliverance could **not but** leave a deep impression on the minds of the **Egyptians**. A tradition of their **prince's escape from the mighty** army of the Assyrian **king** survived among them **down to** the time of Herodotus, and was related to him by **the** Egyptian **priests.** The story, as they had it, was naturally imperfect, since none of the antecedent circumstances could be known to the Egyptians, and the awful and mysterious nature of the event had impelled those who first recorded it to clothe it in something of an allegorical **form.**

Sethos, the Egyptian priests told Herodotus, was a pious priest of Vulcan, who, on his succession to the government, offended the military class among his subjects by revoking some of the privileges usually accorded them. In revenge for this neglect the warriors refused to **come to** his **aid** when Sennacherib king of the Assyrians **marched** his vast army into Egypt. On this the **monarch, greatly** distressed, entered the inner sanctuary, and before **the** image of his god bewailed the fate that impended over him. As he wept, **he** fell asleep, and dreamed that the god came and **stood at** his side, bidding him be **of** good cheer, and **go** boldly forth to meet the Assyrian host, which should **do** him no hurt, as **he** himself would send those who **would help him.** Sethos then, relying on the dream, **collected such of the Egyptians** as were ready to follow him, and **with these** marched to Pelusium, and **there pitched his camp. As** the two armies lay here opposite each other, there came in the night **a** multitude **of** field-mice, which devoured all the quivers and bow-strings of the enemy, and the thongs by which they managed their shields. Next morning they commenced their flight, and great multitudes fell, as they had no arms with which to defend themselves. There stands to this day, Herodotus adds, in the temple of Vulcan, a statue of Sethos with a mouse in his hand, and an inscription to this effect, "Look on me, and learn to reverence the gods."

The shrew-mouse among the Egyptians was the emblem of prophetic power. The statue, with a mouse in its hand, erected shortly after the destruction of the Assyrian army before Pelusium, expressed allegorically the sense of the Egyptians that a wonderful interposition of the Divine power had been manifested on their behalf. It is easy to see how Herodotus, communicating with the priests of a later age through a half-instructed Greek interpreter, may have taken the allegorical sign for a reality, and introduced the incident of the mice into the story through a natural misunderstanding of what he saw and heard.

It is a curious fact that Sennacherib's clay cylinder omits all notice of that expedition into Palestine which ended so disastrously for him; it does not even allude to the taking of Lachish, though, as already mentioned, a series of pictures on the walls of Sennacherib's palace depict some of the events of the siege.

After Sennacherib's flight from Egypt he abstained from making any further attempt against the nations south of the Lebanon, but his misfortune did not prevent his carrying on new wars in the southern and north-western portions of the empire, and in hitherto unconquered regions in the south-west. In the intervals between his campaigns he erected a magnificent palace at Nineveh, which differed from the old model in being more commodiously planned, and having better proportioned halls, rooms, and courts. The character of the pictures on the walls is also somewhat different. Fewer allegorical figures appear in them, and more realistic representations of everyday events. Sennacherib has less room for the gods in his brick and marble life history than had the earlier kings; perhaps because he remembered how they had failed him once. The events of ordinary days are depicted as well as scenes of war and the chase. We see the long procession of servants bringing dishes from the kitchen for the king's dinner —game, and dried locusts stuck on sticks, and trays of fruits and cakes. We are also shown minutely the process of building the palace, the making of the bricks, the quarrying of the stone, the carving of a colossal winged bull, and its transport down the river to its position on the top of the mound at the palace gate.

When all the sculpturing and decorating were completed, Sennacherib seems to have been well satisfied with the work, and to have felt anxious that his costly piece of autobiography should fairly last its time, and have many readers, for he caused this final inscription to be engraved on the walls of the palace when all the other inscriptions and pictures were set in their places.

"This palace will grow old and fall to pieces in the course of time. I wish my successor to raise it out of its ruins, to replace the inscriptions on which my name is written, to clean the bas-reliefs, and put them back in their places. May Assur bless him and hear his prayers if he does this; but if he cuts out my name, may the great god, the father of gods, cut him away from the succession—may he deprive him of sceptre and throne, and break his sword away from his hand."

It would almost seem as if some foreboding of the events that followed must have been in Sennacherib's mind when he dictated those words, for it is certain that the calamity he wished to guard against quickly came.

We know little of the circumstances that preceded his violent death, but it could hardly have occurred as it did without some previous time during which the splendid palace was filled with an atmosphere of intrigue and treachery, and a Damocles' sword hung over the monarch's head as he sat at the sumptuous feasts we see preparing. The treachery was rifest in his immediate family. Two of his sons, Adrammelech and Sharezer, plotted against their father's life, and slew him with the sword as he was worshipping in the temple of his god Nisroch.

They did not long profit by their crime, for they were driven from the throne they had usurped by a younger brother, a few years afterwards, but they retained power long enough to leave a record of their **unnatural conduct, which remains to this day.**

They caused the portrait of their **father** Sennacherib to be effaced from the bas-reliefs of his **own palace** wherever it occurs, thus openly defying the curse he had recorded there, perhaps but a very short **time** before his murder. Some of the marbles from which Sennacherib's face has been broken away are now in the British Museum. We look with a strange interest at these silent witnesses **of the angry** passions of people dead so many centuries ago, trying to picture **to** ourselves **the** days when **Sennacherib** and his traitor sons sat daily at table in the palace banqueting-hall, while the marble face unmutilated looked at them from the wall; and then that other day when the original of the portrait lay a murdered corpse in **the temple,** and the **two sons stood** before the slab and had the features cut away. Was it because they **could** not bear to see the sculptured face of their dead father staring at them as they feasted in the palace he had built?

CHAPTER XVII.

THE BURDEN OF NINEVEH.

AFTER a brief reign Sennacherib's traitorous sons Adrammelech and Sharezer were driven into exile, and their younger brother Esarhaddon was acknowledged king by the whole nation. The first years of his reign were disturbed by civil wars with his banished brothers; but when peace was restored to the interior of the empire after their death, he had leisure to undertake expeditions into the distant provinces, where the tributary kings had taken advantage of the disturbances in the capital to reassert their independence.

Esarhaddon has left a clay cylinder recording the campaigns of the first ten years of his reign. The same names recur that figure in previous annals. A king of Sidon revolts, and when his city falls into the hands of the Assyrian troops, seeks safety in flight to an island in the sea. Esarhaddon relates how he traversed the sea like a fish, and took the fugitive monarch prisoner. Babylonia is completely conquered, and punished for its revolt by the death of its king. Another year's expedition is said to take

Esarhaddon and his army to "the extreme confines of the earth," on the other side of the desert. From the description given of the country and the journey thither, across 140 miles of sandy waste, "the extreme confines of the earth" is supposed to mean South-eastern Arabia, to which region no previous Assyrian monarch had ever penetrated.

Emboldened by the success of these campaigns, Esarhaddon, in the last years of his life, again carried the Assyrian arms into the countries which had witnessed his father Sennacherib's discomfiture and ignominious flight. Unfortunately the clay cylinder ends with the tenth year of his reign; we only hear of his expedition into Egypt, and complete conquest of Tirhakah, the Ethiopian king, by a short notice of these events in the annals of his son Assurbanipal. Tirhakah was put to flight, and Egypt broken up into districts, over which Esarhaddon placed rulers of his own choosing. Thebes fell into the hands of the conquerors, and suffered all the calamities described by the prophet Nahum: "Populous No, situate among the rivers, whose rampart was the flood, and her wall the flood ... Yet was she carried away, she went into captivity: her young children were dashed to pieces, and all her great men were bound in chains."

The downfall of Egypt drew after it signal punishment and humiliation for Judah and Jerusalem, whose heathen-minded king Manasseh, the unworthy son of Hezekiah, had allied himself in the closest manner with the Egyptian princes who had ruled the Delta under Tirhakah. Esarhaddon does not appear to have gone in person against Jerusalem; but on his return through Palestine by the coast route, after his conquest of Egypt, he despatched a detachment of his army into the interior of the country, commanded by captains of the host, who "took Manasseh among the thorns" (by treachery, Josephus says), bound him with fetters, and carried him captive to Babylon, where Esarhaddon was then holding his court. There, in the very centre of the heathen worship for which he had deserted the service of Jehovah, himself a victim to the heathenish spirit of cruelty which he had encouraged when he relit the fires of Tophet and deluged the streets of Jerusalem with the blood of the prophets, the conscience of Manasseh awoke, "and he sought the Lord his God, and humbled himself greatly before the God of his fathers," entreating the Lord (Josephus tells us) to "render his enemy humane and merciful to him."

The prayer of Manasseh was heard; the heart of an Assyrian king was for once moved with compassion. The grief and humility of the Jewish captive touched Esarhaddon; he gave Manasseh permission to return to his own land, and restored to him a certain amount of kingly authority. To the end of his life Manasseh conscientiously used his recovered power to undo, as far as possible, the evils he had wrought in his early years, and show his gratitude for the miracle (the softening the heart of an Assyrian king was indeed a miracle) that had been wrought in his behalf.

Esarhaddon died after a reign of seventeen years,

and was succeeded by a son, Assurbanipal, in whose reign the empire of Assyria attained its highest point of outward prosperity, though to the eyes of Jewish prophets, who saw that the measure of its sins and iniquities was daily being filled up, and that the splendidly adorned capital was becoming more and more "a city of bloods," it was evident that the gigantic Assyrian tree was already bending and tottering to its fall. The great victories gained by Assurbanipal in almost every quarter of the then known world could not save it; they only hastened the catastrophe by reducing the strength of the army and by rousing the hatred of fresh nations against the overweening conqueror. The boughs of the gigantic cedar "were multiplied," and his branches "had become long," but decay was at work in the great trunk; and to some prophetic ears among the captive people torn from Samaria and Judea, "the noise of the whip, and the rattling of the wheels, and the prancing of the horses" of the coming destroyer were already audible.

Assurbanipal exceeded his predecessors as much in the magnificence of his buildings as in the extent of his conquests. The ruins of his palace at Nineveh have furnished some of the most beautiful of the marbles now in the British Museum; and as the subjects depicted on them are more various than those sculptured in earlier times, they are the principal sources of our knowledge of the habits, customs, daily occupations, and amusements of the Assyrian court.

The one domestic scene that occurs in the long

series of Assyrian sculptures is found on a slab from Assurbanipal's palace. It presents him reclining at his ease in a vine-covered arbour of the royal gardens with his queen, who sits opposite to him on a chair of state, surrounded by her attendant maidens. Birds are singing in the branches of the trees in the garden round; and in strange contrast to these images of peace and luxury, there hangs, close behind the queen's back, from a branch of a palm-tree, a ghastly decapitated head, evidently that of a war-captive or criminal, which looks as if it had been newly placed there, for it is still clothed with flesh, the lip is pierced with an iron ring, and the hair streams down: a curious evidence of the state of manners in the "bloody city, full of lies and robbery," which could admit such an ornament for the favourite retreat of the king's private hours.

The preponderance of hunting scenes in Assurbanipal's marbles shows, that, if he had his moments of repose, a life of active adventure was what was most congenial to him. Lions or wild bulls were his principal prey; and to provide him with a sufficient number of victims for a day's sport it was customary to bring wild beasts from a distance in wooden cages to the royal pleasure-grounds, and to set them free as the monarch approached in his chariot or on horseback, just at the right moment for him to despatch them with his arrows without overmuch trouble or risk to himself. The sculptures represent sometimes as many as eighteen lions lying dead or wounded after a single day's sport; the carcases were afterwards brought into the city and a kind of religious ceremony held over them, when the king, attired in his royal robes, came out before the people and poured libations of wine in honour of the hunting god Nergal.

Assurbanipal's love of destruction was unfortunately not appeased by unlimited slaughter of wild beasts. Cruel as were most of the Assyrian kings, this last conqueror among them exceeded all the others in the savage punishments he inflicted on his vanquished enemies. The bas-reliefs of his palace descriptive of his numerous campaigns are full of horrible representations of wounded captives thrust through with the spear; of others having their tongues torn out by the roots; of prisoners advancing to execution with the bloody head of a brother or friend fastened round their necks, or being struck on the face by the executioner before he despatches them. Fit pictures for the adornment of "the bloody city," "the dwelling-place for lions, the feeding-place for young lions; where the lion tore for his whelps and strangled for his lioness, and filled his holes with prey and his dens with ravin."

A son of Assurbanipal, named Saracus, succeeded peaceably to the throne. Unlike his predecessors of the Sargonide dynasty, he appears to have been a man of weak and indolent character, who preferred the peaceable enjoyment of the vast hoards of treasure which his ancestors had collected in their palaces, to the constant warlike expeditions by which former kings had kept alive the terror of their power in the minds of the surrounding nations.

After some years of indolent rule, shut up in his father's palace at Nineveh, he was roused from his apathy by finding himself besieged in his capital by the king of the Medes at the head of a powerful army. During the latter part of Assurbanipal's reign the Medes had exchanged their weak government of confederate chieftains for the rule of a single king, and had grown into a powerful nation, able to retaliate on the Assyrians the frequent invasions and humiliations to which they had been subject while Sargon and Sennacherib were at the head of the Assyrian empire.

The fall of Nineveh was, however, retarded for a few years by a sudden and terrible event, which for a time made all the civilized nations of Asia companions in misfortune, and obliged them to turn their arms from attacking each other to withstand a common enemy. A vast horde of Scythians, driven by famine from their own sterile homes in the North, poured through the passes of the Caucasus into Media, and quickly spread themselves over Assyria, Syria, and Palestine to the borders of Egypt.

This was the "evil out of the north" breaking forth on "all the inhabitants of the land" of which the prophet Jeremiah had been forewarned in his vision of a "pot seething in the north." All the civilized people of Asia and Europe, friends and foes alike, cowered under the terrible destruction—"the great day of the Lord, the day of desolation, the day of clouds and thick darkness," that had now come upon the earth.

The Median king was forced to retire from the

siege of Nineveh to protect his own country, as far as he could, from the barbarians, who plundered and burned all before them. The reprieve did not, however, afford the Ninevites opportunity for regaining their strength, for the Scythians entered their territories, and inflicted great calamities upon them.

In a few years the northern invasion had spent its fury. It came like a sudden tempest, sweeping over the lands, and breaking down every obstacle before its resistless strength; and, like a tempest, it sank away almost as suddenly as it had burst forth. Some of the Scythian tribes retired with the booty they had collected to their northern homes. Great numbers died the victims of their own excesses; numbers more were slain by the inhabitants of the countries they had overrun, whose courage revived when they found that the seemingly exhaustless river of invaders had ceased to overflow them.

Saracus himself appears to have displayed some energy after the departure of the Scythians, and to have set on foot some building at Nineveh; but it was a falling kingdom he now had to govern, and time for restoration was not given. The Median king no sooner found himself released from the danger that had threatened to overwhelm him, than he again recurred to his projects of conquest against Nineveh. The Babylonians—so often vanquished, but never utterly subdued by the Assyrians—took the opportunity of their enemies' extremity to rise in rebellion against them, and sent a large army to the assistance of the Medes. After a siege of some duration Saracus, finding himself utterly unable to make head against the power of the allies, resolved to put an end to his own life rather than fall into the hands of enemies who had the memory of so many ages of cruel oppression to wipe out in blood. He is said to have burnt himself alive in the most splendid of his palaces, where he built a funeral pile of all the treasures that his ancestors had heaped together. The sandal-wood and the ebony, the seal-skins, and the purple and saffron stuffs, and the gold and silver of which Sennacherib and Sargon boast in their inscriptions, that was the end of it all.

After his death the Medes and Babylonians entered Nineveh, and destroyed it with fire and sword, levelling its splendid palaces, and leaving it a heap of ruins.

The oppressed people of the surrounding nations heard the news of the fall of their great enemy with a mixture of triumph and fear, which the prophet Ezekiel graphically describes. The great fir-tree, envied of all the other trees in the garden of Eden, fell; the mountains and all the valleys were full of his branches; his broken boughs lay by all the rivers of the land. And on the day that he went down to his grave the Lord God "caused a mourning." Lebanon mourned, "and all the trees of the field fainted for him," "the nations shook at the sound of his fall;" if he could fall, which of them might feel secure? Yet the trees of Eden, the choicest and best of Lebanon, rose up relieved from the great shadow that oppressed them, and were comforted.

Judah and Jerusalem, the choicest and best, rested

under the rule of the good king Josiah. For a few years the valleys and cultivated fields of the Holy Land, so often trampled into dust by the rushing wheels of Assyrian war-chariots and the tread of its armies, blossomed in security and peace.

No attempt ever seems to have been made to rebuild Nineveh after its complete destruction by the Medes. It remained for ever afterwards "empty, and void, and waste," as the prophet Nahum saw it in his vision; so completely forgotten that the precise locality of its renowned walls and palaces became a matter of dispute, till recent researches restored their mutilated and fire-blackened remains to the light of day once more.

The doom the prophet Nahum had pronounced, averted now by no repentance or prayers of its people, was at length fully accomplished and remained fixed. "Woe to the bloody city! Behold, I am against thee, saith the Lord of hosts. I will show the nations thy nakedness, and the kingdoms thy shame. I will make thee vile, and will set thee as a gazing-stock. And it shall come to pass that all that look upon thee shall flee from thee, and say, Nineveh is laid waste: who will bemoan her? Draw the waters for the siege, fortify thy strongholds, go into clay, and tread the mortar, make strong the brick-kiln. There shall the fire devour thee, the sword shall cut thee off; it shall eat thee up like the cankerworm. There is no healing of thy bruise, thy wound is grievous. All that hear the bruit of thee shall clap their hands over thee, for upon whom hath not thy wickedness passed continually?"

CHAPTER XVIII.

THAT GREAT CITY BABYLON.

" A GREAT eagle with great wings, long-winged, full of feathers, which had divers colours, came unto Lebanon." The prophet who describes the gradual rise of the Assyrian empire under the figure of a fir-tree transplanted from the garden of God, and nourished by the concourse of waters round its roots to such luxuriant growth that all the other trees of the garden languished under its shadow, uses a different emblem for the sudden uprising of the Babylonian kingdom into the power the Assyrian had forfeited. A great eagle with long wings, full-feathered, is seen rising in the sky, bringing shadow and trembling once more to the nations that for a brief space had rejoiced in the freedom and light which the fall of the overshadowing shroud of Assyria had given them. For a brief moment the trees of Eden were comforted, and then the dusky lowering wings and sharp beak and talons of the new destroyer brought more terrible ruin than had yet overtaken them.

The contrast between the two figures exemplifies a difference in the two powers that strikes us as we follow the course of their influence on the destiny of the Jews. The Assyrian is the rooted tree of luxuriant branches, one gradually stretching beyond the other in extent; it is not one bough that grows and surpasses all the others, it is the whole tree. So in all the notices of the Assyrian power in the Bible it is the king of Assyria, rather than any individual man, that is particularized. Sargon's name is not even mentioned in Kings or Chronicles, and the names that do appear, with the exception of that of Sennacherib, hardly seem to individualize their owners, one succeeds the other with so little comment. The Assyrian annals themselves leave the same impression on our minds. It is the history of a power, not that of the individual wielders of it, we are learning.

The names change on the cylinders, and we mark how one king after another stretches his sceptre a little further over the earth, but their deeds are the same in war and peace; the change from father to son seems to make no other difference than the change of name on the marbles of the palaces.

The Babylonian power, on the contrary, comes before us with the character of one man impressed upon it; the life of a single king comprises nearly all its triumphs and the erection of all its architectural wonders. It is best figured, not by the slow growth of a rooted tree, but by the swift movements of a living creature. The prophets of Israel announce this king by name as chosen by God to perform a certain work, and rule for a certain period over the earth. "Thus saith the Lord, Now have I given all these nations into the hand of Nebuchadrezzar the king of Babylon, my servant." "Behold, I will bring against Tyrus Nebuchadrezzar a king of kings." "I will make the multitude of Egypt to cease by the hand of Nebuchadrezzar king of Babylon."

The comparatively speaking few remains and records of Babylon concur in placing Nebuchadnezzar in the same conspicuous light as the sole creator of Babylon the great, as it was when visited by the writers of ancient times who have described its glories. The researches that have been made on the site of the ancient Babylon and in its neighbourhood have not produced such a rich harvest of interesting relics as that which rewarded the excavators in the mounds of Nineveh.

The desolation of the two sites seems equal. Nineveh is "empty, and void, and waste," and Babylon has become, as Jeremiah foretold, "heaps"—a desert tract, whose formerly level surface is broken on every side by shapeless hillocks of dust and fragments; but on examination the ruin of one city exceeds that of the other. The mounds of Nineveh are graves, which on being opened can still give back some relics of the dead that were laid within them, and move the living with wonder at the vastness of the skeletons they entombed; but the heaps of Babylon can testify to little save to the thoroughness with which the besom of destruction has swept them through and through.

Almost the only thing they have kept safe is the name of Nebuchadnezzar, which is found to recur again and again, graven on the fragments of the sunburnt bricks which build up the melancholy heaps of ruins that cover the country for miles of the district where the great city once stood.

Conspicuous among these heaps are three that tower up to the height of considerable hills, and are distinguished by special names among the Arabs who frequent the neighbourhood. One high, oblong mass is called by the most ancient name of the city of Babylon itself—Babel, the gate of God; and though there is little to identify it beyond the name of Nebuchadnezzar graven on the bricks of a few feet of straight wall, which shows here and there where the accumulated rubbish of ages has been worn away by wind and rain, it is supposed to be the ruins of the great temple of Belus, which Nebuchadnezzar built, and which Herodotus and other ancient visitors to Babylon praise so highly.

A second hill, crowned by some broken walls built of very fine yellow brick, is called the "palace" by the Arabs; it is a vast mound covered with broken bricks and tiles, and bears on its summit, besides the yellow walls, a colossal figure of a lion standing over a man prostrate with outstretched arms, rudely carved in black basalt. Between the broken walls and the black lion stands a single tamarisk tree, whose presence among the ruins impresses the Arabs so much that they declare it to be a tree of a peculiar species never met with elsewhere, and look upon it as a relic from the gardens of the ancient city. At the foot of the wall some slabs of stone have been found graven with the inscription, "This is the great palace of Nebuchadnezzar king of Babylon, who walked in the worship of the gods Nebo and Merodach, his lords."

These pale yellow walls then, and the rudely carved lion, once formed part, and are all that remain, of the house where Nebuchadnezzar lived; where he dreamed his dream, "At rest in mine house, and flourishing in my palace;" where Daniel and the three holy children conversed with him; on whose roof he was walking when he looked round and said, "This is great Babylon that I have builded." The scanty remains afford no clue to the original plan or appearance of the house we should so much like to be able to picture to ourselves, but the fragments of brilliantly painted tiles that abound on the hill, the fineness of the brickwork, and the size and shape of the mound, confirm some of the particulars on which ancient writers have enlarged in their descriptions of Babylonian palaces, and dispose us to rely on the accuracy of their accounts.

The third hill is a still more complete ruin than the other two. Its vast irregularly shaped mass has yielded nothing to the excavators but a few bricks marked with the names of early kings. This leads to the conclusion that here stood the ancient palace, probably coeval with the foundation of the city by Nimrod, which Nebuchadnezzar in one of his inscriptions says he repaired and raised above the level of the river, and which he afterwards abandoned for his new palace.

About nine miles from the site of the ancient city

there is a fourth pile, which, standing alone on the plain, and towering to a great height into the sky, forms the most conspicuous object in the whole circle of ruins. Its pyramidal shape and large dimensions, and the vast fragments of jagged old wall that still crown its summit, so struck early travellers that it was long believed to be the remains of the Tower of Babel itself. It was afterwards identified with the temple of Belus, till the discovery of some clay cylinders within its walls bearing the title of the god Nebo, and calling the temple the "Wonder of Borsippa," proved it to have been dedicated to a different god, and to have formed part, not of Babylon, but of a town mentioned by ancient writers as lying near it.

It presents rather the appearance of a natural hill with a ruined tower on its summit than a structure raised by the hands of man; but its sloping sides have been deeply furrowed by wind and rain, and here and there in the ravines portions of the ancient walls of unburnt brick are laid bare. From careful examination of these remains, Sir H. Rawlinson has been able to make out the original plan of the building, and considers that a reconstruction of the temple as it looked in Nebuchadnezzar's time may be given with a very near approach to certainty.

This hill of broken bricks and tiles was once a temple tower, similar in form to those which Urukh and Ilgi erected in the primitive cities on the Persian Gulf. It stood, as did the moon-god's temple at Ur, on a high platform, and consisted of seven stages, decreasing in size as they mounted upwards, and crowned with a sacred tabernacle or shrine at the top. The mere piling up of masses of unburnt brick, though it satisfied the ambition of the early kings, did not afford sufficient display of wealth or taste for such a monarch as Nebuchadnezzar. The bricks of the Borsippa mound are found to have traces of colour on them, and confirm the accounts which ancient writers have left of the style of ornamentation used for the later Babylonian temples. Being designed for the worship of the heavenly bodies, the seven stages were meant to correspond to the seven celestial spheres—of the sun, moon, and five planets; and as each sphere had a particular colour appropriated to it, the stages of the temple were painted to mimic each the colour of its planet. The sphere of Saturn—the most distant of the then known planets, almost out of the influence of the sun's rays—was black, that of Jupiter orange, that of Mars blood red, the sun's gold colour, Venus' primrose, Mercury's blue, the moon's silver.

In these well-assorted gradations of colour the great temples rose. The black sphere of Saturn, built of bricks coated with bitumen, rested on the raised platform planted with trees and paved with richly coloured tiles. Jupiter's orange, with Mars' blood red, relieved the gloom of the black, both stages being faced with bricks of their colour. In the centre of the building the sun's sphere, built of unburnt brick, was faced with plates of solid gold, which must have had the effect, when the sun shone on it, of a ring of fire circling the building. The primrose sphere of Venus quenched the fiery rays in a pale sunset glow; while Mercury's stage—built of bricks fused by strong heat to a dim blue colour, —like a section of heaven itself divided two luminaries, for the seventh stage mimicked moonlight with a coating of silver, only a little less brilliant than the sun's gold. Above all, like a star in the horns of the moon, the richly-decked glittering shrine was lifted into the blue of the sky.

In a country where there were no mountains or natural elevations of any kind, where the well-watered level land presented always a monotonous surface of luxuriant green to the eye, brilliantly coloured artificial hills like these temple structures, towering up in grand proportions to such a height as to serve as landmarks for all the country round, must have afforded a welcome variety in the landscape.

The use of a great deal of colour in the ornamentation of the buildings seems to have been a marked feature in the new Babylon which Nebuchadnezzar constructed, and must have made it contrast strongly with the grey cities built of unburnt brick of earlier times. The walls of the houses as well as those of the temples were decked in rainbow hues, and walking through the royal quarter of Babylon—"the golden city," as the Jewish prophet called it—must have been like passing down a long picture gallery.

Nebuchadnezzar's palace is described by ancient writers as having been entirely covered outside with paintings of hunting and battle scenes, interspersed with inscriptions written in blue letters on white enamelled ground; and the numerous fragments of glazed tiles painted in rich colours, with trees, flowers, and animals, that cover the heap of ruins where the palace once stood, prove the correctness of their account. The smaller ancient palace repaired by Nebuchadnezzar, and the houses of the nobility, said to have been two or three stories high, were no doubt ornamented in a similar fashion. Somewhere in the royal quarter of the city stood the celebrated hanging gardens, erected by Nebuchadnezzar to gratify his Median queen, who, coming from a mountainous country, could take no pleasure in the monotonous scenery round her new home. Here plantations of trees, shrubs, and rare flowers flourished high up in the air, raised from the ground by successive tiers of lofty arches, ponderous enough to sustain the weight of earth in which they grew. The river running through the centre of the city in ancient times must have greatly added to its beauty, by giving back a second series of rainbow-hued walls and fantastic gardens to the gaze of those who promenaded along the tops of the low, broad walls which Herodotus says flanked it on either side: and besides the river there was an immense lake, constructed by Nebuchadnezzar in the neighbourhood of his two palaces, which served as another looking-glass for the wonders of the place to repeat themselves in.

An inner wall of great strength surrounded the principal part of the city, which, as it was entirely rebuilt by him, may be called Nebuchadnezzar's Babylon. Beyond lay a vast space, partly covered with streets, partly laid out in parks, gardens, and fields, where enough corn could be grown to feed the city during a siege. Enclosing all, a great square, ten miles in extent every way, rose to the height of 80 feet, the outer walls accounted one of the wonders of the world. They were built of unburnt brick, and defended by double rows of towers, between which a chariot and four could drive and turn round. Twenty-five brazen gates in each wall opened into the city.

Gorgeous with all manner of colours—with towers literally of gold and silver cleaving the soft southern sky, with sheen of sunlight reflected from its hundred brazen gates, with various foliage of exotic trees and shrubs shading its broad streets and glittering waters —must have been the Babylon over which Nebuchadnezzar looked, when satisfaction in the work he had completed rose to overweening pride in his heart and brought sudden punishment.

Outside the walls of the great city stretched a wide featureless level plain, which in Nebuchadnezzar's time, and while the Jews were captives there, was the best cultivated and most fruitful region in the world.

To a native of Babylon, the broad expanse of flat green fields, divided by slender watercourses, with their fringes of dark rushes and white willows, would no doubt appear the perfection of beauty; but it would look very wearisome to the Jewish captives toiling on the city walls, all of whose pleasant associations were with the vine-clad hills, and deep valleys, and oak-glades of Judea, and who would turn away their eyes in disgust from the parti-coloured sham temple-hills that alone broke the monotonous level.

The extraordinary fertility of the soil was a principal source of wealth to the Babylonians; but the city also carried on an extensive commerce, second only to that of Tyre. The same sins of covetousness and over-luxuriousness for which the Tyrians were remarkable prevailed among the Babylonians. They coveted an "evil covetousness," and spent the wealth they restlessly toiled for in vain-glorious show and the indulgence of every kind of pleasure. The women were "tender and delicate,"[1] and the men luxurious and effeminate in their style of living, indulging in soft and rich clothing, wearing ornaments—earrings in their ears—and "exceeding in dyed attire upon their heads, all of them princes to look at."[2] Their houses were full of costly furniture, gold and silver drinking vessels, soft couches, and silken hangings for the walls and windows.

Nebuchadnezzar set an example of extreme lavishness in the use of the precious metals, such as perhaps was never indulged in by any other monarch; for he records that he covered the walls of some of the buildings he erected with plates of gold. This excess of luxury did not, however, bring with it any softening of the fierce passions that are supposed to belong to a half-civilized people. The Babylonians seem to have been as cruel as the Assyrians in the

---

[1] Isaiah xlvii. 1.   [2] Ezek. xxiii. 15.

punishment they inflicted on their enemies, and in their treatment of war-captives. "They showed no mercy, and laid the yoke very heavily even upon the ancient."[1] They made their lives bitter to them. "A bitter and hasty nation," Habakkuk calls them, "terrible and dreadful; their horses swifter than leopards, more fierce than the evening wolves." "Proud men," who "enlarged their desires as hell," and as death could not be satisfied.[2]

Amid so much evil one better characteristic stands out. From the early times, when the first Chaldean settlers practised the arts of civilized life, in Babel and Ur and Erech, and began to watch the motions of the heavenly bodies from the tops of their temple-towers, the Babylonians were distinguished by a desire for knowledge, and a high respect for those who made its pursuit the object of their lives. The title "wise man" seems to have been regarded as the highest honour, and those who attained to it formed a class apart, whose members held a special office in the state, and were consulted even by such despotic monarchs as Nebuchadnezzar and Belshazzar. They were called Chaldeans, because they alone of the later Babylonians preserved the use of the ancient language of Chaldea, which, after the conquest of the primitive cities by Arab tribes and the settlement of bodies of foreigners in Babylonia under the Assyrian kings, had been superseded in general use by a different dialect.

This ancient dead language was to the Baby-

---

[1] Isaiah xlvii. 6.   [2] Habakkuk i.

lonians what Latin was to the Europeans in the Middle Ages. All scientific investigations were carried on in it, and acquaintance with it elevated a person at once into the learned class. This was "the tongue" in which Daniel and his companions were instructed during the three years they lived in Nebuchadnezzar's palace. Daniel attained great proficiency in it, and in the sciences to which it was the key, and, after his interpretation of the king's dream, was made a prince over the Chaldeans.

Unlike the learned class among the Egyptians, the Babylonian wise men were not a priestly caste. Some were priests, and some devoted themselves entirely to learned pursuits, especially to the studies of astronomy and astrology, which had to a certain extent a sacred character. The heavenly bodies were held by the Chaldeans to be closely connected with the gods, if not gods themselves. The planets, the abodes of the great gods, rained down, they believed, influence on the earth each according to the character of its presiding deity. "The stars in their courses" were to them real warriors fighting for or against nations and individuals. Acquaintance with their aspects and motions was held to confer the power of divination, the gift of interpreting dreams, and other occult powers. The Chaldeans began the practice of casting nativities, and of predicting events by the position of the heavenly bodies, a practice that long outlived the creed that gave rise to it. "Astrologers, star-gazers, monthly prognosticators," Isaiah calls them, whose supposed powers, he warns them, will be found unavailing when the day of calamity arrives.

In spite of the false bent which their views of the nature of the heavenly bodies gave to their researches, the gazers from Chaldean watch-towers made great advance in the true science of astronomy, as is proved by the evidence of astronomical tablets stamped on clay which have been found among the ruins of the ancient cities.

At a very early period they distinguished the planets, "the wanderers," from the fixed stars, and understood the general laws of their motions so far as to state by anticipation their positions in the heavens throughout the year. They predicted eclipses of the sun and moon, catalogued the fixed stars and divided them into groups, to which they gave the names we use for the constellations now. It is even thought that they must have invented some sort of telescope, for the tablets show them to have been acquainted with the satellites of Jupiter and Saturn, which could not have been visible to the naked eye even in the clear air of Chaldea. They certainly made sun-dials and water-clocks, and had calculated correctly the length of the solar year. Between their real and their supposed knowledge, the wise men occupied a very conspicuous place among their fellow-citizens and before the king, who never entered on any important undertaking without summoning them to stand before him and assist him with their advice.

CHAPTER XIX.

THE EAGLE WITH GREAT WINGS.

THE condition of Babylon during the long period of Assyrian supremacy varied with the greater or less energy of the monarch reigning at Nineveh. Sometimes the Babylonian sovereigns succeeded in maintaining their independence for a while; again they were subdued and forced to acknowledge themselves tributaries to the empire. On some occasions, as a punishment for continual revolts, the native princes were altogether set aside, and the province ruled by governors chosen at Nineveh. Esarhaddon incorporated Babylonia into the empire, and was living at Babylon when Manasseh was brought to his court—the first of the Jewish royal captives who saw the high walls and languished in the palace dungeons that were to echo to the groans of so many princely Hebrew prisoners.

During the reign of the last king of Assyria, while the empire was falling to decay, Babylon rapidly increased in strength and riches; but when danger first threatened Nineveh from the Medes, the Babylonians did not waver in their allegiance. They remained faithful during the season of terrible calamity brought on Assyria by the invasion of the Scythian hordes; but when the Median king appeared in Mesopotamia a second time, and prepared to invest the capital city before it had recovered from the ravages of the barbarians, the people of the southern provinces, Babylonians and Susianians, bethought themselves of seizing so favourable an opportunity for recovering their independence.

An army of united Susianians and Babylonians collected with the purpose of approaching Nineveh from the south, while the Medes advanced on it from the north. To prevent a junction of the two threatening hosts, the Assyrian king despatched a portion of his army to Babylon, commanded by an Assyrian noble named Nabopolassar, whom he appointed governor of Babylon, and to whom he entrusted the subjection of the revolted provinces. Nabopolassar succeeded in establishing himself as governor of Babylon; but once in possession of his government, he placed himself at the head of the rebels, proclaimed the independence of Babylonia, and offered his services to the Median king, hoping to be able to secure for himself a portion of the spoil of the expiring empire.

Cyaxeres, the Median king, gladly accepted Nabopolassar's offer of assistance, and agreed to the condition with which it was coupled—that the alliance between the kings should be cemented by a marriage between Nebuchadnezzar, son of Nabopolassar, and Cyaxeres' daughter Amyitis. The young prince and princess were betrothed, and Nabopolassar, accompanied by his son, led a powerful army against Nineveh, took an active part in the siege, and materially assisted in the final overthrow of the Assyrian empire. A division of the provinces subject to Nineveh seems to have followed the triumph of the allies, and to Nabopolassar's share fell not only the district of Babylonia proper, but the tributary nations in Syria and Palestine, whose state of continual disaffection and frequent open revolt made them not very valuable possessions for either king.

The news of the fall of Nineveh does not appear to have roused the Palestinian or Phœnician peoples to any attempt to recover their independence. The Tyrians, the Sidonians, and the inhabitants of the Philistine towns along the coast, had probably suffered too much from the devastations of the Scythians to be in a condition to enter upon a new struggle; and the Jews were at that time ruled over by the good king Josiah, who was then occupied in purging the country from the idolatries with which it had been polluted in the preceding reigns; and who, guided by the counsel of the prophets, preferred to transfer his allegiance to the Babylonian king rather than enter into an alliance with Egypt.

Psammetichus, the king who then sat on the throne of Egypt, was old and disinclined to warlike enterprises, so that the Egyptian party in the Phœnician and Hebrew cities had for a time no foreign support to enforce their pretensions. For some years the supremacy of the new empire established in Babylon was acknowledged by all the old tributaries, and Nabopolassar had leisure to lay the foundations of his new kingdom securely, undisturbed by attacks from foreign powers.

While he was peaceably ruling, his son Nebuchadnezzar served an apprenticeship in warfare under his father-in-law Cyaxeres, with whom he made some campaigns in Lydia in command of a contingent of troops that Nabopolassar furnished to his ally.

The death of Psammetichus, and the accession of his son Pharaoh-Necho to the head of the Egyptian empire, brought a complete change in the political state of all the countries south of the Lebanon. Necho was an enterprising and warlike prince, and having received the kingdom from his father in a prosperous condition and with a full treasury, he conceived the purpose of re-establishing the ancient supremacy of Egypt in Syria and Palestine.

The hopes of the Egyptian sympathisers in the Phœnician and Jewish cities rose high when they heard that Necho had collected a large army and was preparing to march along the sea-coast of Palestine and lay siege to Carchemish, a strong fortified town on the Upper Euphrates, which was the key to the possession of Syria and all the countries lying behind the Lebanon range.

Josiah and all the party that followed him in Jerusalem remained unaffected by the general hopes. The conviction that no good would result from alliances with Egypt, and that the will of the Lord in favour of submission to the king of Babylon had been clearly manifested, was strong in the mind of Josiah. As the sworn vassal of Nabopolassar, he deemed it his duty to oppose the march of the king of Egypt across the valley of Esdraelon. The two armies met at Megiddo, where twice before the fate of Israel had been decided in a pitched battle. Josiah was mortally wounded by a chance shot from an Egyptian bow. The Jewish army fled, and Necho proceeded in triumph to Carchemish, receiving embassies of submission from the Phœnician cities on his way. Carchemish speedily fell before him, and he succeeded in establishing his dominion over the whole country between the Euphrates and Egypt. On his return through Palestine, Necho visited Jerusalem, dethroned Jehoahaz, the young son of Josiah—who had been placed on the throne by that party in the city who, in obedience to the counsels of the prophet Jeremiah, adhered to their allegiance to Nabopolassar—and made Jehoiakim, another son of Josiah who was devoted to the Egyptian interest, king in his stead.

Nebuchadnezzar was probably absent from Babylon when Necho's invasion occurred, or some enterprise of even greater importance than the reconquest of Syria occupied him, for three years were allowed to elapse before any attempt to oppose Necho was made. Perhaps the delay resulted from some jealous fears on the part of the old king, who, too infirm to undertake the conduct of an expedition himself, may have been unwilling to entrust the command of the army to his son, now of middle age, and no doubt impatient of so long occupying a subordinate position in the empire. At the end of three years, however, the necessity of taking an active part against Necho prevailed. A great army was placed under Nebuchadnezzar's command, and he marched to Carchemish, where, on the banks of the Euphrates, Necho awaited him. A great battle ensued; Necho was entirely defeated, and Nebuchadnezzar pressed on, driving the remnant of the broken Egyptian army before him, and seizing on and sternly punishing all the cities and districts that had thrown off the Babylonian yoke.

The great eagle, large-winged, full-feathered, had come to Lebanon and freely wreaked his vengeance on the prey abandoned helpless to his clutches. At Jerusalem the news of Nebuchadnezzar's victory fell like a thunderbolt on the king and the Egyptian party in the city, who for three years had been living in a dream of false security, resenting as an injury to the country, and a proof of want of patriotism, the solemn warnings of coming doom which Jeremiah had continued fearlessly to pour forth—now in the king's palace, now in the gate of the Temple before the assembled people.

The first intimation of the disaster would probably be brought by the fugitives hurrying in to the shelter of the city to escape from the Babylonian soldiers who spread themselves over the land. "The snorting of their horses were heard from Dan; the whole land trembled at the sound of the neighing of the strong ones, for they have come and have devoured the land and all that are in it." With the nearness of the danger, the ferocity of party strife in Jerusalem waxed stronger and stronger. Even while crowds of miserable fugitives thronged the streets, and famine threatened the city, the Egyptian party could not resign their vain hopes, or forego their anger against Jeremiah for his efforts to waken them out of their pleasing delusions. They could not believe that their hero Necho had fallen so utterly that he could be of no further help to them, or that the reed on which they had leaned was really breaking and piercing their hands. The strain of Jeremiah's prophecy grew yet more solemn and emphatic, as he perceived the wilful determination to cherish false hopes that sealed the ears and hearts of his adversaries against him.

With the knowledge of the coming doom upon him, Jeremiah wrote all the prophecies of two and thirty years on a scroll, and on a solemn fast day sent his disciple Baruch to read the writing in the ears of the people at the entry of the gate of the Lord's House. The fearful words arrested the attention of one of the princes of Judah, who brought Baruch into the king's palace, to the scribes' chamber, where many of the princes and chief people were assembled, and ordered him to sit down and recite again all the words of the lamentation in their ears. Fear for themselves, and fear for the prophets who dared to write such distasteful warnings, seized the princes as they listened. "Go and hide thee, thou and Jeremiah, and let no one know where ye be," they said; "assuredly we will tell the king all these words."

The king, Jehoiakim, was seated in another chamber of his palace warming himself by a fire on the hearth, for it was a cold November day, when a deputation from the scribes' chamber came and informed him of what had happened. The interest of the king was so far roused that he ordered the scroll to be brought and read once more before him.

Surely, the princes thought, he will be moved at this time of danger by such words as these to repentance that may yet avert the impending judgments. But Jehoiakim was past warning; the denunciations that should have awakened remorse, only stirred up impatient anger in his heart. He seized the roll before more than a few leaves had been read, cut it into strips with a knife, and threw it into the fire before him. In vain the princes who had brought the roll remonstrated against the blasphemy; the king and the nobles seated round the fire "were not afraid, nor rent their clothes."

In their hiding-place Jeremiah and Baruch again wrote all the words of the book that Jehoiakim had burned in the fire, and added many other prophecies, among them the prediction of the king's death, and sent them with a message to Jehoiakim. Had he burned the scroll because in it was written that the king of Babylon should come and destroy the city? but the king of Babylon was on his way, and would bring even greater destruction to him and his than the first writing had foretold.

The appearance of Nebuchadnezzar with his army before the city gates must for a time at least have put an end to the controversy, and in the midst of much misery brought a certain amount of relief to the prophet Jeremiah and his friends. Jehoiakim surrendered after a short siege, influenced perhaps by Jeremiah's counsels. He was dethroned and put in chains on the entrance of the Babylonian army into the city; but after a time Nebuchadnezzar relented towards him, and reinstated him in his government on his full submission and promise of future fidelity to the Babylonian power. A number of hostages were taken from the king's house and from the houses of the nobility, among them Daniel and the other "well-favoured children of the king's and princes' seed," who were afterwards appointed to study the lore of the Chaldeans in Nebuchadnezzar's palace. The temple was also robbed of some of its treasures, and a considerable body of the poorer citizens were carried away into captivity.

From Jerusalem Nebuchadnezzar marched towards Egypt; but just as he entered the country, news reached him from Babylon of the death of his aged father. The necessity of returning immediately to his capital, lest some usurper should seize on the vacant throne, induced him to make a hasty peace with Necho, and hurry back to Babylon by the shortest route through the desert, accompanied only by a few soldiers, leaving the bulk of the army and the Jewish captives to follow by the easier and longer northern route through Syria. Arrived at Babylon, after his forced march, Nebuchadnezzar found that the Chaldeans had wisely conducted the affairs of the kingdom in his absence, and secured his succession to the throne without dispute. The return of his victorious army laden with spoil and captives soon brought visible proofs of his success as a general before the eyes of his new subjects.

For two or three years after his accession Nebuchadnezzar appears to have remained tranquil in Babylon, occupied in planning and setting on foot the great architectural works that were the glory of his reign. The bulk of the captives brought back by the army were told off to work at the repairs of the great temple of Belus, or set to excavate the vast reservoirs and canals—the "waters of Babylon," which Nebuchadnezzar seems to have regarded as his most important works. The hostages taken from the royal family and the families of the Jewish nobles met with gentler treatment: the most promising among them, the "children in whom was no blemish," were taken into the king's own palace to be instructed in the learned language of the Chaldeans, and fed from the royal table with the highly-seasoned dishes and strong wines that the luxurious Babylonians delighted in, but which were shunned as defilement by Daniel and the three holy children, who resolved to follow the strict enactments of the law they loved, in the heathen land to which they had been carried captives.

It was in this period of his life, the second year of his reign, that Nebuchadnezzar began to dream dreams that troubled his spirit, so that his sleep brake from him. He was the consecrated servant of the God he knew not, chosen to work a certain work in the world, and in the height of his first triumph and first intoxicating taste of despotic power, mysterious intimations from the Supreme Power that was shaping his acts startled and puzzled him.

He had fitful glimpses into a spiritual region, where grander conceptions of the future were presented to him than his self-centred spirit could grasp or retain. The first effect seems to have been to rouse his tyrannical temper to unusual fierceness, as is shown in his conduct to the Chaldeans, the highest and most respected class among his subjects, to whose wise management he had but a short time before owed his peaceable accession to the throne. His threat to put them to death and turn their houses into dunghills, because they could not comply with his unreasonable order to interpret the vision he had himself forgotten, was a display of reckless despotism that must have filled the court and city with dismay.

The inspired wisdom that enabled the youthful Daniel to relate and expound the vision of the great image with head of fine gold, breast and arms of silver, thighs of brass, legs of iron, and feet of clay and iron, saved Nebuchadnezzar from the sin and danger of carrying out the impolitic sentence his fierce temper had tempted him to pronounce, and led to the advancement of Daniel to power and authority in the heathen court. Like Joseph at the court of Pharaoh, Daniel was miraculously raised up and enabled to win the favour of the despotic king, that he might be ready to use his influence to soften the rigours of exile to his brethren in the evil times that were coming on Jerusalem.

During these peaceful years the startling vision of the wide-winged eagle, that had appeared almost without warning in Lebanon and vanished as suddenly, was fading from the minds of the people of Palestine and Phœnicia. The Egyptian partisans recovered the ground they had lost: old hopes and projects were revived in Tyre and in Jerusalem, and again the warnings of Jeremiah were accounted as crimes against his country. In spite of the oath of fidelity to Nebuchadnezzar which Jehoiakim had taken, he allowed himself to be drawn into conspiracies with the Sidonians and Syrians to throw off allegiance to Babylon, and bring back the Egyptian power into Palestine.

In vain Jeremiah set himself as a fenced brazen wall against the projected treachery; in vain he collected the "ancients of the people and the ancients of the priests" in the valley of Hinnom, and broke a potter's earthenware vessel before them as a picture of coming destruction, while he foretold that the streets of the city of Jerusalem should be filled with dead bodies as full as that valley was filled with graves. The high priest Pashur, exasperated at the boldness of his act, smote him and put him in the stocks, in the vain hope of silencing the lips on which had been laid the stern necessity of speaking truths in a time of despair. His unjust conduct only brought on Pashur a more distinct announcement of his own personal share in the miseries awaiting the nation. "Terror on every side" should be the name given him, Jeremiah foretold, for he should be carried away captive to Babylon and die there, with all the people to whom he had prophesied lies. As before, the blind confidence of the king and people could not be shaken up to the very moment when the doom fell.

Tidings of the disaffection at Jerusalem, and of the treacherous negotiations with Egypt carried on by Jehoiakim, were speedily carried to Nebuchadnezzar, but he did not at first think the state of affairs in Palestine sufficiently serious to call for his presence there. By his orders bands of Chaldean soldiers, with mercenary troops of Ammonites and Moabites, were sent to ravage the country. The expected help from Egypt did not appear; the invading armies—half-savage "children of Moab" and "Ammon," supported by Babylonian horsemen—spread themselves unopposed over the open country, burning villages and laying waste fruitful fields, till whole districts were turned into deserts, where wild beasts prowled and birds of prey gathered to feast on the corpses "that had none to bury them."

"The sword to slay, and the dogs to tear, and the fowls of the heaven and the beasts of the earth to devour and destroy," the four kinds of misery which Jeremiah had forewarned them of, stalked through the land. The hunted inhabitants of the valleys and plains fled to the fenced cities for refuge, and again Jerusalem was crowded with starving fugitives. Extreme misery from famine and drought came on all the inhabitants from the lowest to the highest. "The nobles sent their little ones to the water; they came to the pits and found no water; they returned with their vessels empty; they were ashamed and covered their heads."

In the midst of the sufferings which his obstinacy had brought on his subjects, Jehoiakim met his death. According to one account he was slain in a tumult by his despairing people, who hoped to propitiate Nebuchadnezzar by the sacrifice of their rebellious king; according to another, he was slain in a skirmish with a party of the invaders who surrounded the city. His dead body was ignominiously thrown over the wall of the city, and left for many days without burial, exposed to the sun and wind. None lamented for him; there was no one to say, "Ah, my brother! or Ah, my sister! Ah, Lord; or Ah, his glory!" The evil consequences of his sins were then too bitterly felt for even those who had encouraged him most eagerly in his headstrong course to have room in their hearts for pity at his fall.

His son Jehoiachin was raised to the throne, but the state of anarchy and misery in which the country was plunged made his government a mere pretence. At length Nebuchadnezzar was at leisure to turn his attention to the eastern part of his empire. Tyre as well as Jerusalem deserved punishment, and the prospect of rich spoil from the capture of the island city made its reduction an enterprise worthy of being conducted by the king in person. The first object of his attack was Tyre, but finding that he could not take it by assault he left a portion of his army before it and proceeded to Jerusalem.

The city hardly made any show of resistance: after the first assault, Jehoiachin, said by some to have been a mere child at the time, and his mother Nehushta, who had taken a prominent part in the conduct of affairs during his short reign, went and sat as suppliants in the gate through which the haughty Babylonian king at the head of his army passed into the city. The completeness of their submission does not appear to have touched Nebuchadnezzar as much as might have been expected from the occasional flashes of generosity observable in his conduct. His anger against the treachery of the father, whom he had once pardoned, and who had plotted against him, steeled his heart against compassion for the son and wife.

Jehoiachin and Nehushta were placed in close confinement, and sent to Babylon with an immense train of captives, torn from their homes, according to the Assyrian and Babylonian practice, to be transported to a distant land, and made to swell the wealth of the conqueror by their labour, or by their skill as artisans and merchants.

CHAPTER XX.

THE LAND OF CAPTIVITY.

THE scenes attending the deportation of captives which the Assyrian bas-reliefs depict, and which Samaria had witnessed two centuries before, were now enacted in the capital itself. The spoil was collected in great heaps: silver and gold from the temple; household goods from the poorest as well as the richest houses, down to beds and cooking vessels and mill-stones: while the captives, as they were being bound together two and two and told off into the guardianship of the soldiers who were to superintend the sad journey, looked on weeping or sullenly defiant.

When the spoil had been counted, weighed, and such of it as was not set aside for the royal use divided among the greedy soldiery, the march began. The long procession wound its way through the broken city gates—the men bowed down with the weight of the chains that bound them together, the women carrying the children on their shoulders, or the slender package of necessaries for the journey they were permitted to take with them—some braving the blows of their drivers to turn and look again, and yet again, at the sacred roof of the Lord's House standing up still undefiled among the ruins; some marching onward as in a dream, with sullen eyes that were never raised from the blood-stained ground. At the end of the train came a few rude baggage-waggons, in which the mercy of the conqueror assigned a place to some of the more delicate women and children, among whom Nehushta and Jehoiachin would be found.

It is a tradition among the Jews that the beautiful forty-second Psalm was composed by the young king Jehoiachin on this journey. Looking back for the last time over the land of his birth, his own land, he records his vow: "To remember God from the land of Jordan, and of the Hermonites, from the hill Mizar."

He moans out his complaint against the cruelty of his enemies, who taunt him in his grief and try to shake his confidence in God: "My tears have been my meat day and night, while they continually say unto me, Where is thy God? I will say unto God my rock, Why hast Thou forgotten me? why go I mourning because of the oppression of the enemy? As with a sword in my bones, mine enemies reproach me; while they say daily unto me, Where is thy God?"

Among the toilers on foot, the young priest Ezekiel, whom some call the son, some the servant, certainly the disciple and friend of Jeremiah, had a place. The "vision of the Lord" that was to be his consolation in the land of his captivity had not yet visited him, but the tribulation around him did not find him, the faithful recipient of prophetic teaching, unprepared; neither would he turn his back on the city and the Temple with so despairing a heart as others, for the certainty of a mighty deliverer to come, and of the triumphant return of the nation foretold by his master Jeremiah, would support him in the sad moment of separation from all he had reverenced and loved.

The consistent supporters of the Assyrian supremacy, who, like Jeremiah, had suffered persecution from their countrymen in consequence of their fidelity, would no doubt receive some marks of favour from the Babylonian king when he took possession of the city. There is a tradition that he showed special kindness to Jeremiah. The very title of prophet would be a claim to consideration with Nebuchadnezzar, who, according to a tradition of him preserved by Berosus, which is confirmed by the extreme importance he attributed to his dreams, laid claim to a certain degree of divine insight in his own person.

His interest in the aged, sorrow-stricken Hebrew seer would also be increased by his friendship for another Hebrew prophet—the youthful Daniel, of whose wisdom and understanding he had lately had a signal proof. A position among the "wise men" in the Babylonian court equal to that conferred on Daniel would no doubt have awaited Jeremiah if he had chosen to accompany Nebuchadnezzar back to his capital; he preferred to throw in his lot with the remnant of poor people, chiefly those who from their ignorance and weakness were not thought worth carrying away, who still remained in the half-ruined city, and over whom Nebuchadnezzar appointed Zedekiah, uncle of the late king, to rule as viceroy when he withdrew his army from the place. Zedekiah, the half-brother of Jehoiakim, was still a young man when the heavy task of ruling in subjection to Nebuchadnezzar, and wringing the required yearly tribute from the famine-stricken land, was laid upon him. He was not bad at heart like his half-brother Jehoiakim, only weak in will. When not under the influence of evil counsellors, he appears to have turned to the prophet for counsel; and Jeremiah, though foreseeing the persecutions which his enemies would bring against him as soon as the Babylonian king's support was withdrawn, would not desert the last surviving of Josiah's sons while he might still be of service to him and to the expiring kingdom.

Sad as seemed the fate of that procession of captives turning their backs on the Temple and the once favoured land, it was shown to Jeremiah that they were the hope of the nation, and that with them went the favour of the Lord. He saw in a vision two baskets of figs before the Temple; one basket had "very good figs, like figs that are first ripe," the other "naughty figs, which could not be eaten." The first symbolized the exiles then wending their way along the northern road, through the defiles of Lebanon to distant Babylon; the second basket represented the remnant of the people left behind, with whom Jeremiah had cast in his lot.

The miseries of the exiles would be mitigated when they entered Assyria, for in most of the districts through which they passed they would find established countrymen of their own, descendants of the tribes carried away by Sargon—men like Tobit, who had won homes and possessions for themselves in the land of their captivity, and who yet kept themselves separate from the defilements of the heathen, and were ready (as he was when he buried the bodies of the poor Jews on the city wall) to risk the anger of the heathen authorities in defence of the prisoners and the needy among their own countrymen.

The captives carried away by Nebuchadnezzar after his first invasion of Judea were already dispersed about Babylonia, and must have seen the arrival of their fellow-citizens with feelings of mingled sorrow and comfort. Long-parted friends and brothers, parents and children, must have met and clasped hands, hardly knowing whether the tears on their faces were shed for joy at the unlooked-for reunion or for grief at the desolation of the royal city and the sorrows of the captive king.

Arrived at Babylon, they would find how the favour of the Lord had preceded them and provided alleviations to their misfortune through the elevation of Daniel and the three holy children to places of trust and power in the court and city. Like Joseph, they had been sent before to win the affection of the heathen by their wisdom and heavenly gifts, that they might be able to extend protection to their distressed brethren. The prosperous state of the Jews in Babylon at the end of the seventy years' captivity, when many of them had become rich merchants and risen to high position among the citizens, shows that they must have been treated from their first coming more as colonists than as slaves.

Though deprived of the temple service and the rites of sacrifice, they were not without religious instruction. They had priests among them; and the custom of having synagogues in every city where assemblies met for prayer and for hearing the Scriptures expounded, began during the captivity. Numbers of Israelites of the Ten Tribes had been brought into Babylonia after the fall of Nineveh. The more devout among these, laying aside the old jealousy between Judah and Israel, became incorporated with the captives from Jerusalem, so that in every district of Babylonia, and in many parts of Assyria, a little band of worshippers of the true God drew together and became strong and prosperous in their mutual help and close union.

The influence of Daniel over Nebuchadnezzar was not powerful enough to procure any indulgence for the royal captives. Jehoiachin and Nehushta were immediately consigned to a dungeon in the palace prison, where they languished during all the remainder of Nebuchadnezzar's life, till Jehoiachin had grown from a youth to a middle-aged man.

The long file of captives would decrease in extent as the end of the journey was neared. Even the vast area of Babylon could not have contained so great an addition to its inhabitants. In every district they entered a certain number would be left behind, and only a select band—the artisans whom Nebuchadnezzar wished to employ in the city works, the nobles and attendants on the captive king and his mother —would remain to take part in the triumphal entry of the conqueror into his capital.

The lot of the prophet Ezekiel was cast among a band of captives who were settled on the banks of one of the waters of Babylon, Chebar, supposed to be the royal canal, the greatest of the numerous watercourses excavated in Nebuchadnezzar's reign. Ezekiel and his companions were probably employed in the laborious task of digging the canal. The name they gave their settlement, Tel-abib, the hill of grief, seems to imply that a painful, toilsome life was led there. In the fourth year of the captivity their sorrow was lightened by the opening of the vision of the Lord to the eyes of the young priest. The words he was commissioned to speak to his fellow-exiles were at first chiefly words of warning and reproach; but his call from among them to be a watchman over Israel was a witness to them that God was as near them, to reprove and encourage, in the land of their captivity, as when they dwelt within sight of the Temple. Tradition says that a constant interchange of communication was kept up between the exiles on the Chebar and the remnant left in Jerusalem, and that the prophets Ezekiel and Jeremiah exchanged their prophecies, sending the written words of their visions respectively to Jerusalem and Chaldea, that the Jews might hear, as it were, "a strophe and antistrophe of warning and promise."

For some years after the punishment of Jehoiachin Nebuchadnezzar does not appear to have engaged in any new war. The accumulation in his capital of the great number of carpenters and smiths which we are told he brought from Jerusalem enabled him to press on his vast public works with fresh vigour. Ancient writers affirm that the great palace and the Temple of Belus were each completed in fifteen days; and even if there is exaggeration in this statement, the immense number of buildings completed in Nebuchadnezzar's reign show how energetically the business of adding to the capital was carried on, and what vast armies of workmen must have been constantly employed. Captives of all nations—Moabites, Jews, Egyptians, Tyrians, ancient allies, and bitter foes accustomed to confront each other in battle-fields—met in common humiliation at the foot of Nebuchadnezzar's temple-mounds, with their heavy loads of brick, or fine tools for the delicate works of ornamentation. A new Babel of tongues was heard round the old Tower of Babel at Borsippa, as the rubbish of the ancient structure was cleared away and the seven coloured stages rose to completion.

An inscription repeated on four clay cylinders that have been found in the Borsippa ruin, and another, called the standard inscription, because it is so frequently repeated on the bricks and slabs of Nebuchadnezzar's buildings, contain the king's own history of the great works of his reign. His satisfaction in "the great Babylon I have builded" is very apparent. "I finished the great double walls," he says, in the standard inscription, "by the help of the god Merodach, and for the delight of mankind I filled the reservoir quite full of water. ... I strengthened it with bricks burnt as hard as stones in masses like mountains.... I excavated a moat and made use abundantly of great waters, like the waters of the vast ocean, to fortify Babylon against its presumptuous enemies. . . . . Thus I completely made strong the defences of Babylon; may it last for ever.

"In Babylon, the city which is the delight of my eyes, and which I have glorified, the great palace of many chambers and lofty towers called the Wonder of Mankind, built by my father, used to be flooded with water when the reservoir was full. . . . .

"I raised the mound of brick on which it was built, and cut off the waters from its foundation, and set up long beams to support it, and strengthened its gates with plates of iron and copper. . . . . Inside I stored up silver and gold and rare precious stones, whose names were almost unknown, making it the treasure-house of my kingdom. . . . . In a happy month and auspicious day I laid the foundations of my palace on the earth; I completed it, and finished its top, and made it the high place of my kingdom in fifteen days. . . . . I also constructed a strong fort of brick and mortar. Like Shedim, I raised its head for a wonder and for the defence of the people."

The description of the building of the Borsippa tower is still more graphic. "Nebuchadnezzar king of Babylon, shepherd of people," it ran, "the saviour, the wise man who lends his ears to the orders of the highest God; the ruler without reproach, the repairer of the pyramid and the tower. . . . . Merodach the great master has imposed on me to reconstruct his building. The pyramid is the temple of heaven and earth, the seat of Merodach, the spot of his rest. I have adorned it with shining gold in the form of a cupola. . . . . I have completed the magnificence of the tower with silver, gold, precious stones, enamelled bricks, fir, and pine. . . . . This most ancient monument of Borsippa is the house of the seven lights of the earth. A former king built it—they reckon forty-two ages (ago), but he did not complete its head. Since a remote time people had abandoned it, *without order expressing their words.* Since that time the earthquake and the thunder had dispersed its sun-dried clay, the bricks had been split, and the earth scattered. . . . . Merodach the great lord incited me to repair the building. I set my hand to finish it, and exalt its head. I made it as it had been in the ancient days. . . . . O Nebo, be propitious to my works; give victory to my sword; grant me a life to the remotest times; the subjection of my foes; triumphs in many lands; . . . . may Nebuchadnezzar the king-repairer live before thee."

After some years of tranquillity Nebuchadnezzar's peaceful avocations as king-repairer among the towers and temples of Babylonia were interrupted by the breaking out of new plots and combinations against his supremacy in the south-eastern provinces of the empire.

The sufferings that preceded and followed Jehoiakim's death had not sufficed as a lesson to prevent the Egyptian partisans in Jerusalem from recurring to their former line of policy as soon as the actual presence of the Babylonian army was removed from the city. The young, weak-minded king Zedekiah, whom true policy would have led to strict observance of his solemn oath of allegiance to Nebuchadnezzar, was induced, by the vehemence of his counsellors and the flattering assurances of false prophets, to receive ambassadors from the kings of Edom, Ammon, Tyre, and Sidon, who urged him to join in a league with them against Babylon. Jeremiah appeared in the council chamber where the ambassadors were assembled, wearing bonds and yokes on his neck, one of which he sent to each of the allied kings, with a message warning them of the sufferings that resistance to the king of Babylon would inevitably bring upon them. He was boldly opposed by the false prophet Hananiah, who, breaking a yoke from Jeremiah's neck, met his warning with a counter prophecy, that in one year the yoke of the king of Babylon should be broken from the nations of the earth, and the imprisoned king Jehoiachin, with the vessels taken from the Temple, be restored to the city.

"Amen. The Lord do so; the Lord prosper thy words, and bring again all that is carried captive to Babylon, into this place," was the answer made fervently but sadly by Jeremiah, when the flattering words fell on the ears of the king and the delighted councillors. Yet the vision of destruction was too clear before him for him to allow the king and people to trust in a lie. On his return from the council he sent a message to Hananiah to warn him that he was deceiving the people, that he had not been called by the Lord to speak to them, and that his death was decreed before the end of the year.

The sudden death of Hananiah closely following Jeremiah's prediction made a strong impression on the king, and for a time checked the influence of the anti-Babylonian party. The projected alliance with

Sidon and Tyre was not carried out, but the discontent of the Jews against Nebuchadnezzar, and their longing for independence, remained and grew stronger every year, as the more immediate suffering wrought by his last occupation of Palestine was forgotten.

At length the stimulus to open rebellion was given by the arrival of offers of alliance and help from Apries (Pharaoh-Hophra), an enterprising king who at that time ascended the Egyptian throne, and began his reign by entertaining those visions of conquest in the East which old traditions of Egypt's greatness naturally awoke in the minds of ambitious young kings. The Egyptian party again attained entire ascendency over the mind of the vacillating Zedekiah. Even the exiles in Babylon were stirred up to vague hopes and unrest that might have led to outbreaks that would have imperilled the measure of prosperity that had been secured for them.

Jeremiah, whose counsels were no longer listened to in Jerusalem, sent a letter to the exiles, advising them to be tranquil and await patiently for the appointed deliverer. They were to build houses and dwell in them, he said, to plant gardens and eat the fruit of them, and marry their sons and their daughters, and seek peace for the city into which they had been carried captives, for the peace thereof was their peace. The thoughts of the Lord to them were, Jeremiah assured them, "peace, and not evil," and after seventy years He would visit them; but it was not from Egypt that the deliverer was to come.

Even among the exiles there were some to whom

the words of **Jeremiah** sounded as the words of a madman, and who could not be held back from sharing the vain hopes that were leading their countrymen to ruin. Tidings of the pretensions of the new Pharaoh, and of the disaffection he had stirred up in Palestine, at length reached the ears of Nebuchadnezzar, and induced him to collect a large army and prepare for an expedition to the East. The Jewish exiles in Babylonia witnessed his departure from Babylon with melting hearts and fainting spirits, knees knocking together, and feeble hands shaking with apprehension and grief. Tidings of the march of the army eastwards spread through all the Hebrew settlements. Ezekiel, on the hill of grief, heard the news, and saw in a vision the terrible calamities that would befall the eastern lands ere Nebuchadnezzar and his troops returned to the capital. A dark time of suspense and dread came upon the Babylonian exiles, whose hearts clung to their broken kingdom and their holy city as long as a shadow of either remained.

Nebuchadnezzar had other tributaries as well as the Jewish king to punish. When the army reached a certain point in the road, there was a doubt as to whether he should march at once against Jerusalem or attack a stronghold of the Ammonites. It was then that Nebuchadnezzar stood at the "parting of the ways," as Ezekiel describes, to seek counsel of his gods by the secret arts of divination as to which of the two meeting roads—the northern to Ammon, or the southern to Jerusalem—he should follow. "He made his arrows bright" (or shuffled his arrows), "he consulted with images, he looked into the liver." The practice of shuffling arrows, to each of which is attached a slip of writing, and drawing one out blindfold, was long practised by Arab tribes. Consulting images or teraphim and looking into the liver were Babylonian customs of divination. Nebuchadnezzar appears to have possessed strongly the temper of mind fostered by the Chaldean learning, which disposes people to seek guidance by practices of this nature in cases of importance.

The answers on this occasion indicated that Jerusalem should be the first point of attack, and the army poured into Judea, ravaging the country as they marched onward, and driving the peasantry again to crowd for safety into Jerusalem. As day by day the Babylonian troops approached nearer to the gates the hearts of those who had been most confident failed them; for a while Jeremiah was once more consulted and listened to. A solemn assembly was held in the Temple, and all the poor Jews who had been unjustly made slaves by the nobles were restored to freedom.

In the midst of their humiliation and repentance a renewal of hope came. Pharaoh-Hophra, in whom they had trusted so implicitly, at length made an effort to succour his allies. News came that he was preparing to enter Palestine, and that the Chaldean forces had been hastily called away from the neighbourhood of Jerusalem to defend the southern frontier. The Egyptian partisans in Jerusalem passed at once from the depth of despondency to exulting confidence. They repented of their repentance, which was but the fruit of panic, and resumed possession of their liberated slaves. They seized Jeremiah and thrust him into a dungeon, under pretence that he was about to take advantage of the raising of the siege to fly to the camp of Nebuchadnezzar and betray the counsels of the king to him.

Zedekiah, who in his heart revered Jeremiah's counsels and feared to act against them, caused him to be secretly removed from prison and brought to his presence, that he might once more inquire of him, Had any word of the Lord come to him in the new circumstances? any word that could justify Zedekiah in the course he was bent on following. The prophet had only one answer to make, the same that for thirty years he had been vainly uttering in the ears of Jewish kings—There is a word of the Lord, and it is this: "Thou shalt be dethroned by the hand of the king of Babylon." Disappointed to find that nothing could shake the prophet's consistency, the weak king abandoned him to the spite of his enemies, and he was again consigned to a prison, where he remained, occasionally visited by the king, and fed with bread from the king's stores, but at other times subjected to the most cruel treatment from the nobles, till the fall of the city.

CHAPTER XXI.

THE SIEGE.

THE interval of suspense came suddenly to an end. The flash of hope died out into utter darkness. Pharaoh-Hophra made a hasty retreat back to Egypt without effecting anything in behalf of his allies, and the triumphant Babylonian army returned and invested Jerusalem. On the tenth day of the tenth month (January), a day which has ever since been observed as a fast by the Jews, the city gates were closed, and the siege began.

Finding that the natural strength of the place would enable it to hold out for a considerable time, Nebuchadnezzar retired to Syria, and left the conduct of the siege to four of his chief generals. The blockade lingered on for two years and two months. The stores of food were gradually exhausted, and the most terrible expedients of famine were resorted to.

Hunger made the kindly people more cruel than the ostriches of the desert. Children cried for food, and no man broke it to them; mothers boiled and ate the flesh of their own children. The rich nobles and delicate ladies of Jerusalem wandered about the streets searching the dunghills for scraps of food. The city that had once been famed for the beauty of its inhabitants was full of living skeletons, with starting bones, and faces blackened with want.

At length, in the month of July, in the third year of the siege, a breach was made in the walls. At midnight, when the enfeebled garrison had ceased to watch and the streets were empty, the people being all wrapped in the deep sleep of exhaustion, the Chaldean soldiers entered the city unopposed, and marched straight to the Temple. Early the next morning, when the priests and Levites approached the sacred enclosure to offer the morning sacrifice, a cry of consternation that the city was in the hands of the enemy arose, and the slaughter of the miserable inhabitants began in the precincts of the Temple itself—the early worshippers being the first victims.

The royal household in the palace on the opposite hill were roused from slumber by the sounds of conflict, and managed to effect their escape from the side of the city opposite that where the Chaldeans had entered. On foot, with mantles wrapped round their faces to avoid recognition, the unhappy king with his wives and children fled, escorted by a small party of soldiers, through the gate of the royal gardens, and took the road to the Jordan, hoping to cross the river and hide from pursuit in some fortress among the hills.

It was a vain effort; before they had got far from Jerusalem some Jewish deserters, who met and recognised them on the road, brought the news of their flight into the city, and a detachment of Babylonian soldiers was sent after them. The mounted troops speedily overtook the footsore and exhausted fugitives; the little band of soldiers who surrounded the king were overpowered and slain; and Zedekiah and his sons were bound in chains and sent to Nebuchadnezzar, who was then keeping his court at Riblah, a town situate at the end of the valley of the Lebanon, ten days' journey from Jerusalem.

When they reached the Babylonian encampment, Nebuchadnezzar ordered the royal captives to be brought into his presence. The miserable Jewish king looked his last on the light of the sun as he passed through the door of the royal tent, and found himself in the awful presence of the ruler he had offended. He could hardly have hoped for mercy, but the fate that awaited him was more cruel than even his knowledge of an Eastern despot's severity would have led him to fear: a bitterness far exceeding the bitterness of death had been prepared for him. The worst part of Nebuchadnezzar's character—that savage delight in cruelty for which many of the Assyrian kings were remarkable—came out in his treatment of the Jewish prisoners of the royal household. He spoke harshly to Zedekiah, reproaching him bitterly for his treachery in having broken his solemn oath of allegiance to him, after he had given him the kingdom. Then, unmoved by the present abject condition of the fallen king, he ordered Zedekiah's children and friends to be slain in his presence; and when the miserable father had beheld the execution of his last son, he caused his eyes to be put out, lest the memory of that cruel spectacle should ever be effaced by other scenes.

When Nebuchadnezzar had thus wreaked the excess of his cruel rage upon the unhappy Jewish king, he was carried in chains to Babylon and consigned to a prison there. In darkness and solitude for the rest of his life, Zedekiah had time to muse over the prophecies which he had heard with indifference at the time they were uttered. Recognising, as he must have done, the minuteness with which the predictions concerning himself were fulfilled,—how he had seen the king of Babylon eye to eye, and spoken to him mouth to mouth, as Jeremiah told him he would do; and yet how, according to the word of Ezekiel, he had never seen the land of the Chaldees,—he would be encouraged to dwell on the golden thread of hopeful prediction that ran through the messages of woe.

It is not known whether he and his nephew Jehoiachin met in the house of their captivity; but as Zedekiah was certainly taken to Babylon, where Daniel exercised some authority, he cannot have been quite cut off from the society of his countrymen, and from learning what passed among his fellow-exiles. The later prophecies of Ezekiel, full of promise and comfort after the long-foreseen storm had passed, may have been repeated to him in his prison, and the prophet's visions of the new temple that was to replace the desecrated shrine, of the dry bones in the valley of death rising up an exceeding great army, of the desolate land made fertile with "showers of blessings," may have shone before the captive king's blind eyes and blotted out the remembrance of the miseries that, seeing, they had looked on.

The fate of the prophet Jeremiah, after the taking of the city, is involved in obscurity. It is said that Nebuchadnezzar took him out of prison and treated him with great kindness, offering to advance him to honour if he would return with the army to Babylon; but that Jeremiah again preferred to remain in his own country with a few poor people and the deserters to the Chaldean army, who were rewarded by being left in Palestine under the rule of a prince called Gedaliah, whom Nebuchadnezzar set over the country to keep order and collect the yearly tribute.

Gedaliah was a friend of Jeremiah, an old adherent of the Babylonian party, and seemed well fitted for the charge laid upon him. He fixed his residence at Mizpah, a fortress four miles north of Jerusalem. There Jeremiah lived with him, and there he wrote his "Lamentations" over the ruined, deserted city.

The country people, who had hidden themselves in the deserts and mountains beyond Jordan during the occupation of the land by the Babylonian army, gradually returned, and began to rebuild the ruined villages and resume the culture of the fields. There seemed a prospect of some degree of prosperity and peace revisiting the country once more, but unhappily a tumult broke out again. Gedaliah was slain at a feast by a prince named Ishmael, who hoped to seize his authority; and all his followers, including some Chaldean soldiers, were massacred. The perpetrators of the outrage fled for protection to the Ammonites of the desert; but the Jews who had gathered round Gedaliah, dreading the vengeance of Nebuchadnezzar for the governor's murder, resolved to take refuge in Egypt. They consulted Jeremiah on their purpose, but when he endeavoured to dissuade them, and assured them that Egypt would not long be a place of safety—as Nebuchadnezzar would shortly conquer the country—they again suspected him of treachery; and fearing lest he should betray their intention to the Babylonians, they forced him and his disciple Baruch to accompany them in their flight. The fate of the prophet in the hands of these violent men is not known. Some say that, irritated by the warnings, which he did not cease to repeat even on their journey, they stoned him to death at a place called Tahpanhes. Another tradition relates that he arrived safely in Egypt, and on Nebuchadnezzar's conquest of the country was carried to Babylon, where he died at a great age in peace and honour among his countrymen.

As time passed on, when the cup of bitter woe which Jeremiah had seen mingled and been forced to present to his countrymen had been drained almost to the dregs, and the golden hope at the bottom began to appear, Jeremiah came to be regarded less as the speaker of terrible denunciations than as the promiser of that glorious restoration which was the support of all faithful hearts among the exiles. The patriotism and wisdom of his counsels were recognised by his fellow-countrymen, and they caused his prophecies to be collected into a book, and ever afterwards regarded them as next in importance to those of Isaiah.

After the return from the captivity, as years went on, hopes connecting Jeremiah with future glories of the nation, as well as with memories of its past sorrows, grew round his name. It was said that, at the time of the destruction of the Temple by Nebuchadnezzar's army, he had saved the tabernacle and the ark from desecration and hidden them in a cleft in Mount Sinai, and that he would reappear to point out the place of their concealment just before the commencement of the reign of Messiah. It was believed that in the world of spirits he watched over the nationality of his country and interceded for the people. Judas Maccabeus saw him in a vision, "a man with grey hairs, and exceeding glorious." In our Lord's time the hope of his reappearance was so strong among the populace that both John the Baptist and our Saviour himself were taken for him. Even in the early Christian Church a notion prevailed that Jeremiah had never really died, but that he would reappear and share, as one of the two witnesses spoken of in the Revelation, the terrible season of persecution that was to come on the faithful.

The man, "whose sorrow exceeded all sorrow," had so closely interwoven himself with the life of the chosen people and of the Church that no supreme moment of its glory or of its terror could be conceived of without the thought of his presence, seen or unseen, mingling in the anticipation, as supporter in trial or participator in triumph.

For several years after the taking of Jerusalem a series of successful campaigns occupied Nebuchadnezzar. Tyre fell before him after a tedious siege; and he pursued his conquests into Egypt, twice overrunning the country, and on the second occasion dethroning Hophra, and placing a creature of his own on the throne. The immense spoil that fell into his hands after these victories—the accumulated treasures of Tyre, of Thebes, and of Memphis—were sent to Babylon, and enabled Nebuchadnezzar to complete that lavish adornment of his great building which excited so much astonishment among ancient writers.

It was doubtless on his return from one of these campaigns, when his treasury would be overflowing with gold taken from the merchant princes of Tyre, that he set up the immense golden image on the plain of Dura of which Daniel speaks. All the nations and people and languages whom he commanded to bow down before the image had indeed by this time been subdued by him, and lay bound and bleeding at his feet. They had been delivered into his hands, as Jeremiah had foretold.

It was given to Shadrach, Meshach, and Abednego to teach Nebuchadnezzar how little power after all the most despotic ruler can exercise over those to whom faith gives courage to be free; how easily they escape altogether out of his jurisdiction into a region of Divine Providence where no human malice can reach them.

The miraculous preservation of the three holy children brought Nebuchadnezzar to a confession that the God of the Hebrews was the supreme God of all the earth, but it did not bring down his pride or overweening confidence in himself. He still thought to take the government of the earth into his own hands, and patronise the Divine Ruler by persecuting those who would not acknowledge Him at his command. Later, apparently towards the close of his life, he was taught a further lesson. There came a day when the last of the great buildings he had planned, on which he had lavished the treasures won in his campaigns, was completed.

The "golden city" rose perfect throughout — an immense square, extending ten miles on every side, bounded by high walls, which from the centre of the place, where the royal palace stood, showed like a range of clay-coloured hills edging the horizon, their straight grey line broken at regular intervals by a patch of colour, golden and green, where the sunlight was reflected from the brazen gates and the open country beyond. At the foot of these hills stretched corn-fields, fruit-orchards, and gardens yielding food enough to supply the city during a long siege. The inner lower rampart, with its brazen gates and elevated promenade thronged with foot passengers and chariots, broke the level a second time; behind it lay the great reservoir of waters, with the principal buildings of the city clustered round and reflected in it—the parti-coloured palaces, the massive Temple of Bel, the hanging gardens lifting gorgeous flowers and strange vegetation high into the air—all newly-finished, gorgeous with fresh laid colour, shining with bands of silver and gold.

In the evening, when the scorching sun had sunk behind the western rampart, and it was possible to look abroad with comfort, Nebuchadnezzar came up on to the roof of his new palace to contemplate the city he had made. The joyful hum of the social hour, which brought all from the shelter of their houses to enjoy the brief twilight after the overpowering heat of the day, would rise from the crowded streets. Even the exiles and the prisoners would rejoice in the going down of the day : the blind Zedekiah in his cell ; Jehoiachin and his mother Nehushta, who had languished in prison all the while the new city was rising round them; Daniel praying at a window that opened towards Jerusalem.

Nebuchadnezzar stood on the high elevation, and looked over what must have showed like a section of a rainbow circle let down on to the earth, so wondrously were the assorted colours, the seven bands of the temples, the tints of the palaces, blended together in the setting of the blue waters, and the deep winding river that compassed them round. The silver head of the "Wonder of Borsippa" which Nebuchadnezzar had begun and completed in a "happy day," shone like a second moon in the sky to the north ; the old ancestral palace which he had adorned stood opposite ; the great fortifications which he had built up with "stones the size of mountains," were visible in the distance, clear against the evening sky. Every one of these gorgeously coloured buildings, which in their massive strength looked as if they must last as long as the world itself, bore Nebuchadnezzar's name on its every brick and stone, and contained an account of how he had built them, in order that their beauty and his fame might always live together, and no succeeding generation of men fail to know that this was Nebuchadnezzar's Babylon—"The city which is the delight of my eyes, which I have glorified."

As he looked from the palace roof, he repeated the substance of the inscription that all the buildings bore, "This is great Babylon that I have builded," and his heart swelled with even greater pride than when he had first dictated the words, for now all was completed, and no accident could mar his glory, or rob him of his pleasure in it. Then, in that moment of full satisfaction, the malady of which he had been forewarned a year before, in a dream interpreted to him by Daniel, overtook him. From the dizzy height of exultation, where he beheld himself as a god, he was hurled down into the depths of diseased despondency, in which he seemed to himself to have ceased to be a man, and to have become even as one of the beasts of the field.

In his madness the sight of the great buildings to which he had given so much thought in his better days became intolerable to him, and he had to be taken from the dwellings of men and permitted to roam about the fields—probably the enclosed parks within the walls that belonged to the royal domain. There he laid aside the clothes and even the ordinary food of human creatures, and "eat grass as oxen, and was wet with the dew of heaven," till he learned "that the Most High ruleth in the kingdom of men, and giveth it to whom He will."

The promise of Nebuchadnezzar's recovery and restoration to power, held out in the dream which had so truly predicted his illness, was no doubt remembered by the courtiers and the members of the royal family while the king's malady was at its height, and conduced to keep them so faithful to their allegiance, as to carry on the government in his name. There is reason to suppose that the conduct of affairs during Nebuchadnezzar's incapacity was taken by his queen —not the Median princess he had married in his youth, but an Egyptian queen named Nitocris, with whom he had probably allied himself after his conquest of Egypt. Herodotus speaks of a queen Nitocris, to whom he attributed many of the great works that really belong to Nebuchadnezzar, and there are monuments in Egypt bearing the name of Nitocris, that appear to have been erected shortly after Nebuchadnezzar's conquest of Egypt. It seems probable that the Egyptian princess, coming from a country where women were allowed to succeed to the throne, would assume authority during the interregnum caused by her husband's illness. She would naturally turn her attention to the completion of architectural works in her own country, and she seems to have made herself sufficiently conspicuous in her husband's capital for her name to have been remembered and connected with her husband's great buildings down to Herodotus's time.

It has been thought that an allusion to Nebuchadnezzar's malady may be found in the following sentences, which occur in the standard inscription:—
"Four years (?) the seat of my kingdom in the city .... which did not rejoice my heart. In all my dominions I did not build a high place of power. I did not lay up the precious treasures of my kingdom. I did not lay out buildings for myself, and for the honour of my kingdom in Babylon. I did not sing the praises of Merodach, my lord, the joy of my heart in Babylon, the city of his sovereignty and the seat of my empire. I did not furnish his altar with victims, nor did I clear out the canals."

The meaning of these negative clauses is not as yet fully ascertained; and it is perhaps unlikely that Nebuchadnezzar should allude to such a misfortune as his madness in the midst of an inscription, in which he indulges in that arrogant self-laudation for which he must have believed the malady was a punishment.

At the end of three years Nebuchadnezzar's mind returned to him, and he was able to resume the sceptre which his queen had been prudently wielding during his incapacity, and to hold it for the few remaining years of his life.

An ancient writer relates the following anecdote of Nebuchadnezzar's last years. It perhaps embodies the garbled account of the revelations vouchsafed to him in his dreams which was current among the people outside the court who had not Daniel's opportunities of learning the truth. "It is moreover related by the Chaldeans that as Nebuchadnezzar went up into his palace he was possessed by some god, and he cried out and said, 'O Babylonians, I Nebuchadnezzar foretell unto you a calamity which must shortly come to pass, which neither Belus my ancestor nor his queen Beltis have power to persuade the fates to turn away. A Persian mule shall come, and, by the assistance of your gods, shall impose upon you the yoke of slavery, the author of which shall be a Mede, the vain glory of Assyria. Before he should thus betray my subjects, oh that some sea or whirlpool might receive him, and his memory be blotted out for ever; or that he might be cast out to wander through some desert where beasts and birds alone abide. But for me, before he shall have conceived these mischiefs in his mind, a happier end will be provided.' When he had thus prophesied, he expired."

Nebuchadnezzar was succeeded by his son, Evil-Merodach, whose short reign of two years was marked by one beneficent deed. He had conceived an affection for Jehoiachin, the Jewish captive king, whom Nebuchadnezzar had kept in prison for thirty-six years. One of the first acts of his reign was to set him at liberty, and establish him at court in the position of his intimate friend and adviser, making him take precedence of all the other captive kings who, in the course of Nebuchadnezzar's conquests, had been brought to Babylon. It seems probable that this intimacy with Jehoiachin led to other acts of favour to the Jews, and perhaps gave birth in Evil-Merodach's mind to a leaning in favour of the Hebrew religion, which estranged the Chaldeans from him. It is certain that, after a reign of two years, a conspiracy was formed against him, which ended in his dethronement and death. The chief rebel, Neriglissar, one of the nobles whom Jeremiah mentions as having taken part in the siege of Jerusalem, succeeded to the throne, and had an uneventful reign of four years. He built another small but beautifully ornamented temple in Babylon, the bricks of which bear his name, and a title "Rab-mag," which had evidently belonged to him before his elevation to the throne, as Jeremiah affixes it to his name. He left a young son, who, after a few months' reign, was put to a cruel death by a usurper named Nabonadius, who took advantage of dangers which began to threaten the empire from abroad to depose the young king as incapable of managing affairs and seize on the authority himself. The position of the Babylonian kingdom with respect to the neighbouring nations had undergone a rapid change during the short reigns of Evil-Merodach and Neriglissar. While these kings contented themselves with remaining peacefully in their strong capital, a new power had risen up in the far East, whose rapid growth and warlike character awakened the jealous fears of more vigilant sovereigns.

CHAPTER XXII.

WEIGHED IN THE BALANCE AND FOUND WANTING.

A HARDY race of mountaineers from the hill districts of Persia, governed by a wise and enterprising prince, had effected a revolution in the Median state. The Median king Astyages—who had governed his own kingdom of Media, and the provinces of the old Ninevite empire to which he had succeeded, more after the example of the last feeble king of Nineveh than of the founders of the empire—was superseded by his grandson, the Persian Cyrus, who was no sooner firmly established on the throne than he sought employment for his hardy followers in attempting the reconquest of those tributaries of the ancient Assyrian kings that had established their independence under the Median rule.

The most powerful of these tributaries were the Lydians, who, under their fortunate and rich king Crœsus, had not only formed themselves into an independent state, but had risen to such importance as to make them formidable rivals to the new power which Cyrus was building up. Crœsus was the first king to take alarm at the progress of the Persians, and to endeavour to arrest their encroachments by forming the most powerful of the southern and western states into a confederacy for mutual defence. He sent ambassadors to the Grecian states, to Memphis and to Babylon, to represent the common danger, and induce the Grecians, Egyptians, and Babylonians to join their forces to his in the contest between the old governments and the new growing empire which he foresaw approaching.

The Jews living in Babylon must have heard of the rise of the Persians and of the wonderful successes of Cyrus with feelings of tumultuous expectation and joyful hope. The period of seventy years of which Jeremiah had spoken was drawing to a close, and in the warlike and yet merciful and just Persian ruler they could not fail to recognise the deliverer to whose coming their prophets had bid them look forward. The character of the Persians as a nation would gradually become known to the Hebrew exiles; they would hear of their abhorrence of idols, almost as strong as their own; their reverence for law; their belief in one supreme God; the temperate and hardy habits, such as would have beseemed the best of the old Israelites, which they had brought with them from their barren hill-fastnesses. A sense of kinship would awaken in the Hebrew hearts. These were the avengers predestined to repay to the haughty daughter of Babylon all the woes she had poured out on the earth; these were the "blessed" people at whose hands the fierce children of the cruel city were to receive the just reward of their long tyranny.

Crœsus' embassy reached Babylon in the first year of Nabonadius' reign, and was favourably received by the Babylonians, who agreed to join the confederacy against the Persians projected by Crœsus. Nabonadius does not, however, appear to have taken a prominent part in the war between the Lydians and Cyrus that followed. Cyrus' promptitude in marching at once into the enemy's country probably prevented Nabonadius from bringing a force into the field in aid of his ally: and after the entire defeat of Crœsus by Cyrus at the battle of Thymbra, the capture of Sardis, and subsequent annexation of Lydia to the Persian empire, the Babylonians were obliged to content themselves with preparing for an attack by strengthening the fortifications of their great cities—which Nebuchadnezzar had already made almost impregnable—and placing obstructions in the way of an enemy's march through the country by opening fresh watercourses, and building high brick embankments along the courses of the streams.

Some years elapsed after the defeat of the Lydians, during which Cyrus was too much engaged with other enemies to think of punishing the Babylonian king for his alliance with Crœsus; and meanwhile Nabonadius finished his works of defence throughout the country, and laid in stores of provisions in the city of Babylon, such as would enable it to sustain a protracted siege. When at last news of Cyrus' march towards Babylonia at the head of a large army reached the city, little apprehension was felt by any of the inhabitants as to the result of the campaign. If even their armies were defeated in the open field, there would always, the Babylonians believed, remain for them the shelter of their gigantic walls, built up by Nebuchadnezzar with "bricks burnt as hard as stones, in masses like mountains," behind which they could laugh to scorn the efforts of the most persevering foe. Within the defences were wide fields, where harvest could ripen and cattle graze, and vinedressers and gardeners pursue their avocations, undisturbed by any warfare that might rage on the other side; and in the king's quarter of the city were gathered heaps of corn, wine and oil, and luxuries of all kinds, which promised a full supply of every comfort of life for many years.

The Jewish captives were perhaps the only inhabitants of the city who listened to the rumours of Cyrus' approach with anxious interest. To their eyes, as well as to those of the Babylonian citizens, the impregnability of the great city must have seemed certain. The strong walls towering up to heaven shut them in, the massive brazen gates gleamed like ramparts of fire; but the words of the promise were surer than gates or bars, and could not be controverted—"Thus saith the Lord to his anointed, to Cyrus, whose right hand I have holden, to subdue nations before him; I will loose the loins of kings, and open before him the two-leaved gates. I will make the crooked places straight. I will break in pieces the gates of brass, and cut in sunder the bars of iron." How often the captives must have spoken them low to one another during the long period of suspense while the attack was pending—for Cyrus' march from his capital was interrupted by a delay of some months —and again, when news of his actual presence in the neighbourhood of Babylon was brought to the capital, and Nabonadius at the head of his large army marched through the brazen gates to meet his formidable foe.

Cyrus found the Babylonian army drawn up in battle array at a little distance from the city, and an engagement ensued which ended in the total defeat of the Babylonians. The bulk of the army fled to the shelter of the city walls, but the king himself, with a small following, effected a safe retreat to Borsippa, and remained inactive there, with a view perhaps of protecting the vast treasure-store accumulated in the "Wonder of Borsippa" from the Persian soldiers, while they occupied themselves in the apparently useless task of blockading Babylon.

The conduct of the defence and the government of the besieged city fell into the hands of Belshazzar, the young son of Nabonadius, who had lately been associated with his father on the throne, and who had a better claim on the loyalty of the citizens than the elder king, since he was the son of a daughter of Nebuchadnezzar's, whom Nabonadius had married after his usurpation of the crown. He was but a youth, not more than fourteen years of age; and though his mother retained in her mind a recollection of the great lessons taught to her father by the Hebrew prophet, Belshazzar seems to have been brought up in ignorance of the most striking events in his grandfather's life, and never even to have heard that there was in the kingdom "a man in whom dwelt understanding and wisdom like the wisdom of the gods," who, if consulted in time, might have given counsel that would have saved him from destruction.

For the first few months of the siege the proud confidence of the Babylonians in the strength of their defences was warranted by the ill success of the Persians in all their attempts against the city. The citizens walked and drove in their chariots, as was their custom in the cool of the evening, on the broad road between the strong towers on the top of their lofty city walls, and looked down with jeers and smiles of derision on the thin ranks of the besiegers gazing up idly at the mighty ramparts they had no hope of scaling. After a while they observed a change in the appearance of the hostile camp pitched below their walls. Great numbers of the tents had disappeared; the larger part of the army had evidently been drawn away, and only a few bands of soldiers remained stationed at the gates to watch the city.

The confidence of the Babylonians rose higher and higher; weeks and months passed on without any attempt at an attack, and the vigilance at first exercised by the garrison in guarding the gates and the approaches to the river gradually relaxed as their contempt for the enemy increased. The time for celebrating one of the great city festivals drew near; and by way of showing how completely at ease the citizens were, and how abundant were their stores of provisions, Belshazzar and his advisers resolved that the feast should be kept throughout the capital with even a greater show of revelry and enjoyment than was customary on such occasions. A thousand guests were invited to a banquet in Nebuchadnezzar's great palace; the lower ranks of the citizens and the soldiery imitated the example set by the court in proposing to abandon themselves to unrestrained merry-making. Nothing was spoken of throughout the city but the pleasures of the coming holiday.

Meanwhile the soldiers of the Persian army, withdrawn from the immediate neighbourhood of the town, were stealthily engaged on a task for which their wise, far-sighted general had taken care previously to prepare them. During his march on Babylonia, Cyrus had paused for some months on the banks of a small stream midway between Ecbatana and Babylon, and had made his troops employ themselves in digging new channels and turning the waters of the stream into them, so as to leave its original bed dry. No doubt many of the Persian soldiers resented this peaceful occupation as unworthy of warriors, and wondered that so great a commander should thus frivolously waste the time of his army.

When all their efforts before Babylon failed, and Cyrus withdrew them from beneath its walls and caused them to encamp at some distance from the town on the banks of the Euphrates, they began to perceive the reason of the task that had been set them. The battle against Babylon was really to be fought with the spade rather than with the sword. Cyrus had formed a plan of entering the city by diverting the river which ran through it into a new channel, and turning the ancient bed of the stream into a dry deep road, through which his army might march unperceived into the very heart of the place. The skill and experience his soldiers had gained in their former labours enabled them to complete the arduous task of excavating a new bed for the Euphrates in a few months. When the day of the Babylonian festival drew near the work was completed, and all was ready for the proposed attack. It is evident that Cyrus had friends within the city, who kept him informed of all that passed within the walls, and who had not failed to acquaint him with the precise time when the festival was to be kept and with the manner of its celebration. It seems probable that these friends were the Hebrew exiles, who from their long residence in the city would be well acquainted with all its customs, and who had the strongest reasons for wishing success to the Persian leader.

In accordance with this secret information, Cyrus fixed the night of the great festival for his entrance into the city by the road he had prepared, and gave orders that the sluices should be opened and the water of the river diverted into its new course on that evening. In the early part of the holiday, while the religious ceremony was going on, and the streets were thronged with gazers, the river flowed at its usual height, washing the basement of the river walls and the paved steps that led to the numerous landing-places for boats, and after its ten miles' course gurgling out below the massive brazen bars of the great entrance-gate at the further end of the city. As the shades of evening fell, the holiday makers repaired to partake of the sumptuous evening meal and enjoy the long revel in which this particular night of the year was usually passed. The thousand princes of Babylon assembled in Nebuchadnezzar's banqueting-hall, and sat down to their last feast, thinking of nothing so little as of the possibility of approaching danger.

The Hebrews, who had taken no share in the festivity of the day, and who would withdraw with abhorrence from the idolatrous rites and scenes of revelry enacted round them, were probably as alert and watchful as were their forefathers on that other eventful night in their national history when they waited with girded loins and staves in their hands for the "great cry in Egypt" that told them their days of slavery were over. Such of the Jews as lingered in the streets after nightfall, and leaned over the river walls, would observe a gradual sinking of the water in the bed of the Euphrates. The brick embankments stood higher and higher above the level of the water; the mighty river dwindled to a slender stream; the firm ground at the bottom began to be clearly seen; and as soon as the flow of water ceased two other streams—streams of living men—began to ascend from opposite directions the empty river bed, now a broad deep road connecting the city and the country outside, where Cyrus' army, in two detachments, were drawn up opposite the two river gates. Band after band of Persian soldiers descended into the ravine, passed beneath the useless bars of the great gates, and with less noise than the water itself had made, crept onward to the appointed meeting-place opposite Nebuchadnezzar's palace in the centre of the city.

Meanwhile an incident had occurred at the banquet of the princes that had much disturbed their anticipated enjoyment. At the height of the feast, Belshazzar, wishing to add to the sumptuous appearance of the table and give a new impulse to the conviviality of his guests, ordered the beautiful gold and silver vessels which Nebuchadnezzar had taken from the Temple at Jerusalem to be brought forth and distributed among the revellers. Deep draughts of wine were quaffed from them, and songs were raised in praise of the gods in whose honour the festival was celebrated.

In the midst of the revelry, while the song and the wine-cup went round, a sudden change came over the countenance of the young king. His eyes grew wild with fright, and were fixed on the wall opposite, just where one of the numerous lights projected from its polished surface. The sounds of singing and laughter died away. Every head was turned in the direction of the king's, and the revellers sat fixed in their places as if they had been turned into stone; for just under the light, showing clearly on the white enamel of the wall, was a line of mystic letters, and the king cried out aloud that he had seen the fingers of a hand come out and trace them. When the first moments of bewildered terror were past, messengers were sent in haste to summon the wisest of the Chaldean soothsayers into the presence of the king, that they might read the writing to him and explain its meaning. All tried in vain, and the young king's distress increased with every failure. By this time news of what was passing in the banqueting hall had been carried to the women's apartments and had reached the ears of Belshazzar's mother, the last surviving daughter of Nebuchadnezzar. The story brought recollections of her youth to her mind.

She remembered an occasion long ago when the wisdom of the wisest heads in Babylon had been baffled, and when a solution of the difficulty came from an unexpected quarter; and, convinced that she could bring comfort to her son, she sought him in his hall, where all his nobles were still assembled, and addressed him in cheering words. "Let not thy thoughts trouble thee, and let not thy countenance be changed; there is a man in thy kingdom in whom dwells the spirit of the holy gods, whom Nebuchadnezzar thy grandfather found to be excellent in the showing of hard sentences and dissolving of doubts. Let Daniel be called; he will show the interpretation."

Daniel, who was now an old man, had been deprived, in one or other of the revolutions that had occurred since his great patron's death, of the position of head of the Chaldeans, conferred on him by Nebuchadnezzar, but he seems still to have been living obscurely in some part of the vast palace to which he had been taken in his boyhood, and where he had witnessed so many changes. The older Chaldeans and princes would know his face well; the younger would look with curiosity and interest on the once powerful favourite of the great emperor as he was led into the hall. All would hang breathlessly on his words when he turned to the wall, and after refusing the king's offered gifts—"Let thy gifts be to thyself, and thy rewards to another"—proceeded to read and interpret the sentence they had so long gazed at in bewilderment: "Mene, Mene, Tekel, Upharsin. God hath numbered thy kingdom, and finished it. Thou art weighed in the balance, and found wanting. Thy kingdom is divided, and given to the Medes and Persians." Solemn and terrible as were the words, and uncompromising as was the reproof with which Daniel prefaced them, the sentence seems to have been received by the king and his assembled guests almost as if it were a reprieve. Daniel was sent away decked in splendid robes, and elevated to the post of third ruler of the kingdom, which honours the young king had promised to bestow on the sage who could interpret the writing to him.

Belshazzar no doubt believed in the certainty of the doom Daniel had pronounced upon him, but it did not appear to concern him just at that moment. Years hence no doubt the predicted ruin would come, but not now; there was time to finish the revels. The Medes and Persians must come in different guise from that in which he had beheld them in the morning, weak bands slumbering listlessly outside his impregnable gates, before he could seriously fear their taking his kingdom from him. The night was by this time far advanced, and a large part of the Persian army had entered the city by the noiseless shadowy road Cyrus had so cunningly prepared. As they marched onwards detachments of soldiers seized the river-gates, emerged into the open streets, and formed themselves into squadrons ready for attack.

At length a war-cry was raised, and the half-intoxicated Babylonian soldiers poured out of the houses where they had been feasting to find their city already in the hands of the enemy. A messenger fled in haste to the palace to inform the young king that his capital was taken. The bewildered princes, startled a second time from their revel, had no time even to attempt an escape; the besiegers followed close on the heels of the messenger, a band of Persian soldiers rushed in, and in the tumult that followed the king was slain, seated in his banquet-hall with his guests. The wretched inhabitants of the city, roused from slumber or surprised in the midst of feasting, could make no resistance, and a terrible slaughter ensued during the darkness and confusion of the night. Punishment for all the cruelty and wrong wrought on the earth by the haughty queen of empire, long ago foreseen by the Hebrew prophets, had at length come in a watch of the night. "Come down and sit in the dust, O virgin daughter of Babylon; sit on the ground, there is no throne. O daughter of the Chaldeans, thou shalt no more be called tender and delicate. Sit thou silent, and get thee into darkness, for thou shalt no more be called the lady of kingdoms."

The capture of Babylon by Cyrus ended the war, and entirely destroyed the Babylonian empire. The kingdom passed on that night into the hands of the Medes and Persians, as Daniel had said. Nabonadius, when he heard of the capture of his capital and the death of his son, submitted without further struggle, and, more fortunate than his son, was treated with clemency by the conqueror, his life being spared, and the government of a province in Babylonia bestowed on him.

One of the first acts of Cyrus' reign was the

proclamation of an edict, which authorized the Jewish captives to return to and repossess their own land. The feelings of the exiles, when the long-waited-for moment of deliverance actually arrived, are beautifully described in the 126th Psalm: "When the Lord turned again the captivity of Zion, then were we like unto those that dream. Then was our mouth filled with laughter, and our tongue with singing: then said they among the heathen, The Lord hath done great things for them. The Lord hath done great things for us; whereof we are glad."

Joy too great to be realized swelled the hearts of the aged men, who in their early childhood had formed part of the sad procession that passed out between the broken gates of Jerusalem, and turned back to gaze for the last time on the gleaming roof of the Temple on Zion's hill, and who ever since had lived quiet lives of waiting and silence, unwilling to sing the songs of Zion in a strange land: while the younger men and maidens, nourished in musings over the glories of their country drawn from Isaiah's poetry and Ezekiel's visions, as they grasped the glorious prospect of freedom and country, and beheld themselves once more a nation chosen and favoured of the Lord, broke out into triumphant singing and laughter: "The Lord hath done great things for us; whereof we are glad."

Jehoiachin and the blind Zedekiah were both dead. The head of the royal house, when the edict was proclaimed, was a prince named Zerubbabel (begotten in Babylon), who is supposed to have been a nephew of Jehoiachin's.

Cyrus, probably at the suggestion of Daniel, whose wisdom and experience were highly valued by the Persian rulers, appointed Zerubbabel governor of Judea, and leader of such of the Hebrew exiles as chose to avail themselves of the edict and return with him to possess their own land.

A band of 42,360 persons assembled;—"the chief of the fathers of Judah and Benjamin, the priests and the Levites, with all those whose spirit God had raised to go up to build the house of the Lord that is in Jerusalem." They carried away with them from Babylon the sacred vessels belonging to the Temple, which Cyrus restored, either from gratitude for services rendered by the Hebrews to the Persians during the siege, or from reverent sympathy with their feelings, as being himself a devout worshipper of one supreme God, whom it was sin to represent under any visible image.

They set out on their journey with "singing men and singing women" chanting psalms before them, as Miriam and her maidens sang before the rescued Israelites on the shores of the Red Sea.

A vast multitude thus went out in triumph from Babylon, yet it is thought that a still greater number of Hebrew families remained behind in the city, where, according to Jeremiah's advice, they had "planted vineyards and eaten of them, and builded houses, and married their sons and their daughters;" and which, now that it had come into the possession of a people who accepted them as allies, and respected their worship, no longer appeared as a place of exile. The Jewish families who continued to dwell in Babylon, and in the various Hebrew settlements scattered over Assyria and Babylonia, kept up constant intercourse with their brethren in Jerusalem, and were punctual in their visits to the Holy City at the appointed seasons, after the second temple had risen up under the fostering care of Nehemiah, and the sacrifices and festivals began to be observed in their appointed course.

These yearly and half-yearly visits to Jerusalem prevented the colonists from growing indifferent to their nationality, or forgetting the pure teaching of the Law, amid the heathenism that surrounded them. The remnant of the Ten Tribes of Israel who still continued faithful to their religion was gradually absorbed into these Jewish communities, and wherever they settled they became a rich and prosperous people. Yet a longing for a more perfect national union grew up in their hearts as they read the glorious words of Isaiah and Ezekiel, and felt that the restoration they had witnessed did not accomplish all that the inviolable words promised; and with the thanksgiving psalms for the deliverance of the nation from the Babylonish captivity were mingled prayers for the advent of a greater deliverer than even Cyrus, who would gather together the scattered families of the chosen seed, and manifest yet more clearly the favour and presence of God among them. "Sound the great trumpet for our deliverance," they prayed. "Lift up a banner for the gathering of our exiles, and unite us all together from the four ends of the earth."

As the Jewish communities increased in numbers and riches, new colonies were formed in more distant regions, till every important city throughout the East and in Greece and Italy contained at least one little band of worshippers of the true God—one spot where on every recurring Sabbath-day sacred words were read, and prayers to the God of Abraham lifted up.

The Persians, monotheists though they were, soon became corrupted by contact with the gross superstitions and degrading manners of the nations they had conquered. But the Jews, after their period of trial in Babylon, never again fell into the practice of idolatry to which they had formerly been so prone. Wherever they settled, they faithfully maintained their witness to the great truths entrusted to them of the unity and righteousness of God; and though it was not their mission to make proselytes, their silent protest against the errors around them was not lost on the ancient heathen world. Their communities were little spots of light amid the dense surrounding gloom, shaded, yet not altogether hidden, which struggled with the darkness and prepared the way for the recognition of the Bright and Morning Star which was hereafter to arise out of Jacob.

CHAPTER XXIII.

THE MEANING OF THE SIGNS.

WHILE reading of such very remote times as those with which we have been concerned in the preceding pages, we feel naturally curious to know on what authority the various particulars related of them rest; and when we have been referred to papyrus rolls, and graven clay tablets, and writing on walls thousands of years old, our curiosity is apt to be diverted from the remote history which these things reveal to the more recent story of the objects themselves—to the wonderful circumstances which placed them in our possession after the long oblivion that had enveloped them, and to the discoveries which enabled learned men of our own time to unlock the secrets they held for our teaching. When we hear, too, that some of the most interesting of these records are within our own reach—that by visiting the British Museum we may any day walk past pictures taken from copies of that wonderful "Book of the Dead," which was the Bible of the Egyptians among whom Abraham lived, and statues of Ramses the Second that Moses must have seen when they were fresh from the chisel—we perhaps wonder that we have troubled ourselves so little as most of us have to become well acquainted with objects that have such a marvellous double history. A short account of the modern history of some of the ancient records mentioned in this book, and an indication of where they are placed in the British Museum, may incline some of my readers, who have not cared about them before, to look at them in future with more understanding eyes.

On entering the lower Egyptian gallery of the British Museum you have no doubt often noticed, or had pointed out to you, a glass case containing a large but much broken slab of black basalt. It is not nearly so imposing an object as the statues and sarcophagi that surround it, but it deserves to be looked at with even greater reverence and gratitude, for it is the key by which the treasures of knowledge preserved by the other monuments have been unlocked. It is called the Rosetta Stone, because it was found near the town of Rosetta by a French officer of engineers, who, when he was engaged in digging the foundation of a fort, came upon the ruins of an ancient Egyptian temple. It was given up to the English by the French at the capitulation of Alexandria, brought to England by Lord Hutchinson, and deposited in the British Museum. Baron Bunsen says of this stone, that it shares with the "Description de l'Égypte," written by the learned men Napoleon took with his army to Egypt, "the honour of being the only result of vital importance to universal history that accrued from a vast expedition, a brilliant conquest, and a bloody combat for the possession of Egypt." The great value of the Rosetta Stone consists in its containing, what had hitherto been sought for in vain, an inscription in hieroglyphic characters followed by a translation in Greek; the hieroglyphic writing is on the top of the stone, beneath is a repetition of the same words in another Egyptian character, the Demotic (which may be called Egyptian running hand);[1] last comes the Greek translation. Unfortunately no one of the three versions of the inscription is perfect. The Greek sentences were easily read, and proved to be part of a decree issued by the priests of Memphis on the coronation of Ptolemy Epiphanes, and ordered to be engraved and set up in all the principal temples throughout Egypt. It celebrates the victories gained by the young king over rebels, his liberality, his piety, and his public works. The next step was to find out the hieroglyphic and demotic signs that corresponded to the Greek words and letters. It was a difficult task, for the first lines of the hieroglyphic copy of the record and the last of the Greek were broken away, so that only a few sentences answered to each other. The first person who found a clue to the unravelling of the problem was Dr. Young. He observed in the hieroglyphic lines certain groups of signs that were enclosed in oval rings, or in marks like parenthetic signs in the

---

[1] The Demotic writing is properly a corruption of the Egyptian hieratic, or running hand, and was used for the vulgar dialect, hieroglyphics and hieratic expressing the sacred or classical dialect.

demotic, and came to the conclusion that the words so enclosed must be the proper names Ptolemy, Alexander, Arsinoë, Berenice, which he found in the Greek record. The number of groups of signs thus enclosed was found sufficiently to answer to the names in the Greek lines, and the order in which the names occurred showed which Greek name was to be assigned to each ring and enclosed group.

A careful examination of the signs in the rings, and comparison of them with the Greek letters, led Dr. Young to the important conclusion that hieroglyphic signs were not solely, as they had always hitherto been supposed to be, pictures of objects or ideographs (signs put for ideas), but that at least a great number of them were like true letters (signs put for sounds), the object designed standing not for itself, nor for anything it resembled, but for the first sound of its name—as if we were to draw a hand for the sound "h," a bat for the sound "b," a nut for the sound "n." The long names Ptolemy, Berenice, &c. furnished a considerable number of these phonetic signs, whose sounds could be ascertained by comparison with the Greek letters that corresponded to them; and thus the first step was taken towards the discovery of the true value of hieroglyphics, and the manner in which they were used in spelling words. When it was further ascertained that the ancient Egyptian language was the same as the Coptic tongue, till recently spoken by the Copts in Egypt, no insuperable difficulty remained in the way of getting at the meaning of the abundant records graven on

THE MEANING OF THE SIGNS.

Egyptian monuments, which had hitherto presented such a tantalizing problem before the eyes of zealous students of history. The old black stone has been a door that has opened and let us in to a quite new realm of knowledge. It stands fitly at the opening of the long hall lined with graven tablets, and adorned with tablets and statues written over with talismanic characters, whose secrets it has revealed.

It often happens that when a very important discovery is made in one part of the world, it turns out that in some other quarter there has been a student hard at work on the same problem, who, on receiving the new truth, is able to do so much more with it than the first discoverer, that the honour of the invention has ever afterwards to be divided between the two. This was the case with respect to the interpretation of hieroglyphic writing. While Dr. Young and the English *savans* were poring over the Rosetta Stone, a young Frenchman, Champollion Le Jeune, was studying the Egyptian antiquities in France. He became acquainted with Dr. Young's conjecture respecting the phonetic power of hieroglyphic signs, adopted it as a basis for further investigations, and succeeded in producing a complete system of hieroglyphics which late researches have altered but little, and which has been employed with signal success ever since.

When once it was known that the writings on Egyptian tombs and temples were no longer sealed documents, but could be used as material for history, the importance of having them carefully examined and copied by competent persons was strongly felt by all who were interested in historical research throughout Europe. The French and Tuscan Governments undertook two expeditions, under Champollion and Rosellini, which worked jointly with singular tact and success, and produced two of the standard works on the Egyptian monuments. The late king of Prussia, imitating this good example, sent another expedition into Egypt, under Dr. Lepsius, to excavate among the ruins of the ancient cities, and collect antiquities for the Museum at Berlin. They stayed more than a year in Egypt, residing the chief part of the time in the neighbourhood of the Pyramids, and bringing to light many wonderful memorials of the remote times (before Abraham's visit) when the Pyramids of Gizeh were built.

Among the interesting relics which Dr. Lepsius and his associates carried to Prussia, was the entire tomb of a prince called Merhet, who, in the inscription on his tomb, speaks of himself as chief architect to the king who built the Great Pyramid.

What the liberality of a wise king did for the study of ancient history in Prussia has been effected in England by the enterprise, public spirit, and devotion to learning of private individuals. Soon after Dr. Young's discovery, a body of English students—of whom Sir Gardner Wilkinson, Mr. Lane, and Col. Howard Vyse were the most distinguished—visited Egypt, and passed many years in studying the monuments and people. Sir Gardner Wilkinson lived for months at a time in a tomb at Thebes, altered, by the addition of a court and tower to its long grotto, so as to make it a tolerably commodious dwelling-place. The results of the careful researches he here carried on he has given to the world in his celebrated work, "The Manners and Customs of the Ancient Egyptians," which is considered to be the most complete account of any ancient people that has ever been written, and has done more than any other work to make the results of Dr. Young's discovery popularly known.

The most ancient Egyptian relics in the British Museum are to be found in the entrance of the northern vestibule, a passage beyond the great Egyptian hall, facing the north-western staircase, and in the northern end of the great gallery. They consist of two casing-stones of the Great Pyramid, the statue of a proprietor of that remote age, and some slabs and doors of tombs of the same period, whose inscriptions and pictures refer to the funeral rites and illustrate the Ritual teaching. In the upper Egyptian gallery, in a wall-case, is the lid of the mummy-case of the king who built the Third Pyramid, and who is said to have been so zealous a student and guardian of the sacred books, that he sent all over Egypt to search for one of them that even at that early time had been lost. He was also a great lover of the marsh-country where Abraham afterwards sojourned, and where the land of Goshen lay.

The relics which will best help us to understand Egyptian art and manners and customs at the period when Abraham visited Egypt are to be found partly in the north vestibule and partly in the northern end of the great Egyptian gallery. Among them are many tablets with inscriptions and pictures that were put up to persons who were contemporaries of Nehra, and who not improbably may have spoken to Abraham and heard of Sarah's beauty.

The figures on these slabs are so carefully sculptured that the style of dress and ornaments worn at the period can be very distinctly made out, and they are thought to be portraits of the occupants of the tombs, and of members of their families. One figure (No. 562), that of an architect to Osirtasen the First (Abraham's Pharaoh), is represented sitting in an elegant chair, another leans forward on his staff, looking upwards in much the same attitude as that in which Jacob perhaps leaned, when he worshipped, on the top of his staff. Several tablets of this reign represent interesting family groups: in one (under the second window in the vestibule) a husband and wife are seen seated in a double chair before a table of offerings; their two sons, a youth and a little child, approaching bring new presents. The youth brings a bird, the child a flower and a very little bird. In another compartment of the picture the father is seen leaning on his staff and looking at his daughters, who are bringing garlands of fresh flowers. The table, laden with gifts, is evidently a table of funeral offerings; the attitude of the father leaning on his staff, in spite of the exactness of all the details of the figure, suggests that he is not meant to form part of the living group. We feel in looking that the artist intended us to undertand that the father and mother are watching from some far-off region of Amenti the pious acts of the children they have left behind them; and we find ourselves getting a little glimpse into a family history of Abraham's time almost as life-like as those the Bible gives us. The father and mother have died early, leaving four children behind them—two young daughters (the tablet gives their names, Sebeksi and Usersi), over whom the spirit of the father yearns tenderly; and two sons, a youth, Hantef, hardly old enough to be his sisters' protector, and one, the little one of the family, the Benjamin, who timidly approaches the funeral table with his double offering of what he likes best, his flower and his bird. On a mummy-case of this period are extracts from "The Book of the Dead," which, says Dr. Birch, proves that the Egyptians of that time believed in the immortality of the soul.

The relics in the Museum that illustrate the period of the children of Israel's residence in Egypt are still more numerous and imposing. One of the most beautiful is the red granite head of Thothmes the Third, believed by many writers to be Joseph's Pharaoh, which stands in the middle of the great gallery. This enormous head was brought from the temple at Karnac, where it once formed part of a statue erected in honour of Joseph's patron, the greatest of the Eighteenth Dynasty kings. The left ear, the chin, and part of the beard of this head have been broken away by some of the many conquerors of Egypt, who signalized their triumph over the unfortunate inhabitants of the land by mutilating their beautiful public works. Perhaps it was Nebuchadnezzar's soldiers who struck away those fragments of red granite from Thothmes' face; and perhaps Jeremiah, who had previously prophesied that the Babylonian king should break the images of Beth-shemesh, was there and saw them do it. Near this head are two seated statues dedicated to Osiris; in memory one of a prince, the other of a military chieftain in Thothmes the Third's reign, who must—if the chronology be correct that places Joseph's viceroyalty in that time—have been concerned in the great events of the time: the disgrace of the chief butler and the chief baker, the seven years' famine, the sudden rise of Joseph to power, and the arrival of the Hebrews in Egypt. There are many statues in the same division of the gallery of Amenophis the Third, the last powerful king of the Eighteenth Dynasty, the dynasty that remembered Joseph and favoured the Hebrews. His features have an Ethiopian cast, which distinguishes them from other portraits of Egyptian kings in the gallery, and, as he had an Ethiopian mother, it is probable that these statues are true portraits. Soon after Amenophis the Third's death came the revolution in favour of the stranger kings, which indirectly led to the oppression of the Israelites. In the central division of the great gallery are the monuments that illustrate the Nineteenth Dynasty —the Pharaohs that knew not Joseph and oppressed Israel. Near the entrance is a small statue under a glass case of a scribe called Piaai, who, as the inscription tells us, officiated under Ramses the Second. We look at it with interest, thinking that we have here perhaps a portrait of one of Moses' fellow-students or teachers in the priestly lore he followed in his youth. The figure seated on the ground bears in one hand an ear of corn, in the other the symbol of life. It is a memorial tablet symbolically conveying to survivors the hope in which the dead scribe had lain down in his stately tomb—a full ripe ear, gathered in, not to the harvest of death, but of eternal life. The statue opposite Piaai's—of an Ethiopian prince, Paur, kneeling before an altar—conveys the same spiritual thoughts of death; for on the altar before which the figure bends is placed a ram's head, the symbol of the living soul. Several portraits of Ramses the Second, the Pharaoh in whose house Moses was brought up, are to be found in this gallery. The most beautiful is a colossal head of granite, once part of a statue that stood before Pharaoh Ramses' great palace at Thebes, the winter residence of the Egyptian court, where Moses and his patroness must often have resided. The face is quite perfect: when the gigantic statue it crowned was broken to pieces, the head seems to have fallen forward, and remained safely embedded in the soft sand. It was dug up and removed with great difficulty from the neighbourhood of the ruined palace by the celebrated traveller Belzoni, and under the superintendence of the English consul, Mr. Salt, transported to England and presented to the British Museum. The face is handsome and expressive, and is probably a faithful portrait of this haughtiest and cruelest of the Pharaohs, before whom so many slaves and captives trembled, and from whose presence Moses fled to live among the Midianites of the desert.

There is no portrait in the Museum of "Pharaoh's daughter;" but there is in the central gallery a statue of a brother of hers called Shaaemuab, who is supposed by Dr. Brugsch to be the identical Setna of the necromantic story we have quoted—the inquisitive young prince who visited Ptah-neferka's tomb and heard Ahura's story. He bears two standards on his shoulders, and is stated to have been the fourth son of Ramses the Second, and a standard-bearer in the Egyptian army. Men-ptah, the Pharaoh of the Exodus, probably has also a statue in the central saloon, an erect figure in red granite, in the act of walking (No. 61). There is, however, some doubt whether this figure is meant for Men-ptah or his father Ramses, as both names are engraved on the stone. On the north-west staircase, leading to the upper Egyptian gallery, are glass cases containing several very interesting examples of copies of chapters of the "Book of the Dead" that have been taken from mummy-cases: some are as old as Joseph's time; several contain nearly all the chapters of the Ritual, with the little pictures representing the soul's progress in the under world at the beginning and end of each chapter. Almost all have the 125th chapter, which treats of the soul's entrance into the "Hall of the Two Truths," and has for its vignette the celebrated judgment scene.

The mummy-cases in the first Egyptian room are also painted over with sentences from the ancient sacred books, and with representations of the funeral rites, and of the fantastic scenery of Amenti—the strange spiritual beings, protecting spirits or evil genii, "devourers of heads and hearts," who, according to the Ritual teaching, thronged round the unclothed spirit on its entrance into the nether world. In the glass cases in the second room are to be seen examples of the sepulchral vases in which the embalmed heads, hearts, and viscera of the dead were placed under the protection of the four guardian genii of Amenti, whose heads—hawk-shaped, jackal-shaped, man-faced, cynocephalus-shaped—are figured on the covers of the vases.

These and numberless other valuable monuments and relics of ancient times in Egypt have been accumulating for many years, and have been gathered from various sources. Some were taken at the capitulation of Alexandria from the French, who had collected them during Napoleon's occupation of Egypt, and presented to the Museum by George III. Others have been the gift of celebrated travellers—Belzoni, Mr. Salt, Col. Howard Vyse, Sir Gardner Wilkinson, &c.; others have been purchased by the nation from private collectors, or left as bequests.

CHAPTER XXIV.

THE BURIED PALACES.

THE history of the collection of Assyrian antiquities in the Museum, which equals if not surpasses the Egyptian in interest, is wholly different. We are indebted for nearly all the treasures it contains to the exertions of a few individuals whose researches have been carried on in our own time. Thirty-five years ago it was not known that any relics of the great buildings of ancient Nineveh were in existence. Travellers on the banks of the Tigris had pointed out to them certain long ridges of mounds, covered with grass and flowers in the early spring, arid and desolate looking through the long summer, which they were told marked the sites of the ancient cities, but there was little beyond the regularity of their shape to distinguish them from natural hills. Nothing appeared above the soil to attract special attention or give promise of the wonders that the flowers or the hard baked surface covered. M. Botta, who was French consul at Mosul in 1843, was the first person who undertook the task of thoroughly investigating the mounds lying on the east of the Tigris, opposite

Mosul; one of the most conspicuous of which was called by the Arabs **Nebi Yunus**, the prophet **Jonah's** tomb, and believed by them to be the burial-place of that prophet.

For some time the excavations carried on by M. Botta's orders yielded little result—only a few bricks inscribed with cuneiform characters and some inscriptions in stone, rewarded the labour of the diggers.

Meanwhile Mr. Layard, an English traveller, who had acquired an intimate knowledge of the Arabs and of their haunts by living among them as one of themselves and sharing their sports and forays, wrote to M. Botta to encourage him to persevere in his undertaking. On one of his hunting expeditions with the Arabs, Mr. Layard had come across some gigantic and very ancient-looking mounds situated at a place called by the Arabs Nimroud, some miles south of Mosul, and been so much struck with their appearance that the project of examining them more carefully at some time had never passed out of his mind. He now directed M. Botta's attention to this spot, and advised him to pursue his investigations in that direction.

M. Botta was not able to follow this advice, as he could not leave Mosul to superintend work at a distance, but he wrote to Mr. Layard, and kept him constantly informed of the progress he was making.

After some disappointments, and after abandoning the spot where he had first begun to dig for a village north-east of Mosul called Khorsabad, M. Botta's perseverance was rewarded by discoveries that far surpassed any hopes he could have formed. Khorsabad proved to be the site of that palace and city which Sargon (the king who captured Samaria and carried away the remnant of the Ten Tribes) built in the latter part of his reign, and of whose riches and glory he has left an account on his clay cylinder: "At the foot of the Mosul mountains I have built a city," he says, "to exceed Nineveh. The great gods blessed its splendid wonders and its superb streets. There too I erected a palace of incomparable beauty for my royal seat." It was into the midst of this palace of incomparable beauty that Mr. Botta's workmen at length dug down a way. First the sculptured slabs that lined the walls of the great halls and courts were laid bare, then the colossal human-headed winged figures that guarded the palace gates were discovered. Each day's work now disclosed some fresh marvel.

The news of the great success that was attending M. Botta's enterprise was received with intense interest by Mr. Layard, and confirmed a design he had previously formed to set on foot researches of the same kind in the mounds at Nimroud, which had attracted his attention so forcibly some years before. Having obtained assistance from Sir Stratford Canning (now Viscount Stratford de Redcliffe), the English ambassador at Constantinople, he set out from the Turkish capital in the autumn of 1845, and after a quick journey arrived at Mosul. The Turkish authorities there were not only unwilling to give him any assistance, but determined to throw every obstacle in the way of his undertaking. He was obliged to content himself with commencing the work on a very small scale, and conducting it as far as possible in secret. He purchased some tools and weapons, and giving out that he was going on an expedition to hunt wild boars in the neighbourhood, he floated in a raft down the Tigris to the Arab village he had formerly visited, near which lay the ancient mounds that had excited his curiosity. On his arrival he found the place deserted, having been recently plundered by a hostile tribe of desert Arabs. Only a single Arab with his family remained on the desolate scene. The man, however, proved to be the sheik of the village; and when Mr. Layard explained the object of his coming, and promised liberal payment for work done, he willingly undertook to collect a sufficient number of his followers to carry on the excavations. He professed himself well acquainted with the mounds opposite his village, and imparted to Mr. Layard the popular Arab opinion as to their origin and destination. "The palace," said he, "was built by Athur, the kiayah or lieutenant of Nimrod. Here the holy Abraham, peace be with him, brake in pieces the idols that were worshipped by the unbelievers. The impious Nimrod, enraged by the destruction of his gods, sought to slay Abraham, and waged war against him. But the prophet prayed to God, and said, 'Deliver me, O God, from this man, who worships stones, and boasts himself to be the lord of all beings.' And God said to him, 'How shall I punish him?' and the prophet answered, 'To Thee armies are as nothing, and the strength and power of men likewise; before the smallest of Thy creatures will they perish.' And God was pleased at the faith of the prophet, and He sent a gnat, which vexed Nimrod night and day, so that he built a room of glass in yonder palace, that he might dwell therein and shut out the insect. But the gnat entered also, and passed by his ear into his brain, upon which it fed, and increased in size day by day, so that the servants of Nimrod beat his head with a hammer continually, that he might have some ease from his pain, but he died after suffering these torments four hundred years."

The first day's work had the effect of confirming Mr. Layard's convictions of the importance of the Nimroud mounds. A slab of marble, graven with cuneiform characters, was brought to him by the Arabs; and on excavating in the spot from whence they had taken it, he opened out an entrance into the chamber of a palace lined with inscribed marble slabs, which however, from exposure to extreme heat, had been almost reduced to lime, and crumbled to pieces on being laid open to the air. For many months after this commencement Mr. Layard laboured on, sometimes interrupted by the ill-will of the Turkish authorities, and compelled to lay aside the work for a few weeks, then resuming it again with quiet determination. The mounds where he was excavating proved to be the ruins of Calah, one of the ancient capitals of the Assyrian empire, the city where Assurizirpal erected the first sculptured palace.

Mr. Layard's first excavations were made in the

south-west corner of the mound, and led him into the chambers of a palace erected by Assurbanipal. Some of the slabs were sculptured on both sides, and had evidently been originally brought from a much older building. After excavating for some time on this spot, Mr. Layard began a new cutting on the north-west corner of the mound, where the winter rain had worn a deep ravine in the hill that facilitated his entrance. After a few hours' work a slab—beautifully sculptured with an eagle-headed winged figure, bearing a fir-cone and basket—was disinterred. The workmen had lighted on one of the side rooms of that great palace built by Assurizirpal, which we have described in the former part of this book, and were on the road to yet more important discoveries. The next morning, as Mr. Layard was returning from a visit to an Arab encampment in the neighbourhood, he was met by two Arabs urging their horses to the top of their speed. "On approaching me," he says,[1] "they stopped. 'Hasten, O Bey!' exclaimed one of them; 'hasten to the diggers, for they have found Nimrod himself. Wallah! it is wonderful, but it is true; we have seen him with our eyes. There is no god but God!' and both joining in this pious exclamation, they galloped off, without further words, in the direction of their tents. On reaching the ruins I descended into the new trench, and found the workmen, who had already seen me as I approached, standing near a heap of baskets and

[1] See "Nineveh and its Remains," vol. i. p. 65.

cloaks. Whilst Awad advanced and asked for a present to celebrate the occasion, the Arabs withdrew the screen they had hastily constructed, and disclosed an enormous human head sculptured in full out of the alabaster of the country. They had uncovered the upper part of the figure, the remainder of which was still buried in the earth. I saw at once that the head must belong to a winged lion or bull, similar to those of Khorsabad and Persepolis. It was in admirable preservation. I was not surprised that the Arabs had been amazed and terrified at this apparition. It required no stretch of imagination to conjure up the most strange fancies. One of the workmen, on catching the first glimpse of the monster, had thrown down his basket and run off towards Mosul as fast as his limbs would carry him. Whilst I was superintending the removal of the earth which still clung to the sculpture, and giving directions for the continuation of the work, a noise of horsemen was heard. Abd-ur-rahman (the chief of the tribe of Arabs encamped in the neighbourhood), followed by half his tribe, appeared at the edge of the trench. As soon as the two Arabs had reached the tents, and published the wonders they had seen, every one mounted his mare and rode to the mound to satisfy himself of the truth of these inconceivable reports. When they beheld the head they all cried out, 'There is no god but God, and Mohammed is his prophet.' It was some time before the sheik could be prevailed on to descend into the pit and convince himself that the image he saw was of stone. 'This is not the work of men's hands,' exclaimed he, 'but of those infidel giants of whom the prophet, peace be with him, has said that they were higher than the tallest date-tree. This is one of the idols that Noah, peace be with him, cursed before the flood.' In this opinion, the result of a careful examination, all the bystanders concurred."

The figure whose discovery was thus greeted proved to be one of the numerous human-headed lions which adorned the gateways and doors of Assurizirpal's palace. Mr. Layard succeeded in removing four of these enormous sculptures from the Nimroud mounds, where they had so long been buried, and in bringing them in safety to England. They now stand at the entrances of the low room called the Nimroud gallery in the British Museum. The stone slabs ranged along the gallery are portions of the sculptured walls of the great halls and smaller chambers on which Assurizirpal depicted the history of his life. All were brought from the north-west corner of the Nimroud mound, which was excavated by Mr. Layard with so much care that he was able to make out the complete ground-plan of the palace, with all its rooms, courts, and gateways. A second palace, situated in the centre of the mound, furnished even yet more interesting memorials. It proved to be the palace built by Assurizirpal's son—that Shalmaneser who fought so many times with Benhadad king of Syria and his general Naaman, and who after Benhadad's death conquered Hazael and received the submission of

Jehu king of Israel. The obelisk he raised at the entrance of his palace to record his victories was dug out of the mound by Mr. Layard, and now stands in the Nimroud central saloon of the British Museum. There too may be seen four slabs from Tiglath-Pileser's palace at Calah (Nimroud), one of which represents the evacuation of a conquered town. We look with interest at the files of captives setting out on the weary march, with bowed heads and fettered hands; at the rude carts bearing the captive women and children from their homes; at the flocks of sheep and cattle seized by the victorious Assyrian soldiers. We find in them a vivid picture of the scenes that must have attended the deportation of the tribes of Reuben, Gad, and Manasseh which took place in Tiglath-Pileser's reign. The two great human-headed bulls which face Assurizirpal's lions in the Assyrian gallery were brought by Sir Henry Rawlinson from Khorsabad, the site of Sargon's great palace, where was the hall which Sir Henry Rawlinson calls the Hall of Punishments.

The bas-reliefs in the Konyurjik gallery come from the palace Sennacherib built in the latter years of his life; the palace where he stored the treasures he had taken from king Hezekiah, and for whose preservation he addressed a petition to his successor. "This palace will grow old and fall to pieces in the course of time," he says, in an inscription engraved on one of the slabs; "may my successors rebuild its ruins, set up again the towers where my name was written, restore my pictures, clean my bas-reliefs, and put them back in their places. If he does this, may Assur and Istar listen to his prayers."

The slabs from this palace in the Konyurjik gallery are graven with representations of Sennacherib's wars with Merodach-Baladan, before whom Hezekiah displayed his treasures. Other slabs, representing the siege of Lachish by Sennacherib and his army, are to be found in the Assyrian basement-room. There too are many beautiful marbles taken from a palace erected by Sennacherib's son Assurbanipal. Among others should be noticed the one domestic scene of the Assyrian sculptures, where Assurbanipal is represented feasting in a garden-arbour in company with his queen, while birds sing in the branches round him, and a decapitated head depends from a neighbouring tree full in his view. Some of these sculptures were brought to England by Mr. Layard at the close of a second expedition to the site of the ancient cities, which he undertook in 1847. Others have been excavated by Mr. Loftus, Mr. Taylor, and Mr. H. Rassam, who carried on the work of excavation after Mr. Layard's return to Europe. To Mr. Loftus also is due the credit of having extended the search for ancient sites into regions yet more remote and desolate than those visited by Mr. Layard. Mr. Loftus visited and excavated among the ruins of the ancient cities of the first Chaldean empire— Erech, Accad, Calneh, and Abraham's Ur — and brought away from their strange old temples and burial-grounds the bricks, clay cylinders, and sepulchral monuments, from which nearly all our knowledge of the first times of Chaldean history is gathered. Some of these deeply interesting relics are to be seen in the glass cases in the vestibule out of the Nimroud gallery.

Among them is an ancient clay cylinder taken from the moon-god's temple at Ur, which was most probably graven with the minute characters that cover it when Abraham was a child.

Sir Henry Rawlinson, the great interpreter of the records which the enterprise of Mr. Layard and Mr. Loftus have given to the world, has himself only undertaken one exploration. This, however, is one of the highest importance—viz., the thorough examination of the Birs-Nimroud, the so-called Tower of Babel, which proved to be the remains of an ancient Chaldean temple, begun in very remote times, and almost entirely rebuilt by Nebuchadnezzar, who speaks of it in the standard inscription, as the "Wonder of Borsippa." While still a young man Sir Henry Rawlinson was selected, as the best Persian scholar of his time, to take charge of a small body of soldiers who were to be sent to Hamadan (the ancient Ecbatana) to train the troops of the Shah of Persia. After having been there some time, and having exhausted all the hunting and other sports of the neighbourhood, Mr. Rawlinson was led to turn his attention to some enormous inscriptions that were graven on the face of the rocky side of a mountain near Hamadan, called Baghistan or Behistun. These he copied letter for letter with remarkable courage and tenacity of purpose, standing on a narrow foot-ledge facing the inscriptions with his back to a precipice 300 feet sheer down. Indeed, to its inaccessibility we obviously owe the preservation of this record. Sir Henry has shown it to be a series of tablets in three languages, each written in its own form of cuneiform, Persian, Median, and Assyrian, and recording the events which led to the accession of Darius son of Hystaspes to the throne of the Achemenian sovereigns, and much of the subsequent history of his reign. At the time (1846) when Sir Henry undertook to make out this inscription, little was known of the wedge-formed characters; a word or two had been happily guessed at nearly fifty years before by Grotefend, but his researches were for some reason not continued, and neither his book, nor those of other authors who had attempted to deal with the interpretation of the Assyrian characters, had found their way into the distant mountainous region between Persia and Western Asia, where the lonely student set about his difficult work. He first attempted to read the Persian part of the inscription, because he had already noticed that the characters of this portion were much more simple, and that the words were evidently separated by something like a dot. After some months of continuous toil he made out the Persian so thoroughly, that after the publication of his translation and explanation of it, there were probably not twenty words about the signification of which any scholar competent to give an opinion could really doubt. From the Persian Sir Henry

Rawlinson proceeded to the Assyrian—a much more difficult task, since he had here no guiding, such as the modern Persian language and the Sanscrit tongue, closely allied to the Persian, had been to him in making out the ancient Persian inscription. Moreover the Assyrian characters had no separating marks; the groups of wedges, often very complex, had nothing to determine whether they represented letters, syllables, or words. By dint of extreme patience and labour, however, and by picking out the proper names, and forming from them an alphabet, Sir Henry at length succeeded in making out most of the purely historical inscriptions by the middle of the year 1854. The difficulty about the interpretation of the Assyrian language vanished as soon as the phonetic value of the cuneiform characters had been ascertained, for it proved to be so closely allied to Hebrew that any Hebrew scholar could read it when written in Hebrew characters. The most interesting of the inscriptions Sir Henry Rawlinson has deciphered, perhaps, are those on the clay cylinder of Sennacherib, which record the events of the first years of that monarch's reign, including his expedition against Hezekiah, and his enumeration of the tribute paid him by the Jewish king; and the writing on the four little cylinders found in Southern Babylonia, which give the true reading of the name of Belshazzar, and reconcile the biblical account of the king reigning in Babylon at the time of its overthrow by Cyrus with the histories of other ancient writers.

Since Sir **Henry** Rawlinson's discovery many scholars throughout Europe, following in his track, have devoted themselves to the study of the cuneiform character and the deciphering of ancient Assyrian inscriptions. The late Dr. Hincks, also a great student of Egyptian antiquities, and M. Oppert, are among those who have most distinguished themselves in this branch of learning. As a proof of the certainty with which these difficult characters can now be interpreted, it is satisfactory to know that four of the greatest Assyrian scholars—Sir Henry Rawlinson, Dr. Hincks, Mr. Fox Talbot, and M. Oppert—undertook to translate separately the inscriptions on the same cylinder, and that the four versions thus produced are almost identical, varying in a few unimportant phrases only. The record chosen for this experiment was the closely written clay cylinder on which Tiglath-Pileser the First records at such great length and with so much vigour his wars and hunting excursions. Some extracts from it have been given in the preceding pages. Both this cylinder and Sennacherib's celebrated one are to be seen in the British Museum.

THE END.

LONDON:
R. CLAY, SONS, AND TAYLOR, PRINTERS
BREAD STREET HILL.